Clouds Thick, Whereabouts Unknown,

TRANSLATIONS FROM THE ASIAN CLASSICS

COLUMBIA UNIVERSITY PRESS *New York*

Clouds Thick, Whereabouts Unknown

POEMS BY ZEN MONKS OF CHINA

Charles Egan

ILLUSTRATIONS BY CHARLES CHU

Columbia University Press wishes to express its appreciation for assistance given by The Pushkin Fund toward the cost of publishing this book.

COLUMBIA UNIVERSITY PRESS
Publishers Since 1893
New York   Chichester, West Sussex
Copyright © 2010 Columbia University Press
All rights reserved

Library of Congress Cataloging-in-Publication Data
Clouds thick, whereabouts unknown : poems by Zen monks of China / [translated by] Charles Egan ; Illustrations by Charles Chu.
p.   cm. — (Translations from the Asian classics)
Text in English and Chinese.
Includes bibliographical references and index.
ISBN 978-0-231-15038-5 (cloth : alk. paper) —
ISBN 978-0-231-15039-2 (pbk.: alk. paper)
1. Chinese poetry—Translations into English. 2. Chinese poetry—Buddhist authors—Translations into English. I. Egan, Charles. II. Chu, Charles. III. Title. IV. Series.
PL2658.E3C56   2010
895.1′00809212943—dc22
2009030194
∞

Columbia University Press books are printed on permanent and durable acid-free paper.
This book was printed on paper with recycled content.
Printed in the United States of America
c 10 9 8 7 6 5 4 3 2 1
p 10 9 8 7 6 5 4 3 2

References to Internet Web sites (URLs) were accurate at the time of writing. Neither the author nor Columbia University Press is responsible for URLs that may have expired or changed since the manuscript was prepared.

In memory of dear friends,
Charles and Bettie Chu

Contents

Dynastic Timeline

Xia	ca. 2100–ca. 1600 B.C.E.
Shang	ca. 1600–ca. 1028 B.C.E.
Zhou	ca. 1027–256 B.C.E.
Spring and Autumn	ca. 770–476 B.C.E.
Warring States	ca. 476–221 B.C.E.
Qin	221–206 B.C.E.
Han	206 B.C.E.–220 C.E.
Former Han	206 B.C.E.–8 C.E.
Later Han	25–220
Three Kingdoms	220–265
Shu	221–263
Wu	222–280
Wei	220–265
Jin	265–420
Western Jin	265–317
Eastern Jin	317–420
Southern and Northern Dynasties	
Southern	420–589
(Liu) Song	420–479
Qi	479–502
Liang	502–557
Chen	557–589
Northern	386–581
Sui	581–618
Tang	618–907
Five Dynasties	907–960
Song	960–1279
Northern Song	960–1127
Southern Song	1127–1279
Yuan	1279–1368
Ming	1368–1644
Qing	1644–1911

The period of division between Han and Sui/Tang is alternatively known as the Six Dynasties, for six courts that had their capitals in present-day Nanjing.

A Note on Pinyin Romanization

Chinese names and terms in this book are given in Hanyu Pinyin romanization, the most common international standard for transliterating Mandarin. Each syllable may include an initial consonant, and must include a final (a vowel or vowel combination [diphthong]; or a vowel or diphthong followed by -n or -ng). Chinese syllables also have tones—differences of pitch and contour of pronunciation—but as this is a book of translations, these will not be marked.

INITIAL CONSONANTS

Many consonants (**b, p, m, f, d, t, n, l, g, k, h**) are close to their English counterparts. Others require some explanation to avoid confusion.

zh	sounds like the "j" in "jam."
ch	sounds like the "ch" in "charming."
sh	sounds like the "sh" in "shoe."
r	sounds like a cross between English "r" and French "j," as the "s" in the word "measure."
z	sounds like the "ds" in "weeds."
c	sounds like the "ts" in "hats."
s	sounds like the "s" in "sink."
j	sounds like the "j" in "jingle."
q	sounds like the "ch" in "cheap."
x	sounds like the "sh" in "sheep."

There are slight differences between **zh** and **j**, **ch** and **q**, and **sh** and **x** in the position of the tongue and the level of aspiration, but these need not concern readers.

FINALS

VOWELS

-a	sounds like the "a" in "father"
-e	sounds like the "u" in "cup"
-i	sounds like the "ee" in "meet." When there is no initial, a "y" is added, thus "yi."
-o	sounds like the "aw" in "jaw"
-u	sounds like the "u" in "lute." When there is no initial, a "w" is added, thus "wu."
-ü	sounds like the "u" in French "une." When there is no initial, the umlaut is dropped and a "y" is added, thus "yu."

DIPHTHONGS

-ai	sounds like the "i" in "hi"
-ei	sounds like the "ey" in "hey"
-ao	sounds like the "ow" in "how"
-ou	sounds like the "o" in "go"
-ia	sounds like the "ya" in "yahoo." When there is no initial, "y" replaces "i," thus "ya."
-iao	sounds like the "yow" in "yowl." When there is no initial, "y" replaces "i," thus "yao."
-ie	sounds like the "ye" in "yes." When there is no initial, "y" replaces "i," thus "ye."
-iu (iou)	sounds like the "yo" in "yoke." When there is no initial, "y" replaces "i," thus "you."
-ua	sounds like the "wa" in "water." When there is no initial, "w" replaces "u," thus "wa."
-uo	sounds like "wo" in "wonton." When there is no initial, "w" replaces "u," thus "wo."
-uai	sounds like the word "why." When there is no initial, "w" replaces "u," thus "wai."
-ui (uei)	sounds like the word "way." When there is no initial, "w" replaces "u," thus "wei."
-üe	sounds like the "we" in "went." When there is no initial, the umlaut is dropped and a "y" is added, thus "yue."

Most finals consisting of vowels/diphthongs and endings –n or –ng pose no problems, as long as the pronunciations approximated above are followed. Thus -an, -en, -ang, -eng, -in ("yin" when there is no initial), -iang ("yang" when there is no initial), -ing ("ying" when there is no initial), -uan ("wan" when there is no initial), and -uang ("wang" when there is no initial). A few need some explanation:

-ong	the "o" is long, as in ou.
-ian	sounds like the "ien" in "Vienna." When there is no initial, written "yan."
-iong	the "o" is long, as in ou. When there is no initial, written "yong."
-un (uen)	sounds like the "oon" in "boon." When there is no initial, written "wen."
-ueng	only used without an initial, and written "weng."
-üan	sounds like the French "u" followed by the "wen" in "went." When there is no initial, written "yuan."
-ün (üen)	sounds like the French "une." When there is no initial, written "yun."

SPELLING NOTES

The initials j, q, and x *only* take vowels –i and –ü, or diphthongs that start with those vowels. The umlaut over the ü is dropped.

The initials zh, ch, sh, r, z, c, and s can be followed by all vowels and diphthongs *except* those that start with –i and –ü.

The initials zh, ch, sh, r, z, c, and s can end with an "i," but this is not the –i ("ee") vowel sound. Instead, "i" following these initials represents a continuation of the consonant sound, not a true vowel. When the first four are pronounced with this "i," it sounds as if an English "r" was added to the syllable — thus zhi sounds like "jr," and chi like "chr." When added to z, c, and s, only the consonant sound is heard — thus zi sounds like "dz" and ci like "ts."

The umlaut is omitted over –ü most of the time, because the consonants preceding –ü combinations and –u ("oo") combinations are distinct. Thus ju, quan, and yue are clearly syllables with –ü vowels; while zhu, chuang, and zu must be –u syllables. The only initials that can take both –ü and –u combinations are l and n. To represent a –ü final with either of these initials, the umlaut must be marked. Thus lu rhymes with "do" and lü with the French "tu."

Illustrations

> There is no end of beautiful things in the universe;
> The forms under my brush have their own feelings.
> At sunset the sky resembles a slow-flowing river,
> Clouds and mist constantly changing the scene.

Additional works by Charles Chu can be viewed at http://www.littlefrog.com.

Acknowledgments

This project began simply enough more than ten years ago, when Charles Chu and I decided to do a little book together. I would translate selected Chinese Chan (Zen) poems, and he would add a few of his wonderful paintings to illustrate them. The problem, I found, is that Chan poems are anything but simple. My progress slowed, as I began a long learning process. Life intervened as well, and for a long while the project was relegated to the back burner, where it simmered along, given an occasional stir or a few new ingredients. I hope that readers will find that the slow cooking has been worth the trouble.

Many experts have assisted me by commenting on various versions of the work, including Victor G. Hori, Stephen Bokenkamp, John Kieschnik, Dore Levy, Shuen-fu Lin, Haun Saussy, Jonathan Chaves, Paula Varsano, Wan Liu, and Ron Epstein, as well as several anonymous reviewers. I deeply appreciate all their help. Remaining inaccuracies and omissions are, of course, my own. I am also very grateful for the love and support of my family: Farley and Tom Green, Clem Egan, Sandy Egan, Molly and Mike Taylor, Tess and Kenny Emminger, my nephews and niece, and various and sundry Floods, Egans, and Steeles. Many, many thanks to my friends Buzz and Shirley Thompson and their daughter Sophia (who will be delighted to see her name in print, so here it is again — "SOPHIA"). Thanks also to Lee Cole-Chu, Paula Chu, Kevin Chu, Ellen Chu Scala, and Chus everywhere. For help with the illustrations, I am indebted to Rob Scala at Little Frog Gallery (http://www.littlefrog.com/). Jennifer Crewe, Leslie Kriesel, and staff at Columbia University Press have been consistently helpful and professional. Parts of this book were drafted in 2008 in Bangkok, where I stayed with long-time friends Somsak and Rattana Panyakeow and family. My grateful thanks to them, and to all Chinvatanachots, Ekbundits, and others in the greater Chockchainirand family. It was the Chockchainirands' example, when I was a high school exchange student in their home many years ago, that taught me how Buddhism can imbue people's lives with tolerance and grace.

Finally, this book is dedicated to Charles and Bettie Chu. Some of my happiest hours in Connecticut were spent with them in their sunny dining room in New London, discussing Chinese art and literature, admiring Charles's new paintings, or just chatting about this or that. From time to time Charles and I would rush off on expeditions to painting auctions around the Northeast, in search of undiscovered masterpieces at bargain prices. The almost four decades between our ages did not seem like much. Charles and Bettie were a devoted couple, happily married for more than sixty years, despite very different personalities: he extroverted, gregarious, emotional, and subject to wild enthusiasms; she quieter, inquisitive, thoughtful, spiritual, and serene. Charles passed in 2008 and Bettie in 2009, to my sorrow and that of many. Charles did some of the paintings printed here specifically for this book, but others have perforce been selected from his existing works. Bettie often remarked that it was a challenge being married to a character, but it seemed to amuse her no end. Let me conclude in her words:

I am reminded of the time Charles came running into the house, frantically moaning and pointing to his mouth! He raced into the kitchen for a teaspoon of vinegar! Finally we found out that he had been in the garden chewing *jiucai* (Chinese garlic chives), scallion, and garlic blossoms, and "they needed vinegar"! Pop was an artist who was inspired by many moments, and these moments could not be planned or predicted.

Introduction

Poems in the short, fixed-length forms that dominate classical Chinese poetry are designed to encapsulate momentary states of mind of an individual — emotional reactions, philosophical insights, or flashes of religious illumination. All of the traditional Chinese scholarly arts can be termed "lyrical" — not just poetry, but calligraphy, painting, and music as well; artistic creation has since ancient times been viewed as a spontaneous internal response to external stimuli.[1] A poem succeeds when the subject matter and the poet's personal sensibility seamlessly fuse in form and language. Creation opens a window to the artist, and interpretation allows us to look through.

This book is set at the intersection of art and religion, and is about both. Chan Buddhism (Ch. *chan, chanzong;* Zen is the Japanese pronunciation) has attracted enormous interest in recent decades from both scholars and practitioners, yet with the notable exception of the works of Hanshan, relatively little attention has been given to Chinese Chan poetry. This is a shame, as poetry from the monasteries comprises a distinct tradition of rich imagery and profound reflection, spiced liberally with wit and humor. Presented here are poems by both major and minor Chinese figures from the eighth to seventeenth centuries, along with notes to aid reading. Dozens of figures are represented and the span of time is long, yet the selections display a unified vision, as Chan was the motivating force in all the monks' lives.

Followers of Chan Buddhism in the Tang and later dynasties often described it as "a separate transmission apart from the teachings" (Ch. *jiaowai biechuan*) that "does not establish written scriptures" (Ch. *buli wenzi*). They laid claim to a direct link to the truth of enlightenment, through an unbroken line of "mind-to-mind" transmission of masters to disciples that began with the Buddha Śākyamuni. The "teachings" of the sūtras and commentaries were implicitly less direct and thus less useful. Further, the assertion that Chan Buddhists do not establish scriptures of their own suggests that Chan truth was beyond the power of written words to convey. In fact, the two maxims were primarily rhetorical devices, used to distinguish the Chan lineage from other Buddhist monastic orders, in order to gain prestige and to attract patronage and converts. Available evidence for the Song dynasty, for example, shows that Chan establishments and those associated with other Buddhist groups differed very little in terms of sūtra study by monks, the chanting of sūtras as a merit-making device in Buddhist rites, meditation practices, and general monastic organization.[2] The situation for the Tang through Five Dynasties periods is assumed to have been similar (on more limited evidence), and that for the dynasties after the Song certainly was. Moreover, despite their antiscripture and antiwriting stance, Chan Buddhists in China produced an enormous body of texts to present religious thought and practice.

Yet the principles expressed in these maxims and others like them did have a cumulative effect on the nature of the texts produced. Chan Buddhists created a complex language in which indirection, suggestion, ambiguity, and metaphor were prized over straightforward explanation.[3] "Encounter dialogues" (Ch. *jiyuan wenda*) dominate the multiple "transmission of the lamp" (Ch. *chuandeng*) anthologies, as well as the hundreds of "discourse records" (Ch. *yulu*) of individual masters. Each is presented as if it were a verbatim record of an actual oral interaction between a master and a student. Although some type of oral practice was probably current in Chan circles from the late eighth to middle tenth centuries, when the major masters featured in encounter dialogues were active, what it comprised is uncertain; what is clear is that the written texts we have were later *literary* re-creations of how the masters of the past must have spoken and acted.[4] In these texts, typically the student asks a question about Buddhism, which the teacher "answers" after a fashion, but seldom with a logical statement. Instead, the master might respond with a blow or a shout, a gesture, a counterquestion, an illogical or nonsensical pronouncement, a simple image of one or more words, or, increasingly over time, a line of poetry. As a guide to the genre as a whole, it is useful to recognize that the masters and students have vastly different perspectives:

> The best way to understand such features is as a function of the fundamental mismatch of intention between the students and masters as depicted in these texts. The students are generally depicted as requesting assistance in ascending the path of Buddhist spiritual training toward enlightenment. The masters, for their part, are represented as refusing to accede to their students' naïve entreaties, instead deflecting their goal-seeking perspective and attempting to propel them into the realization of their own inherent perfection.[5]

No matter how strange or puzzling the master's answer, each short interaction is presented as containing the key to an enlightenment breakthrough. It could not be otherwise, for a basic Chan principle was that everything an enlightened master says or does reflects the buddha nature, and compassion directs him to provide exactly the medicine the student requires. Moreover, in many instances the student understands the lesson and is enlightened — communication indeed takes place.

A paradoxical approach to language is revealed: though enlightenment cannot be explained in ordinary terms, a special language can be constructed to point the way. The monk Juefan Huihong (1071–1128) wrote, "The subtleties of the mind cannot be transmitted in words, but can be seen in words."[6] The genre of encounter dialogues invites readers to scrutinize the texts for underlying meanings. Some dialogues defy analysis, yet oftentimes much can be learned by placing the master's answer in broader religious, cultural, and literary context — there is method in this madness. For the special language of Chan texts was not created in a vacuum. Ambivalence about the utility of language to completely express meaning long predates the advent of Buddhism in China, and it informs both Daoist and Confucian philosophies.[7] The *Zhuangzi* in particular has often been cited as an influence on Chan rhetoric, and the Daoist sage as a model for the iconoclastic Chan master. Yet more generally, early Chinese views on language also shaped the grand tradition of lyric poetry. As a result, a poetry developed "in which the less is said, the more is meant," characterized by "implicitness over explicitness, conciseness over verbosity, obliqueness over directness, and suggestion over description."[8] Chinese poets had faith that the special code of poetic language could transmit meaning that was otherwise inexpressible; this implied that composition and interpretation are equally creative acts that rely on parallel intuitive leaps. Once meaning is grasped, language becomes dispensable; in Zhuangzi's analogy, "The fish trap exists because of the fish; once you've gotten the fish, you can forget the trap."[9]

The formal characteristics of Chinese poetry, including the enormous common store of metaphoric imagery that developed over time through intertextual collaboration, were designed in large part to escape the limitations of the literal text, to project what is variously termed "meaning beyond the words" (Ch. *yanwai zhi yi*), "suggestiveness" (Ch. *hanxu*), or "resonance" (Ch. *yichang santan* — literally, "one note, three echoes"). Chan Buddhists inherited this legacy, built upon it, and made it their own. Encounter dialogues reveal a strong poetic sensibility — not only when poetic lines are recited but also more generally, in the preference for thought-provoking metaphoric imagery over generalization, the radical economy of expression, and the tendency to view both world and text as only the starting points to true understanding. The language of poetry was very compatible with Chan, and Chan was compatible with poetry.

The Chinese lyric poem, naturally enough, was embraced wholeheartedly by Chan Buddhist monks, not only as a medium for personal expression but also as a characteristic activity of religious practice and proselytizing, and as a means to maintain relationships with secular patrons and friends. Many thousands of poems by monks are extant.[10] In the Tang, a group of "poet-monks" (Ch. *shiseng*) became famous for their literary achievements; meanwhile, several collections in a more vernacular (sometimes earthy) style were developed for teaching purposes in temple settings. The transmission-of-the-lamp anthologies from the Five Dynasties and later periods frequently include poems at climactic points—as evidence of enlightenment, as summations of lessons for disciples, or as final words of wisdom before death. Discourse records of Song and later masters invariably contain multiple chapters entirely devoted to poetic works, and numerous individual and group collections of poems by monks were published separately and widely circulated. Reading Chan poetry is a splendid means to approach religious ideas, and a good part of this book is devoted to explaining how. Yet more generally, the Chan practitioners themselves are held up for view: how did they see the world, not only in terms of religion but also as people living a communal monastic existence? What were they like as individuals, and how were their personalities expressed? And how did they modify traditional poetic language in order to transform religious enlightenment into illuminating poetry?

HISTORICAL AND RELIGIOUS BACKGROUND

The field of Chan studies has been transformed in the last several decades, and much that was once considered fact is now revealed as myth, while new perspectives and approaches are producing startling insights into the evolving tradition. Yet even before describing the new research, certain basic principles of Indian and pre-Chan Chinese Buddhism merit introduction, as they are at the core of Chan beliefs but are seldom fully described in Chan discourse.

THE PRINCIPLES OF MAHĀYĀNA

Chan was a distinctly Chinese development, and the forms it took accommodated Chinese cultural ideas, practices, and attitudes, yet its foundation was the Indian Mahāyāna tradition of Buddhism that was introduced to China in the Latter Han period and flourished beginning early in the Six Dynasties era. Mahāyāna is one of the three major waves of Buddhism exported from the Indian subcontinent, the other two being Theravāda and Tantra. Theravāda, primarily known through the Pāli Canon, underlies Buddhist practice in Sri Lanka and Southeast Asia, while Tantric Buddhism is best known in its Tibetan form.[11] East Asian Buddhism is primarily Mahāyāna, the "Greater Vehicle" (Ch. *dasheng*), so called to distinguish it from Buddhist schools and traditions its adherents considered lesser paths to salvation. The various ideas that coalesced into Mahāyāna begin to appear about the first century B.C.E. as minority opinions within the existing monastic orders. A vast literature gradually took shape, first in Sanskrit and later in East Asian translations and original texts. Yet Mahāyāna was a movement rather than a specific school, and there were no guiding authorities to decide what was included. Paul Williams describes the resulting literature as a shifting mass of sometimes contradictory or mutually critical teachings, and concludes, "There is scarcely a unitary phenomenon here, save in its concern to identify itself as Mahāyāna, as a great, superior path to religious fulfillment."[12]

It is well-nigh impossible to exactly reconstruct the particulars or chronology of "original" Buddhism, because all the relevant religious texts date from hundreds of years later. This much is clear: the young prince Siddhārtha Gautama (depending on the chronology used, died either 480 B.C.E. or 370–368 B.C.E.)[13] abandoned his life of wealth and power and undertook a quest for religious liberation. Under a pippala tree by the river at Uruvelā, he sat down in yogic meditation. Yoga is premised on the idea that the person is a physical-spiritual whole, and so methodical physical practices (asceticism, bodily postures, rhythmic breathing, concentration) can be used to effect spiritual insight. After forty-nine days Siddhārtha was enlightened and became a buddha (Ch. *fo*). He became known as Śākyamuni, the "Sage of the Śākya Clan" (Ch. *Shijia mouni*), or sometimes as the Tathāgata, the "Thus-Come One" (Ch. *Rulai*), and spent the rest of his long life teaching the Buddhist Way (the Dharma, with a capital "D"; Ch. *fa*). In his first sermon at Benares, he proclaimed the Four Noble Truths: 1) life is suffering; 2) suffering arises from craving or attachment; 3) the cessation of suffering results from the cessation of craving; 4) the way that leads to the cessation of suffering is the Noble Eightfold Path—right view, right thought, right speech, right behavior, right livelihood, right effort, right mindfulness, and right concentration. At age eighty, surrounded by his disciples in the Sala Grove at Kushinagara, he passed into *nirvāṇa* (Ch. *niepan*), a state he compared to an oil lamp sinking in upon itself and expiring when its fuel has been consumed. He alone was thereby freed from the cycle of rebirth (Skt. *saṃsāra*; Ch. *lunhui*) that binds living beings and determines their future existences by the law of moral cause and effect (Skt. *karma*; Ch. *ye*).[14]

As taught during the great flowering of Buddhism prior to the advent of Mahāyāna, the process the Buddha used to gain enlightenment was a type of deep spiritual analysis, which disassembles the Five Aggregates (Skt. *skandhas*; Ch. *wuyun*) that make up the person (physical matter, sensations, conceptions, mental constructs like volitions that produce character, and consciousness), leading to the conclusion that the self has no essence, no reality. In other words, the Five Aggregates are discovered to have no inherent existence, and so neither does their ever-changing combination, the person. The self is only a concept. To see things the way they really are brings a cessation of craving, attachment, and self-concern. "Thus the forces which lead to continued rebirth come to an end, and thence ends, to quote the scriptures, 'this complete mass of frustration, suffering' (*dukkha*)."[15]

Several pre-Mahāyāna schools and traditions further systematized the process, to distinguish what really exists from the conceptual constructions of everyday life. The result was the development of *abhidharmas*, bodies of analytical literature that have at their core lists of the basic building blocks that—in different combinations—compose everything. These building blocks, called *dharmas* (with a small "d"), are ultimate realities in the sense that they cannot be further broken down into constituent parts. Most are "conditioned" in that they arise as a result of causes, but they do indeed exist for an irreducible moment before they are replaced by others in a continuous stream. Included are physical and mental *dharmas,* and consciousness itself.[16] *Nirvāṇa,* from the period of early Buddhism on considered identical with enlightenment, is "unconditioned." What did this mean exactly?

Nirvāṇa was not clearly defined in early texts, for it was considered mystical and beyond words, but the various ways it was described suggest it is the perfect opposite of this world, which is characterized by the "three marks" (Skt. *trilakṣaṇa;* Ch. *sanfayin*): impermanence, a capacity to create suffering, and a lack of existence independent of other causes and conditions. Thus *nirvāṇa* is permanent, peaceful (beyond all suffering), and independent of causes and conditions. We should not assume that for early Buddhists *nirvāṇa* meant simple extinction, despite the Buddha's metaphor of the burned-out lamp. Its positive nature was constantly stressed: it is true being, supreme good, final release, the isle of deliverance. Although the personal self as it relates to this world is extinguished, that fact in itself did not mean annihilation in *nirvāṇa.*[17]

Edward Conze sums up the common doctrine of pre-Mahāyāna Buddhism as follows. First, the practitioner recognizes how unsatisfactory is this world, through contemplation of the "three marks" that characterize all objects and factors in our normal experience. Next, his or her personality is gradually transformed by cultivation of a sequence of five cardinal virtues: faith, vigor, mindfulness, concentration, and wisdom. The core of meditative practice is in the middle stages, mindfulness (Skt. *smṛti;* Ch. *nian*) and concentration (Skt. *samādhi;* Ch. *ding, sanmei*). The former is the calm awareness of things as they are, dissociated from the ego and discursive thinking; the latter shifts away from the sensory world altogether to another, subtler realm of higher meditation levels (Skt. *dhyānas;* Ch. *channa, chanding*) and states (Skt. *ārūpyas;* Ch. *wuseding*). Finally, wisdom (Skt. *prajñā;* Ch. *banruo, zhihui*) is gained, which disperses the darkness of delusion and penetrates to the true nature of self and phenomena. Observation of the rising and falling of *dharmas* brings an end to attachment and craving. The practitioner opens the "wisdom eye," which reveals the path to *nirvāṇa*, the "unconditioned," and becomes a saint, an arhan/arhat (Ch. *aluohan, luohan*).[18]

Another pre-Mahāyāna teaching that was a primary influence on Mahāyāna was that of the supramundane Buddha. All early Buddhist traditions appear to have considered the Buddha as more than a human being and attested to the auspicious marks on his body and his miraculous abilities, but the supramundane teaching went much further. The Mahāsaṃghika school taught that the Buddha during his life was devoid of the impurities of this world, and that his ordinary activities—walking, eating, taking medicine, growing old—were mere illusions to conform with worldly ways. He was said to be omniscient, and even though he appeared to sleep he in fact was always in meditation. A collateral development was the rise in status of the bodhisattva (Ch. *pusa*), the enlightenment (Skt. *bodhi*) existence (Skt. *sattva*), or "being of enlightenment." Bodhisattvas are essentially buddhas-in-waiting. There is an extensive and popular literature concerning the Buddha's good deeds in previous lives, when he was a bodhisattva. Since the Buddha was considered supramundane, the bodhisattva took on some of the same qualities. A result was the implicit lowering of the status of the arhat.[19] Williams sums up the Mahāsaṃghika contribution:

> We are not very far here from the Mahāyāna teaching that the Buddha's death was also a mere appearance; in reality he remains out of his compassion, helping suffering humanity. Man's religious goal should be not to become an Arhat but to take the Bodhisattva vows, embarking on the long path to a supreme, totally superior Buddhahood.[20]

The bodhisattva path is the key narrative in Mahāyāna texts. While some allow that the arhat (a "hearer" [Skt. *śrāvaka*; Ch. *shengwen*] of the Buddha's teaching) and the *pratyekabuddha* (one who attains enlightenment without assistance; Ch. *dujue*) are indeed enlightened, both categories of beings are criticized for pursuing individual rather than universal salvation. The *Lotus Sūtra* (*Saddharmapuṇḍarīka*) goes further, explicitly stating that their enlightenment is imperfect and their karma remains incomplete. There is in fact only One Vehicle: the bodhisattva path to perfect buddhahood.

The bodhisattva vows to help all living beings to *nirvāṇa*. Although it is still the cultivation of wisdom that brings enlightenment, compassion becomes the ruling motivation of the universe. Since the spiritual levels and capacities of living beings differ, the bodhisattva develops skill-in-means (Skt. *upāya*; Ch. *fangbian*)—expedient teaching methods—to encourage them to progress on the path. Out of compassion, these are presented only to the degree of complexity or profundity at which the receiver is capable of understanding. It follows that different beings might receive different instruction, and that there are levels of "truth." However, the fact of "pure" or "ulti-mate" truth (Skt. *paramārthasatya;* Ch. *zhendi*) does not mean that "common" or "conventional" truth (Skt. *saṃvṛtisatya;* Ch. *sudi*) is false—both are equally true on the path. For as the bodhisattva progresses through stages to buddhahood (eventu-ally ten were described), a host of supramundane powers are gained to help suffer-ing beings and can be brought to bear to ensure that a certain teaching has a certain result. Infinite realities, even those that are logically incompatible, may be available at the same time, all due to compassion. All the while, the enlightened bodhisattva is aware that the living beings receiving help have no inherent existence, yet endeavors to alleviate their suffering nonetheless. As the practitioner spiritually progresses, myriad instances of skill-in-means are successively revealed and drop away, ultimately leading to their total absence: the pure truth of Buddha.[21]

Mahāyāna proper begins with the *Perfection of Wisdom* (*Prajñāpāramitā*) sūtras. These originated about 100 B.C.E. to 100 C.E. with elaboration of a basic text (the 8,000-verse *Aṣṭasāhasrikā*) that was greatly expanded between 100 C.E. and 300 C.E., then restated in short summaries between 300 C.E. and 500 C.E. (including the famous *Diamond Sūtra* [*Vajracchedikā*] and the *Heart Sūtra* [*Hṛdaya*]), and finally between 600 C.E. and 1200 C.E. was presented in Tantra-influenced texts.[22] The term *pāramitā* (Ch. *boluomi*) literally means "gone beyond" (i.e., to *nirvāṇa*); it is commonly used to describe a series of virtuous practices on the bodhisattva path.[23] Usually six are men-tioned: giving, morality, patience, effort, concentration, and wisdom (the *Daśabhūmika Sūtra* adds four more, skill-in-means, vows, strength, and intelligence, to match the ten stages of the bodhisattva). As the title *Prajñāpāramitā* suggests, these sūtras are pri-marily concerned with the definition of the most important practice, wisdom (*prajñā*). All Buddhist traditions agree that *prajñā* is a state of consciousness that results from analysis. In most early non-Mahāyāna traditions, including those that developed *abhi-dharmas,* it is simply the discernment of the *dharmas,* the constituent parts of every-thing in the world. The *Prajñāpāramitā* literature takes a further step: all *dharmas*—conditioned or unconditioned—are as "empty" of existence as all other objects and factors in our normal experience. To be more specific, *dharmas* have only relative exis-tence like other things and concepts, but no inherent existence independent of causes and conditions. Nothing exists in an independent and permanent sense, and therefore there is nothing upon which to rely, nothing that can induce the practitioner to form attachments. *Prajñā* is both a conceptual recognition and a nonconceptual meditative absorption of this fact. It also came to be regarded as identical with the content of the analysis—the ultimate truth of emptiness itself.[24]

"Emptiness" (Skt. *śūnyatā;* Ch. *kong*) is the sword that cuts through delusion and shows things as they really are. Yet the ultimate truth of emptiness does not mean there is a transcendent realm of emptiness, for emptiness is empty as well.

Emptiness is not a vague absence, still less an Absolute Reality. It is the absence of inherent existence itself related to the object which is being critically examined in order to find out if it has inherent existence. Emptiness is the ultimate truth (*paramārthasatya*) in this tradition in the sense that it is what is ultimately true about the object being analyzed, whatever that object may be. It is not a *thing*, certainly not an inherently existing thing, in its own right.[25]

The systematic application of the emptiness concept by the Madhyamaka school provided the major philosophical basis and methodological approach for the *Prajñāpāramitā* literature. Emptiness is not nihilism, although the Mādhyamika were at times so accused, for nonexistence is a concept that makes no sense without the concept of existence, and such dualities disappear in emptiness. It is helpful in explaining this mind-boggling thought to recognize that both "conventional" and "ultimate" truths are necessary. The conventional world is impermanent and unsatisfying, yet it also happens to be where Buddhist practice takes place. To see the ultimate from the conventional is a difficult task. "Our traditional logic is adapted to a world of relatives. It must lose its bearings where one considers the relations between the relative and the Absolute, the conditioned and the unconditioned, the world of becoming and *nirvāṇa*."[26] To grasp the ultimate, it is necessary to abandon conventional thought processes.

> The *Prajñāpāramitā* now claims that discrimination (*vikalpa*) is the core of ignorance and that the empirical world, with its attendant sufferings, is a thought-construction derived from false discrimination. But "the Tathāgata is one who has forsaken all discoursings and discriminations."[27]

Ultimate truth is nondual: in it there is no distinction between opposites like existence and nonexistence. Using the "four-cornered negation" technique typical of Madhyamaka writing, emptiness is neither existing, nor not existing, nor both existing and not existing, nor neither existing nor not existing. A further point: to say that all *dharmas* are empty suggests that they are all ultimately the same. *Nirvāṇa* is not excepted: it is identical with *saṃsāra* in its emptiness, even though in this conventional world of "dependent origination" the two appear as opposites. Williams writes, "We should not think that this world is empty but *nirvāṇa* is some really existing alternative realm or world. *Nirvāṇa* is attainable here and now through the correct understanding of the here and now."[28]

As a matter of practice, Conze presents Madhyamaka uses of emptiness on five meditation levels. The first three levels use emptiness to distinguish conditioned and unconditioned *dharmas*, in a way not significantly different from the *abhidharma* traditions. In the fourth, emptiness is used to *undo* the previous distinctions. A state of nonduality is attained, which conflates opposites like *nirvāṇa* and *saṃsāra;* in Conze's words, "Emptiness is now regarded as the identity of yes and no, and a vast realm of paradoxes therewith opens before us." In the fifth and final stage, even attachments to logic and words are left behind, and emptiness, the universe, and enlightenment are silently identical.[29]

After the Madhyamaka, the next influential development in Māhayāna was the rise of the Cittamātra tradition (a.k.a. Vijñāptimātra, Vijñānavāda, Yogācāra) in about the fourth century C.E. The Cittamātras accepted the importance of the emptiness teaching, but believed the Mādhyamika had overnegated — there *is* an ultimately existing reality. The principal doctrine is that *dharmas* exist only in the mind, thus the name *citta/vijñāna* (Mind) *mātra* (Only). There is no external reality whatsoever — things are merely concepts — yet the mental flow of perceptions that underlies it is really there. A clear explication is found in the teaching of the Three Aspects. The first is the conceptualized aspect, in which subject (i.e., the experiencer) and object (i.e., that which is experienced) are differentiated and assumed to have inherent existences that they do not in fact possess. This is the ordinary world as it appears to unenlightened people, and it is characterized by the falsifying activity of language. The second is the dependent aspect, which is the nondual substratum of perceptions that is erroneously differentiated into subjects and objects in the conceptualized aspect. It is an ever-changing flow of *dharmas*, beyond language, and is all that really exists. The third is the perfected aspect, which is the dependent aspect that is "empty" of all the subjects and objects of the conceptualized aspect. Through meditation one recognizes the nondual nature of the dependent aspect and experiences a single, undifferentiated flow of perception. In other words, the dependent aspect underlies both *saṃsāra* (the conceptualized aspect) and *nirvāṇa* (the perfected aspect). "This very same flow of experiences can be a basis for suffering in the unenlightened man, but also a basis for liberation in the saint."[30]

The "mind" that is the major topic of the Cittamātra tradition is identical with the flow of perceptions of the dependent aspect. Attaining enlightenment is recognition of the nondual and nonegoistic perfected aspect of this "mind." To this end, the teachings present a detailed explanation of human consciousness in all its forms, and its relationship to the phenomenal world. Eight types of consciousness are described. Perception is the function of the six sense consciousnesses (related to the five physical senses and the mind, which is a "sense" in that it apprehends psychic events and serves to synthesize the experiences of the other five). None of these is permanent; they are rather series of momentary events. The seventh is the "tainted mind" (Skt. *kliṣṭamanas;* Ch. *ranwuyi*), which mistakenly objectifies and posits a self in the eighth, "substratum consciousness" (Skt. *ālayavijñāna;* Ch. *zangshi*, literally "storehouse consciousness"). The substratum consciousness is the source of the other seven; contained within it are "seeds" (Skt. *bīja;* Ch. *zhongzi*) that are "perfumed" and thus activated by phenomenal acts according to the law of karma. The apparent commonality of the phenomenal world around us is the result of collective experiences since the beginning of time; individual difference comes from individual acts. Seen in this way, the substratum consciousness is the basis for *saṃsāra.* Cittamātra writers like Vasubhandu liken it to a great rushing torrent of water that is ever changing yet still the same. It follows that the substratum consciousness was identified primarily with the dependent aspect in its *saṃsāric* dimension—as the basis for the conceptual aspect. Enlightenment occurs when it ceases, when the great torrent is stilled. Yet a purified vision remains, for the seeds of *nirvāṇa* are also to be found in the substratum consciousness: the dependent aspect in its *nirvāṇic* dimension is revealed—the perfected aspect.[31]

An Indian contribution to Mahāyāna that had particularly strong resonance in East Asia was the teaching of the buddha nature (Skt. *tathāgatagarbha;* Ch. *rulaizang, foxing*). It first appeared as early as the mid-third century C.E. in the *Ratnagotravibhāga,* and was a central feature of texts such as the *Nirvāṇa Sūtra* and the *Laṅkāvatāra Sūtra.* All sentient beings are (or have) the buddha nature, and so are already fully enlightened buddhas. Yet this innate embryo of the Tathāgata is obscured by the taints of *saṃsāra.* There is an implicit distinction here between original and actualized enlightenment: the former is quiescent while the latter occurs temporally. The actualization of enlightenment does not "produce" anything; instead, it is a paring away of illusions (caused by ignorance) to reveal the purity that is already there.[32]

The *tathāgatagarbha* doctrine appears to have developed independently of other schools and traditions, but was then absorbed in India by the Cittamātra, which identified the buddha nature with the substratum consciousness. Thus the buddha nature is the source of both *saṃsāra* (when tainted) and *nirvāṇa* (when pure). Yet there are not two types of buddha nature, and it does not change or grow—it is permanent and perfect whether actualized or not. Taints are illusory and do not affect it. To clarify the context for doctrinal discussions of the buddha nature, the *Śrīmālādevīsiṃhanāda Sūtra* uses *tathāgatagarbha* to refer to it when tainted by defilements, and *dharmakāya* when it is pure: "Whoever does not doubt that the Tathāgatagarbha is wrapped-up in all the defilement-store, also does not doubt that the Dharmakāya of the Tathāgata is liberated from all the defilement-store."[33]

The *dharmakāya* (Ch. *fashen*) is the "Dharma body" of the Buddha—the Absolute, Suchness, *nirvāṇa,* ultimate reality. The term is associated with the doctrine of the Three Bodies of Buddha, which became a basic premise of all Mahāyāna. The question whether or not the Buddha disappeared into *nirvāṇa,* posed in early Buddhism, now has a firm answer: yes and no. The "transformation body" (Skt. *nirmāṇakāya;* Ch. *huashen*) of Buddha is unreal and fictitious; it is only a temporary manifestation from time to time sent to spread the Dharma, out of compassion for sentient beings—Śākyamuni was such a one. Yet the *dharmakāya* of Buddha is eternal, and beyond all physical bodies. Conze explains,

> The Dharma-body is eternal, immutable and omnipresent, it acts without interruption everywhere, and its activities never come to an end as long as there are beings to be saved. As Suchness the Absolute is withdrawn from all that seems to be, and as Buddhahood it is spread out through the entire universe.[34]

Intermediate between the physical "transformation bodies" and the limitless "Dharma body" is the potential for various manifestations of Buddha's "enjoyment body" or "communal body" (Skt. *saṃbhogakāya*; Ch. *baoshen*). This is the idealized, perfected body that is revealed, for example, before assemblages of the faithful in the Buddhist paradises; Amitābha is the best known. In sum, in this world and in others, there have been, are, and will be an infinite number of buddhas, yet there is in truth only one Buddha, ineffable and unchanging, underlying them all.[35]

The *Flower Garland Sūtra* (*Avataṃsaka*) is a massive work that builds on the Mahāyāna foundation, and through the philosophical Flower Garland (Huayan) school in China, became a significant influence on Chan. It presents a stunning vision of the Dharma realm (Skt. *dharmadhātu*; Ch. *fajie*) — the universe as seen by a buddha or advanced bodhisattva. To the enlightened mind, all reality is related and interpenetrated by a fundamental unity.

> Each particle of dust contains in itself all the Buddha-fields and the whole extent of the Dharma-element; every single thought refers to all that was, is and will be; and the eternal mysterious Dharma can be beheld everywhere, because it is equally reflected in all parts of this universe. Each particle of dust is also capable of generating all possible kinds of virtue, and therefore one single object may lead to the unfolding of all the secrets of the entire universe. To understand one particular object is to understand them all.[36]

The last and most famous section of the text also circulated separately as the *Gaṇḍavyūha Sūtra*. A notable characteristic is a synthesis of Madhyamaka and Cittamātra ideas: it speaks of both all things lacking inherent existence and a pure untainted awareness or consciousness as the ground of phenomena.[37] This is evident from the following quote from the text:

> Endless action arises from the mind: from action (arises) the multifarious world. Having understood that the world's true nature is mind, you display bodies of your own in harmony with the world. Having realized that this world is like a dream, and that all Buddhas

are like mere reflections, that all principles [*dharma*] are like an echo, you move unimpeded through the world.[38]

The Buddha as he is in himself is the universe itself: the *dharmadhātu* is identical with the *dharmakāya*. Yet out of compassion for sentient beings infinite transformations are possible, and miracles should be no surprise. "If all lacks inherent existence, or all is Mind, then not only are these images, these magical interventions, as real as anything else, but also, as mind, or lacking in inherent existence, they reveal the true nature of things as much as anything else."[39]

MAHĀYĀNA IN CHINA

The development of Buddhism in China proceeded in a vastly different way than in South and Central Asia. Texts arrived piecemeal, and were introduced initially without complete knowledge of the scholastic traditions and doctrinal controversies that produced them, their relative importance in the canon, or even their chronological place. The pioneering translators also had to contend with cultural obstacles: for example, Buddhist monastic institutions asked practitioners to "leave home" and remain celibate, which runs directly counter to the Confucian axiom that to produce descendants is an act of filial piety. To make the new religion seem familiar and less threatening, Daoist terminology was frequently employed to explain Buddhist concepts, but this introduced subtle changes in meaning that channeled the evolving tradition in new directions. A host of competing doctrinal schools were founded, which tried to bring clarity to the mass of material by ranking the spiritual importance of the sūtras and by creating commentaries, discourses, and even new or expanded sūtras to fill ideological gaps and to define the teachings.[40] An extraordinarily influential text in this regard is the *Awakening of Faith in the Mahāyāna*, which reflects the tendency of Chinese exegetical writing to bridge difference through synthesis.

The *Awakening of Faith* influenced virtually every school of Chinese Buddhism, including Chan. Despite its brevity (less than a dozen pages), the text has inspired more than 170 commentaries.[41] Once attributed to the Sanskrit poet Aśvaghosha (ca. first to second century C.E.), it is now generally accepted as a Chinese work of the middle sixth century C.E. The major focus is the Tathāgatagarbha doctrine, presented both as a means to enlightenment and as a description for all reality. Variously termed the One Mind, Mind, the Mind of the sentient being, the essential nature of Mind, etc., the *tathāgatagarbha* "includes in itself all states of being of the phenomenal world and the transcendental world."[42] In its Absolute aspect, it is identical with the Dharma realm (*dharmadhātu*), and is beyond perceiving subject, objects, language, and thought itself:

> That which is called "the essential nature of the Mind" is unborn and is imperishable. It is only through illusions that all things come to be differentiated. If one is freed from illusions, then to him there will be no appearances (*lakshana*) of objects [regarded as absolutely independent existences]; therefore all things from the beginning transcend all forms of verbalization, description, and conceptualization and are, in the final analysis, undifferentiated, free from alteration, and indestructible. They are only of the One Mind; hence the name Suchness. (32–33).

"Suchness" is defined in terms that make Madhyamaka and Cittamātra approaches complementary. It is "truly empty" in accordance with the "four-cornered negation" — when practitioners are freed from their deluded minds, "they will find that there is nothing to be negated." It is also "truly nonempty" in that once illusions are dispersed, "the true Mind is eternal, permanent, immutable, pure, and self-sufficient," and "is endowed with undefiled and excellent qualities" (34–36).

The *tathāgatagarbha* in its phenomenal aspect is the storehouse consciousness of the Cittamātra tradition, wherein "'neither birth nor death (*nirvāṇa*)' diffuses harmoniously with 'birth and death (*saṃsāra*),' and yet in which both are neither identical nor different" (36). Thus it is the starting point for both liberation and suffering. "Original enlightenment" is its essential nature; free from thoughts, it is analogous to empty space that pervades everywhere, or a bright mirror undefiled by worldly reflections. Such is its natural state, yet "because of not truly realizing oneness with Suchness, there emerges an unenlightened mind and, consequently, its thoughts" (43). Mental agitation is the cause of ignorance. The relationship between ignorance and enlightenment is compared to the wind stirring up waves upon the ocean: when the wind (of ignorance) ceases, the waves (aspects of deluded mind like the subject [self], objects and concepts, discrimination and attachments, karmic suffering) also cease, but the ocean (of wisdom) remains (55).

Since nonenlightenment is obscuring original enlightenment, the actualization of enlightenment is necessary. The inception of this process is natural to the human condition, for ignorance and Suchness permeate each other in the storehouse consciousness. Thus even when one is in a state of nonenlightenment, "Through the force of this permeation, [Suchness] causes the deluded mind to loathe the suffering of *saṃsāra* and to aspire for *nirvāṇa*" (58). Obviously, removing the stream of deluded thoughts is the key: "If a man gains [insight into] that which is free from thoughts, then he knows how those [thoughts] which characterize the mind [i.e., deluded thoughts] arise, abide, change, and cease to be, for he is identical with that which is free from thoughts" (40).

Exactly because he is already enlightened, as soon as deluded thoughts are recognized as such they will disperse.

The last chapters are practical, and include directives for proper meditation that reflect the text's premise that ignorance is the result of thought activity, while original enlightenment is immutable and still. In a list of six *pāramitā*, the terms "cessation" (Skt. *śamatha;* Ch. *zhi*) and "clear observation" (Skt. *vipaśyanā;* Ch. *guan*) substitute for "concentration" and "wisdom," and present a concrete approach:

> Should there be a man who desires to practice "cessation," he should stay in a quiet place and sit erect in an even temper. [His attention should be focused] neither on breathing nor on any form or color, nor on empty space, earth, water, fire, wind, nor even on what has been seen, heard, remembered, or conceived. All thoughts, as soon as they are con-jured up, are to be discarded, and even the thought of discarding them is to be put away, for all things are essentially [in a state of] transcending thoughts, and are not to be cre-ated from moment to moment nor to be extinguished from moment to moment; [thus one is to conform to the essential nature of reality (*dharmatā*) through this practice of cessation]. (96)

When "cessation" becomes habitual and can be carried to all activities of life, then one is absorbed into the *samādhi* of Suchness and realizes the oneness of the Dharma realm. This *"samādhi* of one movement" (Ch. *yixing sanmei*) is the foundation of all other *samādhi* (e.g., visualizations).[43] Yet without "clear observation" it remains in-complete: *śamatha* focuses and brings tranquility to the mind, while *vipaśyanā* verifies the truth of the teachings through insight. Tiantai school founder Zhiyi (538–597) described the relationship between the two: *śamatha* is the hand that holds the clump of grass, while *vipaśyanā* is the sickle that cuts it down.[44]

The *Awakening of Faith* flows directly from Indian and Central Asian roots, yet the choices of material presented and their explications paralleled existing Chinese approaches to spirituality. Both Daoists and Confucians taught that the innate nature of human beings is beclouded by external influences, yet a "return" to innocence and purity can be accomplished through individual reflection.[45]

CHAN DEVELOPMENT

Discussions of the development of Chan have until recently been based primarily on sources produced by the mature tradition itself. This has resulted in an overemphasis on the transmission lineage of masters, and often an uncritical acceptance of the Chan version of chronology and key events. That is to say, the transmission-of-the-lamp anthologies have too often been taken as historical records, rather than as proselytizing texts aimed at Song dynasty and later Chinese audiences. At the turn of the twentieth century, a magnificent collection of books, documents, and artworks was discovered behind a false wall at the Dunhuang Buddhist caves in Gansu, where it had lain hidden for a thousand years. Among the materials were many Chan texts of the eighth to tenth centuries, which have provided scholars unfiltered access to the doctrinal positions and disputes, the personalities and interpersonal relationships, and the organizational aspects of groups in the Chan evolutionary period. For the last several decades a group of experts has researched the Dunhuang texts, and their conclusions for the evolutionary period are so at odds with the accepted narrative that they in turn have inspired a comprehensive ongoing reappraisal of the Chan tradition. John McRae—himself a major contributor to the research—has recently written a lucid summary of the work to date, *Seeing Through Zen*.[46]

McRae begins by deconstructing the basic lineage usually presented in the transmission-of-the-lamp anthologies, reproduced here:

Lineage Diagram of Chinese Chan Buddhism[47]

Seven Buddhas of the Past

↓

Śākyamuni

↓

INDIAN PATRIARCHS:

Kāśyapa

(first Indian Patriarch)

↓

Ānanda

⋮

↓

CHINESE PATRIARCHS:

Bodhidharma

(= twenty-eighth Indian and first Chinese Patriarch)

↓

Huike

↓

Sengcan

↓

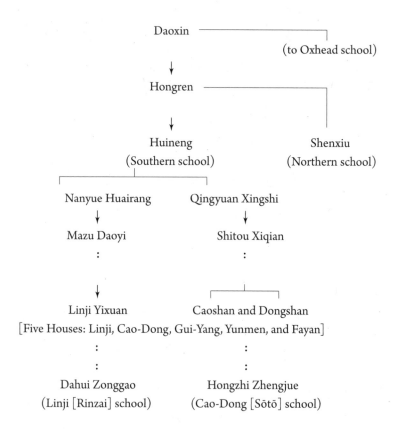

Daoxin ——————————————
                        (to Oxhead school)

Hongren ——————————————

Huineng   Shenxiu
(Southern school)   (Northern school)

Nanyue Huairang   Qingyuan Xingshi

Mazu Daoyi   Shitou Xiqian
    :   :

Linji Yixuan   Caoshan and Dongshan
[Five Houses: Linji, Cao-Dong, Gui-Yang, Yunmen, and Fayan]
    :   :

    :   :

Dahui Zonggao   Hongzhi Zhengjue
(Linji [Rinzai] school)   (Cao-Dong [Sōtō] school)

McRae makes multiple inferences based on the basic lineage diagram, which suggest that while it served the needs of the evolving Chan tradition very well, it reveals very little about the actual state of affairs in the periods it covers. It was more polemical statement than historical record, a claim to the superiority of Chan over other schools, for it represented followers as the direct recipients of Śākyamuni's original and thus truest teachings. Moreover, as what is "transmitted" is complete enlightenment (or Buddhist "emptiness," for "nothing" is actually transmitted), Chinese masters were granted the same religious status as the Indian buddhas and patriarchs. There is also a shift away from Indian methods, which present spiritual practice as an essentially solitary meditative endeavor. In contrast, the heart of the Chan lineage chart is the spaces or lines between the names, which indicate dynamic encounters between masters and their students. Encounter dialogues constituted a cohesive force; the authority of the master (and Chan in both its spiritual and its political dimensions) is valorized in every dialogue or exchange associated with him, up to and including his formal bestowal of approval of the student's enlightenment (Ch. *yinke*, also called *xinyin* [mind seal]). That the encounters were idealized, or even patently fictional, does not lessen their importance to the tradition and may in fact increase it. For the process by which the dialogues and exchanges were augmented, edited, or improved over time was one of collective ownership and participation, and the finished product became part of the legendary lore by which Chan masters came to be identified throughout Chinese culture. McRae concludes that what distinguished Chan from other schools or forms of Buddhist training was that it was "genealogical," both in its self-understanding as a school and in the design of its practices.

> By saying the Chan practice is fundamentally *genealogical,* I mean that it is derived from a genealogically understood encounter experience that is *relational* (involving interaction between individuals rather than being based solely on individual effort), *generational* (in that it is organized according to parent-child, or rather teacher-student, generations), and *reiterative* (i.e., intended for emulation and repetition in the lives of present and future teachers and students).[48]

What was a boon to the tradition can be a headache for the historian, for the lineage model is a profound distortion of the subject matter. The lineage is a selective understanding of tradition, and affirming a single line effectively blocks other viewpoints. Power and privilege are protected by lineage. We also must recognize that the line begins at the end: the individuals at the end of the list have the most to gain by tracing their "roots" back to the source. In other words, lineages are retroactively produced and controlled.[49]

McRae thus sets the lineage diagram aside and provisionally proposes a new model to describe the phases of Chan development through the Song dynasty, grounded in recent research. His outline is reproduced here, followed by synopses of the phases.

Simplified Chart of the Phases of Chinese Chan[50]

Proto-Chan	Bodhidharma (d. ca. 530)
(ca. 500–600)	Huike (ca. 485 to ca. 555 or after 574)
	Treatise on the Two Entrances and Four Practices
Early Chan	Hongren (601–74)
(ca. 600–900)	Shenxiu (606?–706), Huineng (638–713)
	Shenhui (684–758)
	Northern, Southern, Oxhead factions
	Platform Sūtra of the Sixth Patriarch
Middle Chan	Mazu (709–88), Shitou (710–90)
(ca. 750–1000)	Linji (d. 867), Xuefeng Yicun (822–908)

	Hongzhou and Hubei factions, antecedents of the Five Houses
	Anthology of the Patriarchal Hall
Song Dynasty Chan	Dahui (1089–1163), Hongzhi (1091–1157)
(ca. 950–1300)	Five Houses, Linji and Cao-Dong schools
	Blue Cliff Record

PROTO-CHAN

It is inaccurate to say that Chinese Chan begins with Bodhidharma; rather, the tradition chose him as First Patriarch. It was an advantage that many of the early figures who appear in the Chan lineage were historically obscure, for they became vessels to be filled with legend and doctrine. The hagiography of Bodhidharma evolved over a millennium, and includes multiple contradictions.[51] The same is true of his disciple, and Second Patriarch Huike, who was said to have chopped off his own arm to prove his dedication to the master's teaching (one source says bandits removed it for him). What is reliably known is that the two men were teachers of a group (or groups) active in north China that taught the Tathāgatagarbha doctrine and was characterized by ascetic practices and a particular dedication to meditation. It is reasonable that the tradition embraced them, as "Chan" is an abbreviated form of *channa,* the Chinese transliteration for *dhyāna*—meditation. Chan was, first and foremost, the Meditation School of Chinese Buddhism.[52]

One of several texts attributed to Bodhidharma does indeed show similarities with the doctrine of later Chan, the *Treatise on the Two Entrances and Four Practices.* The heart of the text is the "entrance of principle," a restatement of Tathāgatagarbha doctrine similar to that in the *Awakening of Faith.* It includes a puzzling reference to being frozen in "wall contemplation" (Ch. *biguan*). A very literal interpretation is probably what led to the legend of Bodhidharma meditating for nine years while facing a cave wall. McRae suggests that *biguan* here correlates well with Tiantai founder Zhiyi's term *biding,* "wall concentration." Zhiyi uses the walls of a room as a metaphor for excluding distractions during meditation practice, and the reference in the Bodhidharma text may be as simple as that.[53]

The equal importance placed on the "entrance of practice" suggests a doctrinal tie with later Chan. The *Treatise* describes the attitudes one should adopt during daily activities, in a progressive series leading to "Practice of accordance with the Dharma: to eradicate wrong thoughts and practice the six perfections, without having any 'practice.'" Introspective yogic meditation is now paralleled by correct living in the world; either means may lead to Buddhist truth. McRae concludes, "We will see that the bimodality between principle and practice, or rather between an abstract description of one's inner attitude and the progressive elaboration of one's ongoing activities, is a recurrent theme throughout the Chan tradition — one that will help us to organize the sometimes unruly creativity of later periods."[54]

EARLY CHAN

The Early Chan phase featured multiple loosely defined Buddhist groups that had major disagreements on matters of doctrine and practice. Yet everyone involved placed enormous emphasis on meditation techniques to allow unmediated access to the Absolute — in order that "they could see into their own natures and with direct apprehension become buddhas." Thus they can be considered participants in a single reform movement that sought to counter Buddhist scholasticism.[55]

The connection between the Bodhidharma/Huike followers and Early Chan is unclear, particularly since Third Patriarch Sengcan remains a cipher — most of what is "known" about him was manufactured long after his death. About the next two on the usual list, Daoxin and especially Hongren, considerably more can be said. The two were active for half a century, from 624 to 674, at monasteries on adjoining peaks at Huangmei, in Hubei Province. Hongren lived on the eastern peak, and the approach of both men became known as the "East Mountain teaching." Daoxin and Hongren were meditation teachers, pure and simple; there are no references to indicate they advocated sūtra study and practices common to other schools. There is also no evidence that monastic labor was required of residents, contrary to the claim of the later tradition. Students of various religious interests came to Huangmei for relatively short-term training before carrying on their monastic careers elsewhere. Among them were Shenxiu — soon to become the major Chan figure in north China — and the future Sixth Patriarch Huineng.[56]

After Hongren's death, the East Mountain teachings continued to exert influence through his students, but the center of operations shifted to the two imperial capitals of Chang'an and Luoyang, inaugurating an era of explosive growth. It was at that time that a lineage model was first adopted. Late in the seventh century, Hongren's students compiled a written record of the master's teachings, the *Treatise on the Essentials of Cultivating the Mind*. The central lesson of this extraordinary text is to "maintain awareness of the mind" (Ch. *shouxin*), which is merely to keep the buddha nature (the One Mind) continuously uppermost in one's mind during all activities of life. It employs a vivid metaphor of the sun obscured by clouds to describe the relationship between the *tathāgatagarbha* and defilements. Two specific meditation techniques are described, one implicitly focused on original enlightenment and the other focused on the mental activity that obscures it. Yet both demonstrate the composed attitude implicit in *shou-xin*. The first is to visualize the perfect orb of the sun just as it sets, and remain fixed on that one point without distraction. The other is to focus on consciousness itself, as the following beautiful passage describes:

> View your own consciousness tranquilly and attentively, so that you can see how it is always moving, like flowing water or a glittering mirage. After you have perceived this consciousness, simply continue to view it gently and naturally, without it assuming any fixed position inside or outside of yourself. Do this tranquilly and attentively, until its fluctuations dissolve into peaceful stability. This flowing consciousness will disappear like a gust of wind.[57]

The Chan tradition has not been kind to Shenxiu, though he had been fully in the mainstream of its development. He suffered the ignominy of excision from the lineage, and worse, he was parodied in the *Platform Sūtra of the Sixth Patriarch* and its interpretations. Yet during his lifetime his ideas were the central matrix for Chan development, and his fame as a religious teacher reached even to the imperial court, where he received the public reverence of Empress Wu Zetian herself. Shenxiu taught a radically new message: the Buddhist scriptures are only "skill-in-means" or "verification of Chan meaning," for the Buddha was not interested in mundane matters "but used each and every utterance to describe the practice of Buddhist meditation." Thus Shenxiu viewed the scriptures and conventional religious practices only as metaphors and interpreted them entirely in terms of spiritual cultivation. Even mundane daily activities were brought into the sphere of religious practice and became subject to interpretation. The attitude of constant awareness required to understand the true meanings he termed "contemplation of mind" or "viewing the mind" (Ch. *guanxin* or *kanxin*). Activities as diverse as temple repair, the offering of incense, or taking a bath, if understood correctly, may lead to buddhahood in the here and now. The doctrinal approach is new, while the specific meditation practices he espoused generally follow the lines of Hongren's treatise.[58]

Readers with background in Chan/Zen may wonder why there has not yet been mention of the schism between the "Northern" Chan of Shenxiu and the "Southern" Chan of Huineng over "gradual" versus "sudden" enlightenment. Here again the myth-making of the later Chan tradition needs to be examined. The terms "Northern Chan" and "Southern Chan" were not coined until several decades after Shenxiu's death in 706 C.E., and the doctrinal positions of the two "schools" (if they can be called that) on the gradual/sudden question were much closer than is usually described. Finally, no version of the text that describes the gradual/sudden dichotomy most directly, the *Platform Sūtra of the Sixth Patriarch,* has been found that dates earlier than about 780 C.E.—100 years after the events it purports to relate.

"Gradual" enlightenment, obviously, is reached in stages; much of the Indian source material affirms it. "Sudden" enlightenment was generally understood in two aspects, following the monk Daosheng (ca. 360–434), who first described it in China: the Absolute is indivisible and empty, and so must be grasped all at once or not at all; and from the practitioner's point of view, enlightenment must occur at a sudden point in time, just as a fruit suddenly drops from the tree only when it is ripe.[59] Daosheng was certainly influenced by Daoist ideas, yet the concept of "sudden" enlightenment has Indian roots as well: Tathāgatagarbha texts imply it, and the idea of interpenetration in the *Flower Garland Sūtra* suggests that even a first-stage bodhisattva is fully enlightened.[60]

Beginning in 730 C.E. and for some decades afterward, a charismatic Buddhist preacher named Shenhui publicly accused followers of Shenxiu of gradualism. He claimed the meditation practices advocated by the Shenxiu group were merely "freezing the mind to enter concentration" or "fixing the mind to view purity," and argued they were dualistic and thus taught that enlightenment could be attained gradually. Instead, he called for a dynamic state of mind in which meditation is inseparable from wisdom. This seems to reflect an absolutist position that denies the relevance of cultivation, though in other recorded statements Shenhui hedges—he allows that gradual practice can be melded with sudden enlightenment.[61] It was Shenhui who first used the terms "Northern" and "Southern" Chan, respectively to refer to Shenxiu and his followers, and Huineng and his. As he had been a student of Huineng, his championing of Southern Chan was probably motivated at least in part by personal interest in redesigning the accepted lineage.[62]

The gradual/sudden dichotomy is a major topic of the new Chan research and the scholarship is voluminous and often technical, but there is general agreement that Shenhui mischaracterized the practices of the Shenxiu group, and that so-called Northern Chan did not teach gradual enlightenment.[63] As both Shenhui and Shenxiu accepted the Tathāgatagarbha doctrine, clearly the dispute was about the actualization of enlightenment. Shenhui implicitly rejects the time-honored "cessation" and "clear observation" method Shenxiu inherited as a two-step process (though the *Awakening of Faith* specifically states they are not separate).[64] In particular, he criticizes Shenxiu's concept of "detachment from thought" (Ch. *linian*) as an intentional manipulation of mind to stop thoughts arising, in order to view the pure mind—this would constitute not only gradualism but also a passive quietism, and an unseemly attachment to purity.[65] Instead, he advocated "no-thought" (Ch. *wunian*), an active state of mind in which thought remains, but without conceptualization and attachment. "For Shenhui, no-thought is itself sudden awakening, and as such there must be knowledge at work within it."[66] His various criticisms can be refuted by reference to texts Shenxiu and his group produced,[67] but they were influential enough to change the terms—if not the substance—of Chan discussion. This is evident in the landmark text of Early Chan, the *Platform Sūtra of the Sixth Patriarch.*

There is no evidence that Sixth Patriarch Huineng (638–713) played any role in the composition of the *Platform Sūtra,* nor does the historicity of the events described stand scrutiny. Huineng is recorded as one of Hongren's ten major disciples, and he taught Chan in Caoqi in his home province of Guangdong in the far south, but that is about all we know for certain. The *Platform Sūtra* is a masterpiece of religious litera-ture, but literature it is. The earliest text extant was found at Dunhuang and dates to about 780 C.E., while the version popular in later dynasties shows many additions and changes.[68] Authorship is now generally ascribed to members of the Oxhead school of Chan (a faction independent of both "Northern" and "Southern" Chan),[69] who wished to resolve the crisis Shenhui had precipitated.[70]

Following Shenhui, no-thought is the major teaching in the *Platform Sūtra:* "If you recognize your fundamental mind, this is the fundamental emancipation. And if you attain emancipation, this is the *samādhi* of *prajñā,* this is nonthought."[71] No-thought (also called "no-mind" [Ch *wuxin*]) is itself enlightenment, and the mind thereby gains perfect freedom of thought: "If in seeing all the dharmas, the mind is not defiled or attached, this is nonthought. [The mind's] functioning pervades all locations, yet it is not attached to all the locations" (46). Again following Shenhui, the traditional ces-sation/clear observation method is rejected, in favor of a unified method combining meditation and wisdom: "Meditation and wisdom are of one essence, not different. Meditation is the essence of wisdom, and wisdom is the function of meditation. At times of wisdom, meditation exists in that wisdom; at times of meditation, wisdom exists in that meditation" (56).

The text uses the metaphor of a lamp and its light to show the complementary na-ture of meditation and wisdom: "The lamp is the essence of the light, and the light is the function of the lamp" (56). The use of polarities like meditation/wisdom, essence/function, stillness/activity, and cessation/clear observation is typical of discourse on Chan meditation (and Chinese philosophy in general). Such pairs of terms are useful to show both surface contrast and underlying commonality and integration.[72] Similar polarities characterize Chinese poetry, as we shall see.

The unified method is termed the "*samādhi* of the single practice" (Ch *yixing san-mei*), which is defined as "to always practice the single direct mind in all one's actions, whether walking, standing still, sitting, or lying down" (56). Ideas of interpenetration derived from the *Flower Garland Sūtra* inform the Chan use of the term: "since [the] Principle of the absolute (*li*) manifests itself in each and every phenomena (*shi*), one must start from the absolute to understand the phenomenal world."[73] Meditation per se is not necessary, and the *Platform Sūtra* reinterprets it metaphorically (rather as Shenxiu might have done!):

> Good friends, what is seated meditation (*zuochan*)? In this teaching, there is no impediment and no hindrance. Externally, for the mind to refrain from activating thoughts with regard to all the good and bad realms is called "seated" (*zuo*). Internally, to see the motionlessness of the self-nature is called "meditation" (*chan*). (60)

This is all easier said than done, of course. Fortunately the text throws the less adept practitioner a lifeline by allowing the (limited) usefulness of cultivation: "Good friends, the correct teaching is fundamentally without either sudden or gradual—it is human nature that is either clever or dull. Deluded people cultivate gradually, while enlightened people suddenly conform [to the truth]" (57). This does not indicate that gradual enlightenment is possible, only that sudden enlightenment may occur after a period of gradual cultivation; nor does it show any *direct* connection between cultivation and enlightenment, which would constitute gradualism. Instead, within the logic of the sudden teaching, it is an attempt by the Oxhead authors to bridge the schism between Northern and Southern Chan.[74]

The same is true for the most famous part of the *Platform Sūtra,* the poetry competition between Shenxiu and Huineng to choose Hongren's successor. As the story goes, Hongren called on his followers to submit poems to show whether they had been "enlightened to the great meaning." Whoever could do so would be named the Sixth Patriarch. The body of monks deferred to their instructor, Shenxiu. He composed a verse, but in a state of great indecision could not bring himself to submit it to the master. So he secretly wrote it on the wall of a corridor and waited to see what the Fifth Patriarch's response would be.

> The body is the *bodhi* tree;
> The mind is like a bright mirror's stand.
> Be always diligent in rubbing it—
> Do not let it attract any dust. (31)

The next morning, Hongren publicly praised the verse, but privately told Shenxiu he had failed to see the fundamental nature. Meanwhile, an illiterate woodcutter named Huineng had been at work in the temple hulling rice. He heard Shenxiu's verse, composed a response, and asked someone to write it on the corridor wall.

Bodhi is fundamentally without any tree;
The bright mirror is also not a stand.
Fundamentally there is not a single thing—
Where could any dust be attracted? (33)[75]

The master publicly rejected the poem but in secret preached the *Diamond Sūtra* to Huineng, who experienced a great enlightenment. Hongren then made him the Sixth Patriarch and gave him the robe of Bodhidharma.

The traditional interpretation is that Shenxiu's poem teaches gradual enlightenment while Huineng's teaches sudden enlightenment, but this conclusion is not borne out by analysis. First, Shenxiu's poem refers to a constant practice of cleaning the mirror, not a gradual or progressive one. Second, Huineng's poem is an inversion of Shenxiu's poem and could not stand alone—the two constitute an indivisible pair, a polarity. Third, the terminology used in *both* poems has roots in *Northern* Chan sources. McRae concludes the poems present a threefold logical structure, typical of Oxhead thought. The constant teaching is first posited as a profound expression of Buddhism in formal terms; the second poem then undercuts it by means of the rhetoric of emptiness; yet the true meaning is the nonduality of the polarity.[76]

MIDDLE CHAN

Layman Pang asked Mazu, "Who is the one who is not companion to ten thousand *dharmas*?" Mazu answered, "After you have swallowed all the water in the West River in a single gulp, I'll tell you." At these words the layman was suddenly enlightened.[77]

The break between Early Chan and Middle Chan is not between Northern and Southern Chan, but between doctrinal exposition and encounter dialogue. Sometime during the latter half of the eighth century the locus of Chan instruction appears to have shifted from the lecture hall or the ordination platform to the back rooms of the monastery. Public sermons that might then be transcribed and disseminated gave way to individual oral lessons. Thus while Middle Chan was the period of the most famous masters and stories in the Chan tradition, a relative dearth of contemporary documentation means that little can reliably be said about the approach. Encounter dialogue texts suddenly appear fully formed and in great quantity in the *Anthology of the Patriarchal Hall* of 952, more than 150 years after many of the exchanges purportedly described. An earlier partial text produced within the Hongzhou faction of Mazu Daoyi, the *Transmissions of Treasure Grove* of 801, does *not* include encounter dialogues. Middle Chan is a puzzle to which pieces are still missing. McRae suggests several precedents for the genre in Early Chan sources that utilize such elements as questions and answers, ritualized call and response, anecdotes and dialogue, or metaphors, but none appears to be a direct precursor. Understanding of the genre perforce must be primarily from internal evidence in the texts themselves.[78]

That encounter dialogues are literary re-creations can be shown in several ways. First, although the *Anthology of the Patriarchal Hall* describes events that occurred in the south and was compiled there, the vernacular language in which it is written follows the standard of the capital at Chang'an in the northwest.[79] Second, as T. Griffith Foulk suggests, "the use of metaphor, symbolism, dramatic devices, realistic settings, and the verbatim quotation of private conversations and unspoken thoughts—are typical of fiction." He further points out that the descriptions of the monastic environment of the Tang masters often contain anachronistic details that are characteristic of Song dynasty monasteries.[80] Third, the style can best be described as "performative," in the sense that it is designed to engage the reader in an act of interpretation; such a style is characteristic of literary texts. Bernard Faure writes, "The performative nature of Chan texts derives from their strategic or tactical use, which appears to take precedence over their actual content."[81] Finally, and most obviously, revisions and additions to the stories can be traced in the various transmission-of-the-lamp anthologies.[82] Of course, the presence of literary elements does not mean that the exchanges did not occur in some form. Nor should we forget that the veracity of the anthologies was unquestioned within Chan, and that Song and later practitioners, collectively and individually, developed on the "historical" foundation inscribed there.

The new Chan paradigm began in the communities of Mazu Daoyi (709–788) and Shitou Xiqian (700–790) in the second generation after the Sixth Patriarch Huineng. While Mazu led the Hongzhou faction in Jiangxi in central China, Shitou was based at Mount Heng in the southern region of Hunan. Mazu was the more important figure in terms of setting the parameters for Southern Chan thought and practice, but the two were retroactively given more-or-less equal status to validate the lineages of the five Chan "houses" of the late Tang and Song: Linji and Gui-Yang were traced to Mazu, while Cao-Dong, Yunmen, and Fayan were said to descend from Shitou. Many of the most famous masters were their followers: Baizhang Huaihai (749–814), Nanquan Puyuan (748–845), Zhaozhou Congshen (778?–897), and Linji Yixuan (d. 867) descended from Mazu; Dongshan Liangjie (807–869), Caoshan Benji (840–901), and Yunmen Wenyan (862/4–949) from Shitou. In the generations after Mazu and Shitou, both communities expanded regionally—apparently with official support—survived the chaos of the Buddhist persecution of 845 and the depredations of the Huang Chao Rebellion of 875–884, and began the long road to Chan dominance of Buddhist institutions in the Song.[83] Meanwhile, the independent Baotang faction of Chan flourished in

Sichuan in the southwest,[84] Oxhead and Northern Chan teaching continued, Shenhui's Heze faction still had followers, and non-Chan schools remained active. The short- and long-term success of Southern Chan resulted from a superior message combined with the organizational strengths of its lineage system.

Doctrinal variation and change during the Middle Chan period is extraordinarily difficult to assess and awaits further research, due to the complexities of encounter dialogue rhetoric and the imprint of Song dynasty mythmaking. Clearly the teaching styles of various masters differed, but that is not doctrinal difference. Some special teachings attributed to one or another of the five Tang dynasty Chan houses, like the Cao-Dong "Diagrams of the Five Positions," are most likely Song interpolations.[85] So for the purposes of this book at least, we can accept that Middle Chan doctrine was a more-or-less unitary phenomenon. Mazu starts where the *Platform Sūtra* leaves off, with "a system totally oriented to the experience of awakening, to the complete depreciation of cultivation," and a belief that "Everything that occurs to the individual is an expression of the functioning (*yong*) of the essence (*ti*) of the inherently enlightened Buddha-nature."[86] However, the Hongzhou school's premise that "the everyday mind is the way" is so open-ended that it ironically set a very high standard for practitioners. Moreover, it presented the danger that the "self" (including the passions) is understood as a spontaneous and complete expression of buddha nature, and that nothing needs to be done to actualize enlightenment.[87] Notable in Song dynasty Chan is a renewed focus on method and process (e.g., the development of *gong'an*/*kōan* and "silent illumination"—see below). There were other moves to harmonize cultivation and enlightenment in the intervening years.

In the transmission-of-the-lamp anthologies, encounter dialogues are embedded in birth-to-death hagiographies of the individual masters, and Tang examples became the models for later ones. Although some factual biographical material is included, religious teaching takes precedence over historical accuracy. Chan presents the enlightened masters themselves as the locus of the Way, and thus models for emulation. A standard format emerged, which indicates that despite differences in family background, temperament, or training, there is a common path leading to enlightenment, and an accepted career arc once enlightenment is attained. Key to interpreting the hagiographies is the bodhisattva ideal: portents accompanying his birth presage his spiritual destiny; his sudden enlightenment (precipitated in typical Chan fashion, with a completely ordinary experience) constitutes his perfection of wisdom; his subsequent drive to teach is motivated by the bodhisattva's compassion for living beings; and his death—the most spiritually important moment of his life—is equivalent to his passing into *nirvāṇa*.[88] Selections from the hagiographies for many monk-poets are presented later in this book.

Many older histories of Chan Buddhism present periods of incipience, flourishing, and decline, corresponding to what have been termed here "Early Chan," "Middle Chan," and "Song Dynasty and Later Chan." It has often been argued that Song and later practitioners had lost the creative spark of the great Tang and Five Dynasties masters. However, if we are to point to a "golden age" of Chan, it should be the Song. The Chan lineage controlled the majority of large "public monasteries" throughout the period, and Chan monastic disciplinary codes were so influential that even other Buddhist schools followed them. Chan teachers also gained wide popularity and maintained close ties with the Song elite.[89] As for creativity, the transmission-of-the-lamp anthologies that established the iconoclastic Tang masters were a product of the Song, and great numbers of other Chan texts were written — which ironically have often been dismissed as "Chan of the written word" (Ch. *wenzi chan*), falling victim to the tradition's own rhetoric. Chan ideas also permeated the intellectual atmosphere, influencing philosophy (Neo-Confucianism in particular), art, and literature.[90] Chan dominance in the Song occurred precisely because it "developed powerful new rhetorical modes and polemical strategies and produced an appealing body of quasi-historical mythological lore which served to spread its message and sustain its claims to spiritual leadership."[91] In later dynasties, the Song model for Chan organization continued uninterrupted, and if Chan thought appears to have been less often on center stage, it is because it was already fully integrated into the intellectual and social fabric.

Life in the monasteries controlled by the Chan lineage is illuminated by extant Chan disciplinary codes. Although such a code was attributed to Mazu's disciple Baizhang Huaihai (749–814), there is no contemporary evidence for it, and it is likely another Song myth.[92] The earliest complete extant code is the *Pure Regulations of the Chan Garden* compiled by Changlu Zongze in 1103. An earlier but incomplete code is the *Regulations of the Chan Gate* in the *Record of the Transmission of the Lamp of the Jingde Period* of 1004. Both developed from a tradition of *Vinaya* (monastic rules) codes that stretches back to Indian Buddhism. The two texts and others were carried to Japan by pilgrim monks and formed the basis of the Zen monastic practice there that continues to the present.[93]

Although the basic Buddhist precepts against killing, stealing, sexual misconduct, false speech, and intoxicants are of course the core of the codes, matters of monastic discipline, organization, and administration make up the greater part of the chapters. From the institutional perspective, there were two overarching goals: maintain social harmony within and uphold the reputation of the temple and its monks without. Thus a premium was placed on control of the individual monk. First, an extraordinarily specific list of rules of conduct, with a set punishment for each infraction, put clear bounds on behavior. Second, a full schedule of activities—including meditation sessions, physical labor (Ch. *puqing*), communal meals, and instruction by the abbot—governed virtually every moment of the day. There were set procedures and etiquette even for seemingly minor activities, like wearing the monk's robe or taking a bath. Third, a rigorous hierarchy of all temple residents, augmented by a large bureaucracy of monk-administrators to oversee every activity, maintained clear lines of authority. Ideally all would benefit, because the routine operation of the temple and the security of habit would head off potential conflicts and allow each monk to focus on religious progress. Yet the picture of ritualized discipline of Song monastic life is in stark contrast to the myth of the spontaneous, egalitarian existence of Tang practitioners depicted in transmission-of-the-lamp anthologies.

Another point about Song and later monastic life: despite popular stories depicting Tang masters like Danxia Tianran (739–824) burning Buddhist icons for warmth or Linji Yixuan declaring, "If you meet the Buddha, kill him," Chan monks were not mountaintop philosophers who had transcended traditional religious practices. The full panoply of Buddhist deities was worshipped in temples associated with the Chan lineage, sūtra study and chanting were faithfully practiced, and a broad spectrum of religious ceremonies was performed for the public. Moreover, a look beyond Chan orthodoxy shows heterodox strains exerting influence from the margins. These include an unsettling fixation on death rituals, a cult of bodily relics of holy masters (Skt. *śarīra*; Ch. *sheli*), including flesh bodies—mummies (Ch. *roushen*), and an abiding faith in miracles.[94]

Only three of the five Chan "houses" were active in the Song. Yunmen produced a number of remarkable Song masters, most notably Xuedou Zhongxian (980–1052), co-compiler of *The Blue Cliff Record*, but was otherwise minor in the period. Cao-Dong began the dynasty nearly moribund, until it was revitalized by Furong Daokai (1043–1118) and Hongzhi Zhengjue (1091–1157). Song Chan was from beginning to end dominated by Linji, which was further divided into several sublineages. Two competing teachings came to characterize Song Chan: the Linji "public case" method and the Cao-Dong "silent illumination" method. The dialectic between these two to a great degree set the stage for the development of Japanese Zen.

The term "public case" (Ch. *gong'an*, Jp. *kōan*) originally referred to legal records and the precedents they set. In Chan, the "precedents" in some way reflect higher religious truth. Virtually all exchanges that involve enlightened masters, and even pithy quotes from the sūtra literature, can loosely be considered "public cases," but the term specifically refers to a more limited number of anecdotes that appear in major Song and later *gong'an* collections, like *The Blue Cliff Record*, *The Records of Serenity*, and *The Gateless Pass*. Although the use of *gong'an* in Linji practice stretches back at least to the beginning of the Song period, the method described by Dahui Zonggao (1089–1163) became standard.

Dahui saw the sudden actualization of enlightenment as the heart of Chan. He conceived it as the culmination of a physical and mental struggle during which the practitioner overcomes doubt. Dahui writes, "These days, most of those who study the Way do not doubt themselves, but instead doubt other people. So I say to you, only after great doubt can there be great enlightenment."[95] Gong'an are only "skill-in-means" to this purpose, and so have no ultimate meanings or answers; as Wumen Huikai (1183–1260) wrote in The Gateless Pass, they are "brickbats to batter the gate." Day and night the practitioner contemplates the gong'an, especially the key word or phrase (Ch. huatou), to the point that habitual modes of thinking are totally blocked and an anxious period of doubt sets in. When all doubt is centered on the huatou, it will grow until it shatters and disappears. Dahui compares this moment to the bottom of a lacquer bucket suddenly bursting outward, revealing the sun.[96] He writes,

> Observe this story [huatou]. "A monk asked Zhaozhou, 'Does a dog have the Buddha nature?' Zhaozhou answered, 'No [wu].'" This one word, "no," is a weapon that will crush a multitude of perverse perceptions. Do not try to understand it through having or not having [youwu]; do not try to understand it with reason. Do not rely on the mind to think it through or figure it out; do not be fixated on raising the eyebrows and blinking the eyes. Do not try to make your way on the path of words; do not just float in idleness. Do not simply assent to its source; do not verify it in writings. But all day long, in whatever you are doing, always keep it before you and keep yourself alert to it. "'Does a dog have the Buddha nature?' [Zhaozhou] answered, 'No.'" Without leaving your daily activities, try to work at it in this way. In ten days to a month, you will see for yourself.[97]

In contrast, Furong Daokai and Hongzhi Zhengjue saw the meditation experience as the heart of Chan. "Silent illumination" (Ch. mozhao) is a practice wherein one returns to an inherent "silence" beyond words and the "illumination" of innate wisdom. Hongzhi Zhengjue explains in his "Lancet of Seated Meditation":

> Essential function of all the Buddhas,
> Functioning essence of all the Patriarchs;
> It knows without touching things,
> It illumines without facing objects.
> Knowing without touching things,
> Its knowledge is inherently subtle;
> Illumining without facing objects,
> Its illumination is inherently mysterious.
>
> . . . .

The water is clear right through to the bottom,
A fish goes lazily along.
The sky is vast without horizon,
A bird flies far far away.[98]

Bielefeldt writes, "Zhengjue celebrates the detached clarity of the state of *samādhi* — the 'subtle' and 'mysterious' cognition in which the mind has become a boundless space, a limpid pool, through which the object passes effortlessly without a trace."[99]

A key question is whether or not the focus on "silent illumination" meditation meant Cao-Dong discounted the importance of the actualization of enlightenment. Dahui Zonggao clearly thought so, and though he and Hongzhi Zhengjue were personally close, he excoriated "silent illumination" meditation in a series of letters and pronouncements. Morton Schlütter writes, "In Dahui's view, Silent Illumination uses the mind to control the mind, suppressing thought and inducing a state of unreflective calm, devoid of wisdom. This kind of practice is a soteriological dead end and can never lead to enlightenment."[100] The parallel between Dahui's criticism of Cao-Dong "quietism" and Shenhui's disparagement of Northern Chan is striking.

Yet as during that earlier controversy, it appears the criticism was misplaced. Dahui does not take into account the frequent Cao-Dong exhortations to practitioners to exert themselves to gain liberation. Cao-Dong meditation was judged to be a failure when it was merely quietistic; it was only complete when a quality of enlightenment was present. Moreover, certain Cao-Dong statements do imply a moment of enlightenment, as when Hongzhi Zhengjue writes in the "Lancet of Seated Meditation," "when silence and illumination are both operating and complete, the lotus flower opens and the dreamer awakens." While Song dynasty Cao-Dong practice generally emphasized inherent enlightenment over the actualization of enlightenment, a breakthrough to wisdom was still considered necessary.[101] Bielefeldt writes, "while there is surely good reason to recognize more than one approach to, or style of, Chan in twelfth-century China, there is less reason to suppose that the differences ever crystallized into a sustained sectarian dispute, let alone that they reflected mutually exclusive contemplative systems."[102]

In Japan, Linji (Rinzai) and Cao-Dong (Sōtō) did develop as competing schools, and the gulf grew wide between them. Rinzai dismisses the mindless quietism of Sōtō as a "ghost cave" of the spirit and instead favors the dynamic practice of *kōan* study; Sōtō rejects the utilitarian striving to "make a buddha" of Rinzai and teaches the less psychologically limited practice of *shikan taza*, or "just sitting."[103] Although Song Chan informed the beginnings of Japanese Zen, the impulse to view Chinese developments through a Japanese prism should be strenuously avoided.[104]

Buddhist sūtras frequently include religious verse sections, called *gāthās* (Ch. *qietuo* or *qie*), that summarize content in an easily memorizable form. Although Sanskrit *gāthās* conform to strict metrical rules and demonstrate verbal euphony, Six Dynasties Chinese translators were content merely to transmit the meaning in equal verse lengths of four, five, six, or seven characters. Chinese *gāthās* from the sūtras are doctrinal and discursive in nature, do not rhyme, and may contain (to the poet's ear) odd rhythms.[105] A *gāthā* genre developed within China that initially did not depart far from the early translations; it was designed to present philosophical/religious discourse in easily digestible form for a mass audience. The resulting works are not "poems" as that term was understood. The poem (Ch. *shi*) was a development of the literati, characterized by lyric purpose, concrete imagery, erudite language, strict meter and rhyme, primarily pentasyllabic and heptasyllabic line lengths, auditory effects, and complex use of metaphor and allusion. Beginning in the mid-eighth century, scholar-poets like Wang Wei and Meng Haoran and high-profile monk-poets like Jiaoran, Guanxiu, and Qiji popularized *shi* poetry on Buddhist themes to a wide literati audience; at about the same time, composition of *shi* poetry became a common part of practice in Chan monasteries—based on the evidence of the transmission-of-the-lamp anthologies. While influential *gāthās* of the traditional variety continued to be written,[106] *shi* became the dominant medium for Buddhist versifying, and the term *gāthā* was broadened to describe Buddhist-inspired *shi* compositions as well. Buddhist *shi* developed into a distinct subgenre, which incorporated to varying degrees the proselytizing function of the *gāthā*.

Buddhist *shi* in turn influenced the direction of secular poetry. Buddhist ideas and terminology were incorporated in poetry criticism and played a major role in defining the overall Tang aesthetic of "a fusion of feeling and scene" (Ch. *qingjing jiaorong*), which presents the successful poem as a seamless unity of the poet's thought and the environment described. The key Buddhist term in this context is "realm" or "world" (Ch. *jing*; Skt. *viṣaya*), which refers to the objects of perception/cognition. Each sense has its realm (e.g., the eye has a realm of seeing, the ear has a realm of hearing), and the mind has a realm of thinking (Ch. *yijing*), wherein all other sense realms are unified. The influence of the Cittamātra view of consciousness is clear. As applied to poetry, the best early description is from *Standards for Poetry*, attributed to the major poet Wang Changling (698–757?):

There are three realms of poetry: 1) The object realm. To write a landscape poem, [consider] a realm of springs, stones, clouds, and peaks displayed in all its peerless beauty.

Spiritually [activate] it in [your] mind and lodge [your] body in it. View the realm in [your] mind, and see it brilliant and pure in [your] hands. Then exert thought to completely grasp the images in the realm. Thus [you will] succeed in describing the likeness of the object realm. 2) The emotion realm. [Experience emotions like] pleasure, joy, sadness, or anger [e.g., inspired by the landscape], and array them in [your] thought and lodge them in [your] body. Then [by means of] the rush of thought, [you will] profoundly attain [expression of] the emotion realm. 3) The mental realm. Display both [objects and emotion] in [your] thought, and contemplate them in your mind. Then [you will] attain the truth of the mental realm.[107]

The first realm is an artistic depiction of objective reality, and the second is an artistic expression of a subjective response to it. The "mental realm" is presented as superior, for it transcends objectivity and subjectivity in favor of a unified vision. The implication is that through poetic inspiration the poet communes and merges with his surroundings, in a process akin to enlightenment. Jiaoran (730–799) employs the term "realm" more than two dozen times in his poems and critical works. He writes, "The mind realm of cold flowers and grasses/The Empty Gate of the moon on green mountains"; "Worldly matters are dust on the flowers/Focus the mind on the realm of emptiness"; and "My mind sees the realm where all is not."[108] Commenting on the metaphoric aspect of Buddhist poetry, he says that the literary concepts of *jing* (tranquility) and *yuan* (distance) refer not to the physical environment, but to a quietude and remoteness of mind.[109]

As literary criticism developed in the late Tang and Song, the Chan-poetry analogy was broadened and popularized, attaining its most comprehensive rendering in the works of Yan Yu (fl. ca. 1200), who stated that the way of poetry lies solely in wondrous enlightenment.[110] Yet the attempt by Yan Yu and those influenced by him to cover all poetry, to rank poets and periods, and even to indicate the relationship between study of models (cultivation) and poetic inspiration (enlightenment) took them far from the original intent of Chan ideas and terms. The Chan-poetry analogy was just that—an analogy.[111]

For the purposes of discussing specifically Buddhist poems, it is preferable to start again with the definition of the mental realm. Jiaoran writes, "When the realm is pure, ten thousand images are true."[112] "Truth" here should be understood as "seeing things the way they really are," and is the by-product of an enlightened mind. Everyone's experience comprises realms of perception and cognition, but for the unenlightened they are false and misleading. These are the "six dust realms" (Ch. *liuchen jingjie*)—eyes, ears, nose, tongue, body, and mind. Thus from the Buddhist perspective, describing a mental realm in a poem is not necessarily a good thing. In the early twentieth century,

Wang Guowei offered a new take on mental realms in poetry. He distinguished poetry that presents a "self realm" (Ch. *youwo zhi jing*) from a superior type that describes a "selfless realm" (Ch. *wuwo zhi jing*).

> In the world with a self, it is "I" who looks at the external objects, and therefore, every-thing is tinged with my color; in the world without a self, it is one object that looks at other objects, and therefore, one no longer knows which is "I" and which is "object."[113]

In both the merging of subject and object is a feature, but the former projects emo-tion onto the external object while the latter presents subject and object as equals that reflect each other. With caveats, Wang's definition of poetry of the selfless realm may serve for Chinese Chan Buddhist poetry. First, selflessness must be understood in its Buddhist sense. Not all poetry that sublimates the self in pure contemplation of the surroundings is Buddhist. At some level, explicitly or implicitly, Buddhist doctrine should underpin the presentation. Second, selflessness should not imply that the poet be reduced to a passive observer of the surroundings, as Wang's definition might sug-gest. There is nothing passive about enlightenment—no-mind is characterized by its dynamism. Distancing the poet and foregrounding the surroundings is a technique fre-quently employed in Chan poems (often called "the insentient speaking the Dharma," Ch. *wuqing shuofa*); however, it should be remembered that the surroundings are no more "real" than the self. It is the quality of enlightenment that is featured, experienced by the poet and recognized in the environment. A strong poetic personality/voice is not precluded.

POETIC CODES

Chinese poetry developed to allow unobstructed expression of personal states of mind that are catalyzed by experience of the world (either the real world or the learned world of history, mythology, religion, and so on). When the experienced world has been internalized and filtered, it becomes a completely personal vision. The prefer-ence for concision led to the omission of most pronouns, numbers, syntactical con-nectives, tense markers, and many adverbs in favor of nouns, adjectives, functive verbs, and selected adverbs; and the preference for implicitness led to the omission of most abstractions and generalizations. The result is a poetry that is radically undergram-maticalized and ambiguous, yet imparts a sense of vividness, immediacy, timeless-ness, and seemingly unmediated "reality." Metaphoric imagery and allusions, thematic subgenres and period styles, techniques of metrical and rhetorical presentation, and the poetic forms themselves (which provide structures for composition and interpretation) effectively became a specialized type of communication, a shared "code" for writing and reading poetry.[114]

Because their training, worldview, and topics of interest differed significantly from those of the mainstream secular poets, Chan poets made changes and additions to the "code," thus effectively creating a separate and distinct "Chan code" of poetic language. Images as simple as the moon, clouds, boats, reflections in water, plum and lotus, bamboo and pine, monkeys and herons took on complex connotations based in Chan ideas, famous verbal exchanges, and Chan and Buddhist texts. While the resulting language in fact allowed great flexibility and range of expression, its specialized nature could be an obstacle for the uninitiated, which is one major reason traditional secular critics often undervalued Chan poetry as literature. Another is that the overall tone of Chan poetry—variously described as "pure" (Ch. *qing*), "cold" (Ch. *han*), or "even and pale" (Ch. *pingdan*)—conflicted with the preference in secular poetry for indirect expression of strong emotion.[115]

IMAGERY

Chinese poetic images appeal to the senses, primarily the visual, and are most often drawn from the natural world. Apart from surface meanings there may be multiple levels of metaphoric associations. Northrop Frye's distinction between the simple sign and the literary archetype is useful.[116] The former affirms a one-to-one literal correspondence outward to the world. The latter suggests an inward one-to-many verbal connection to the rest of the work in which it appears, and simultaneously to all other uses of it in literature. With the archetype, meaning is hypothetical: a range of possible associations is suggested by comparison with the context of the poem and the literary tradition. The image becomes the focal point for dynamic intratextual and intertextual dialogue. To cite a typical Chinese example: based on early precedent-setting texts, the blossoming plum tree in poetry suggests at least two primary referents, the palace lady and the noble scholar in difficulties. Each carries a host of further qualitative associations through comparison of attributes. The former suggests beauty, youth, purity, delicacy, vulnerability, transience (the blossoms); dependence (the plum as domesticated tree); fertility (the plum as fruit tree); and so on. The latter suggests integrity, endurance, independence (as the plum tree blooms in winter), or perhaps the vigor of moral principles in old age (evident through comparison of the fresh blossoms with the gnarled and cracked tree).[117] Allusions function similarly to metaphoric images, though at a higher level of complexity. There are two basic types: direct verbal allusions to earlier texts and general allusions to people, events, and stories from the past (e.g., the lovely story of the plum blossom that dropped onto the forehead of a sleeping Han dynasty lady, creating a fashion sensation). With both types all the associations of the source are brought to bear on the present text. The ambiguity of undergrammaticalization and the multiple associations of poetic images and allusions are very much in keeping with the Chan reluctance to make firm declarations about "pure truth." Potentially, a poetic line may carry multiple meanings simultaneously—a feature any Chan master would applaud.

The variety of Chan metaphoric imagery is virtually unlimited, and this book has no pretensions to comprehensiveness. Chan rhetoric was the collective product of centuries of effort by the Chan school to declare independence from its predecessors and competitors. As Robert Buswell notes, "One way to assert that independence was to express Buddhist doctrines in a new way, using language more in keeping with the Chinese preference for concrete, laconic descriptions over the abstract, periphrastic formulations more common in Indian philosophy."[118] Korean Sŏn master Chinul (1158–1210) provides a useful contrast in this regard, with lists of Indian and Chan terms for the "true mind" (Ch. *zhenxin*) of enlightenment. While the sūtras use the abstract and conceptual terms *bodhi, dharmadhātu, nirvāṇa, tathatā,* and the like, the "language of the patriarchs" uses substantive metaphors:

> Sometimes it is referred to as "oneself," for it is the original nature of sentient beings. Sometimes it is named "the proper eye," for it makes visible all phenomena. At other times it is called "the sublime mind," for it is empty yet numinous, calm yet radiant. Sometimes it is named "the old master," for it has been the supervisor since time immemorial. Sometimes it is called "the bottomless bowl," for it can survive anywhere. Sometimes it is called "a stringless lute," for it is always in harmony. Sometimes it is called "an inextinguishable lamp," for it illuminates and disperses delusion and passion. Sometimes it is called "a rootless tree," for its roots and trunk are strong and firm. Sometimes it is referred to as "a sword which splits a wind-blown hair," for it severs the roots of the defilements. Sometimes it is called "the unconditioned kingdom," for the seas are calm there and the rivers clear. Sometimes it is named a "wish-fulfilling gem," for it benefits the poor and distressed. Sometimes it is called "a boltless lock," for it shuts the six sense-doors. It is also called "a clay ox," "a wooden horse," "moon of the mind," and "gem of the mind." It has such a variety of different names that I cannot record them all.[119]

Bernard Faure suggests that Chan monasteries defined a new domain, a "*utopian* space . . . a place ruled (in theory) by the law of emptiness and functioning as a kind of negative field in which all worldly values were canceled, dismissed, or inverted."[120] Chan poems can be considered another form of sacred "space," for the primary metaphor is spatialization. Many describe idealized visions of the *dharmadhātu*—not the world as it seems to most of us, but as the enlightened person sees it. In this "mental realm," everything is connected and significant. Certainly as a result of the Huayan influence, the poems reveal a heightened sensitivity to the meanings of ordinary objects, for since the *dharmadhātu* is present and complete in everything, virtually anything can be a trigger to enlightenment.

To exemplify the use of specialized Buddhist metaphor, this well-known poem by Hanshan (Tang dynasty) will suffice:

My mind is like the autumn moon,
As fresh and pure as a jade pond.
But nothing really compares with it—
Tell me, how can I explain?

The moon and the pond each carry both general and Buddhist associations. In general usage, the full moon (it is always full in Chinese poetry, unless otherwise specified!) connotes family unity and returning home, due to its perfectly round shape and its associations with holidays on the lunar calendar like the New Year and the Mid-autumn Moon Festival. The spring of pure water in landscape poetry carries philosophical overtones, as the source of a stream is metaphorically the source of Dao. These meanings still resonate in Buddhist usage, but are subtly transformed. The moon and pond form a polarity with a multivalent enlightenment message. On one level, the bright round moon obviously alludes to the light of *prajñā* wisdom that dispels ignorance. The *Platform Sūtra* says: "Good friends, sagacity is like the sun, and wisdom is like the moon. Sagacity and wisdom are always bright, but through being attached externally to sensory realms, the floating clouds of false thoughts block the self-nature, rendering it obscure."[121] The shining jade pond is a combination metaphor: as the *Awakening of Faith* has it, still water is the enlightened mind, revealed when the wind (of ignorance) dies and the waves (modes of mind) cease (compare also the ceasing of the rushing torrent of the Cittamātra tradition); the water then becomes a bright mirror, reflecting things as they really are (the enlightened mind as mirror is also described in the *Awakening of Faith*).

The moon and pond together carry additional associations. Chinul related the "moon of the mind" to the true mind of enlightenment.[122] To extend this metaphor: for the individual the moon may represent original enlightenment and the pond actualized enlightenment; on a cosmological level, the moon could be the *dharmakāya* in its absolute aspect, and the pond (which reflects the ten thousand things) in its phenomenal aspect. The unity and interpenetration of the two is emphasized by the fact that traditional Chinese mirrors are perfectly round; thus the moon is a mirror above, and the pond is a mirror below.

Another meaning of the polarity is suggested in the *Perfection of Wisdom*, which says the enlightened being "understands all dharmas to be like a sleight of hand, a mirage, the moon in the water, the void, an echo, a *gandharva* city [mirage], a dream, a shadow, the reflection in a mirror, or a transformation." The Chinese commentary to this passage in Kumārajīva's (344–414) *Discourse on the Great Wisdom* notes,

> As for its being like the moon in the water, the moon is really in the sky, but its reflection appears in the water. The moon, like the mark of the real Dharma, is as if in the "sky" of the reality of the true Dharma nature. In the "water" of the mind of all gods and men there appear the marks of the ego and all that belongs to the ego, and for this reason it is said to be like the moon in the water. Moreover, if a small child sees the moon in the water, he is glad and wishes to grab it, but when an adult sees this, he laughs.[123]

Here, the focus is on the insubstantiality of the reflections, to show that all phenomena are empty of inherent existence. Similarly, Panshan Baoji (fl. late eighth–early ninth century) had this to say: "The moon of the mind is solitary and round, and its brightness engulfs the ten thousand things. Its brightness does not shine on the mirror, for the mirror does not exist. When brightness and mirror are both forgotten, what is it that is left?"[124]

When Hanshan says that "nothing" compares to his mind, he is alluding to emptiness, and simultaneously restating the line in Huineng's *Platform Sūtra* poem—"At root there is not a single thing." The allusion brings to bear on this poem all the complex associations of the East Mountain poetry competition. Thus Hanshan has "returned home" to the peace of the enlightened mind, which both exists and does not exist. Yet these analogies aside, the poem concludes, enlightenment cannot be put into words—tell me, how can I explain?

COUPLET STRUCTURE AND PARALLELISM

Most Chinese poetry is uniformly regular in meter, comprising occasionally quadrisyllabic but most often pentasyllabic or heptasyllabic lines.[125] Each line in a *shi* contains a caesura (pause) in the middle, before the final disyllable (in quadrasyllabic poems) or trisyllable (in pentasyllabic and heptasyllabic poems). The equivalent or roughly equivalent halves encouraged the use of simple topic-comment structures to complete the line: the topic in the first half and the comment in the second (or vice versa, as presentation is frequently inverted). Sometimes two very short topic-comment structures are placed together in a single line. A continuous structure over two lines is also an option, but when it is employed the end of the first line always coincides with a sensible dividing point. Thus a Chinese poetic line generally imparts a sense of semantic completeness and metrical balance, which implicitly suggests that the "world" being described is also complete and balanced.

Yet the couplet, not the line, is the basic structuring unit of Chinese poetry. Even when two lines superficially appear to describe different things or events, the fact that they adjoin each other in a couplet means they must be interpreted in relation to each other. For example, a couplet by Du Fu (712–770) written during the An Lushan Rebellion reads, "Nation broken, mountains and rivers remain/The city in spring, grass and trees thick." At first glance, the second line describes a very pleasant scene — but that is not Du Fu's meaning at all. Instead, the lush growth in the city is incredibly sad, for it shows the place is an overgrown ruin. Thus couplet structure provides the poet with another tool for implicit suggestions. Rhyme at the end of each even-numbered line further sets off couplets from one another.

A special type is the parallel couplet, in which the two lines follow the identical syntactical pattern but use words with opposite or complementary meanings. Thus a noun in line one is paired with a noun in the same position in line two, verb is paired with verb, and so on. As Chinese writers developed quite specific semantic categories from which to choose words (e.g., "celestial objects" for sun, moon, stars, etc.), the process of interpreting a parallel couplet was simultaneously one of equivalence and contrast. The significance of parallelism is far more than rhetorical; Chinese literati of the Six Dynasties period (222–589), when the practice matured, considered it the proper linguistic means to reflect the innate bipolar symmetry of nature itself. As the critic Liu Xie (ca. 456–ca. 522) wrote in *The Literary Mind and the Carving of Dragons*:

> Nature, creating living beings, endows them always with limbs in pairs. The divine reason operates in such a way that nothing stands alone. The mind creates literary expressions, and organizes and shapes one hundred different thoughts, making what is high complement what is low, and spontaneously producing linguistic parallelism.[126]

Six Dynasties poets explored the potential of parallelism most fully in the genre of landscape poetry. Mature Chinese landscape poetry is "verse inspired by a mystic philosophy which sees all natural phenomena as symbols charged with a mysterious or cathartic power."[127] The poets used parallel couplets both to describe the landscape and to suggest its underlying dynamism and pattern; a landscape poem became an experience of Dao.

Chan poetry is largely landscape poetry, with the difference that the "mysterious power" of Dao is replaced by that of the Dharma. Couplets, and particularly parallel couplets, take on new roles in light of Buddhist thought. At the simplest level of interpretation, the parallel couplet presents contrasting pairs of things, events, or qualities—a world of stark duality. Wang Wei (701–762), himself a practicing Buddhist, wrote the famous parallel lines, "Walk to the place where waters end/Sit and watch the time clouds rise." Here movement is contrasted with quiescence, or perhaps walking meditation with seated meditation (walk/sit); substantiality with insubstantiality, or wisdom with ignorance (waters/clouds); ending with beginning (end/rise); and even space with time (place/time). The first line might also describe cultivation (reaching the source) and the second enlightenment (the rising of clouds). Yet on a deeper level, through poetic equivalence, all these opposites are conflated. That is to say, since each given pair is in tense, static opposition, it effectively becomes a unified whole. Time is suspended, and even the verbs become mere descriptives, brimming with potential energy. The couplet as a whole presents a unified scene that is simultaneously static and unchanging, and dynamic and moving—what better expression of nonduality could there be?

POETIC FORMS

The Chinese *shi* forms are divided into "ancient-style verse" (Ch. *guti shi*) and "recent-style verse" (Ch. *jinti shi*). Besides line length (either pentasyllabic or heptasyllabic), meter, and a rhyme at the end of each couplet, there are few rules for "ancient-style verse." Parallelism is often used but not required, and indefinite length obviated the development of any set interpretive pattern. Instead, a loose tripartite pattern was adopted: an introduction, usually no more than four or six lines; a longer middle section of description (or, in some cases, narration); and a short conclusion or summary. Chan monk-poets did not extensively use the forms, probably because they encouraged too much wordiness for poets who wanted to "say more by saying less."

The great majority of Chan poems follow the "recent-style verse" forms of the late Six Dynasties and Tang, which feature short fixed length and strict patterns of the tones intrinsic to Chinese syllables. Fixed length had enormous implications, as it encouraged standard interpretive structures and approaches to develop. The eight-line "regulated verse" (Ch. *lüshi*), in pentasyllabic and heptasyllabic line lengths, comprises a one-couplet introduction, a body consisting of two couplets, and a one-couplet conclusion. Syntactic parallelism must be observed in each of the two middle couplets; as each couplet is parallel (and in an implicit interpretive sense, the two couplets also parallel each other), time is reduced to a dynamic stasis, a lyric "moment" in the poet's mind. The introduction directs one from the real world into the poetic "world" and the conclusion directs one back out again, and in so doing may suggest real-world relevance for the poet's lyric experience. "Regulated verse" focuses only on what is absolutely essential. The reader is invited to build a unified interpretation that takes into account every image, and the relationships among images.

Wang Wei's pentasyllabic *lüshi* entitled "A Visit to Gathered Fragrance Temple" presents a commonly recurring theme in Chan poetry: the journey up a mountain as the quest for enlightenment.

> I don't know Gathered Fragrance Temple,
> And so mile after mile, enter cloudy peaks.
> By ancient trees, no walking path;
> In deep mountains, whence the bell?
> The sound of a spring gurgles on high rocks;
> The color of the sun chills green pines.
> Toward dusk, by the curve of an empty pond:
> Quiet meditation tames poison dragons.[128]

The poem reads as a simple landscape description—until the surprising final line. "Poison dragons" is a cautionary Buddhist term for the worries and aggravations (Skt. *kleśa*; Ch. *fannao*) caused by desires. The reader is drawn to reassess the previous lines in the poem for underlying meanings. As the journey begins, the poet is already lost: he does not know the location of the temple (i.e., Buddhist truth), nor can he see where he is going, as he is surrounded by obscuring mists (of ignorance). His situation worsens in the second couplet: he finds himself in a dark grove with no path to follow. Suddenly, from deep in the mountains he hears a ringing temple bell. This is his "guide" to the temple, and to the Dharma. The poetic "world" is consequently transformed in the third couplet: mist and darkness are replaced by clarity and light. He hears the splash of water (purity, wisdom, etc.) from a spring (a stream's source—and metaphorically original truth); and he sees the light of the sun (enlightenment) on the pines. Lest such a reading seem a trifle forced, note that the light of the sun unexpectedly *chills* the pines. Enlightenment is often couched in terms of coldness of mind: a euphemism for *nirvāṇa* is "the pure and cool" (Ch. *qingliang*). Finally, the poet sits in meditation by the bright mirror of an "empty" pond (the mind of *śūnyatā*) and successfully tames the "poison dragons." The conclusion is in fact anticlimactic, after the dynamism of the third couplet. The attentive reader will have noticed that the poet never does visit the physical temple—sightseeing was never the point.

The "recent-style verse" forms also include the pentasyllabic and heptasyllabic quatrains (Ch. *jueju*). Only half the length of their respective "regulated verse" cousins, *jueju* rely more heavily on projection. Editor and critic Gao Buying (1875–1940) explains:

The number of characters in *jueju* is not large, so if the meaning becomes exhausted then the spirit will be withered; if the language is obvious then the flavor will be short. Only continual suggestiveness can make people lower their heads and imagine endlessly. This is the Greater Vehicle.[129]

Poets adopted methods of thought-provoking closure for *jueju*.[130] The first couplet is usually declarative and descriptive, and is frequently parallel. It is designed to set up the conclusion by raising an expectation that demands resolution: a question might be posed that needs an answer, or a cause presented that inevitably will have an effect, or a process begun that must have an end. The second couplet is where all the key "action" takes place; it is usually propositional and verb-centered, and seldom parallel. It fulfills the expectation of the first couplet. Yet this does not mean that Chinese quatrains are predictable: rather, the best examples add a "turn" (Ch. *zhuan*) to a new direction. The poem is unified and resolved, but in an unexpected way, causing readers to "lower their heads and imagine endlessly." Consider the following untitled poem by Gong'an Zuzhu (fl. 1163–90), included in this anthology:

Moonlight shines on the mountain valley;
The sound of a spring falls down a steep cliff.
Between the shimmer of water and the color of mountains
One stick of rotten, dead wood.

A structure takes shape through repetition: equivalents of the images from the first two lines reappear in the third line. Our expectation is that the pattern will continue, though on the metaphorical level how could the polarity of the moon and the spring of water be augmented? Then comes the shocking fourth line, which demands to be integrated with the rest of the poem. The rotten piece of wood overwhelms all the beautiful yet intangible sensory images (light/sound) that came before—it becomes the only "real" thing in the poem. The image does not in fact challenge the rest of the scene but is a natural consequence of it, for the old or dead tree is a frequent metaphor for an enlightened individual. One source is the *Zhuangzi*, where the question is asked, "Can you really make the body like a withered tree and the mind like dead ashes?"[131] Similarly, the *Nirvāṇa Sūtra* describes a hundred-year-old tree: "This tree is old and decayed, its bark and leaves have all fallen off. All that remains is what's really real. The Tathāgatha is also like this."[132] In Chan texts, there are many variations on the "dead tree blossoming again," which describes the dynamic nature of no-mind. This poem appears aimed at integrating enlightenment in its individual and cosmological dimensions.

Certainly the Chinese Buddhist poet best known to American readers, and perhaps overall the most famous Chinese poet in the Western world, is the Tang recluse Hanshan (Cold Mountain). The collection attributed to him, E. G. Pulleyblank and other scholars have argued, was in fact by multiple authors from the early to late Tang.[133] Portions of the corpus have been translated at least a dozen times, by such luminaries as Arthur Waley, Gary Snyder, and Burton Watson, and a large number of modern studies of the poems are available.[134] Although the poems make for delightful and often thought-provoking reading, this abundance of interest does not much predate the second half of the twentieth century and is due to considerations other than the collection's centrality to either general Chinese poetry or Chan poetry. In the West, Hanshan's introduction coincided with tumultuous times when his ultimate outsider persona proved highly attractive, while in the People's Republic since 1949 his poetry has inspired scholars looking to discover the traditions of the folk as an alternative to literati culture.[135]

To generalize, there are two axes of difference that can place a poem in the spectrum of Chan poetry: linguistic style and literary function. Linguistic style ranges from "vernacular" (Ch. *tongsu*) to "imagistic" (Ch. *qingjing*, literally "pure realm").[136] "Vernacular" poems, naturally enough, often employ vernacular expressions, but more broadly present material using strong syntax—often complete sentences—with an abundance of personal pronouns and grammatical specifiers. Direct and "talky," such poems tend to explain rather than suggest. A poem attributed to Wang Fanzhi exemplifies the style:

Back before I was born,
It was dark and I knew nothing.
The Heavenly Lord caused me to be born,
But born for what purpose?
Having no clothes makes me cold;
Having no food makes me hungry.
Return me, you Heavenly Lord!
Return me to the time before birth.[137]

The "vernacular" style of language in Chan *shi* poetry grew out of the *gāthā* tradition and is consistent with a general trend in Chinese Buddhist writing to employ direct, vernacular expression.[138] Yet it is in strong contrast to the mainstream style of classical *shi* poetry described in the previous section—spare, undergrammaticalized, and suggestive. Most Chan monk-poets favored the mainstream style, and with the addition of Chan poetic code elements, wrote in an "imagistic" way. That said, the two styles are not mutually exclusive: imagistic Chan poetry might contain some vernacular expressions (orthodox secular poetry also adopted words and phrases from contemporary spoken usage), and vernacular Chan poetry might be interspersed with imagistic, even parallel couplets. Moreover, within the works of individual poets (or in the case of legendary recluses like Hanshan, the poetic corpora attributed to them!), there can be a range of linguistic styles. Thus Qiji (fl. 881), known for his elegant and limpid poetry, could write, "The Big Dao is a big laugh!"[139]

The literary function implicit in Chan poetry is on a continuum from "proselytization" (Ch. *chuan daoqing*) to personal "religious reflection" (Ch. *shu daoqing*). Where a particular poem might fall along it largely depends on audience. Three audiences can be posited: a general audience made up of people of different social and educational levels, who were to be persuaded to follow the teachings and support the monasteries; other monks and masters within the monasteries; and literati patrons and friends. By and large, Hanshan's poems, as well as those by his sometime colleagues Shide and Fenggan and those by Wang Fanzhi, are both "vernacular" and "proselytizing" in order to cater to the general audience. There is some contemporary evidence that they were indeed used in temples for instruction. For all their seeming aloof eccentricity, Hanshan and the others are teachers quite concerned with explaining the tenets of their religion. It is notable that some of their works make mention of karma, evil destinies in reincarnation, and even Buddhist hells—topics seldom mentioned in Chan discourse, which is focused on the attainment of the "pure truth" of enlightenment in the here and now. Poems on such topics can be seen as a form of "expedient means" for those not ready for the higher teachings.

Theoretically, poetry of "religious reflection"—traditional lyric poetry (*shuqing shi*) with religious content—is written for no one but the poet himself. As Northrop Frye writes, "The lyric is the genre in which the poet . . . turns his back on his audience."[140] This is doubtless true for composition, but the poem was also an instrument of communication through communal interpretation. In China, poetry was very often composed and enjoyed in group settings, or shared *ex post facto* to build social and personal relationships. That many poets had one eye open to an audience is undeniable. As for educated readers or hearers, a "message" was acceptable if it was imparted solely through lyric means. Within the monasteries, poetry was clearly a major activity, used in part for proselytizing by masters (e.g., many poems are entitled "Instructions for my disciples" and the like) and proof of spiritual progress by students. Yet most of the "proselytizing" seen here is not the same as that in many works by Hanshan, Wang Fanzhi, and similar poets. There is little attempt to explain. Instead, the poet presents a state of mind, and it is up to the reader or hearer to interpret it correctly. Each poem presents a unified scene, and its integrity is not sacrificed to discursive concerns; the poet's response is integrated with the scene, and a range of meanings and associations becomes evident to the reader/hearer upon interpretive reflection. As these are poems written by Chan adherents for other Chan adherents, there is often a quality of "inside baseball" to them—allusions to the Chan poetic code are frequently included that seem abstruse to us (and doubtless were to many traditional Chinese readers as well). Like encounter dialogues, poetry could be a form of test set by masters to challenge students. Conversely, when students presented their poems for inspection, the master—now a literary critic—would decide whether to assign a passing grade. Due to the premium placed on use of the vernacular in general Buddhist teaching, poems of "religious reflection" by monks often make use of more vernacular expressions than does secular poetry.

As for poems by Chan monks written for the literati audience, these are also mostly imagistic lyrics of religious reflection, though less of the abstruse quality is apparent. The literati were an important source of patronage for the monasteries, so it is no surprise that monks would want to write poetry in the style of the dominant class. Moreover, Chan monk-poets often came from educated families, were actively engaged with scholars and officials, or perhaps merely aspired to educated status—the ability to write "proper" poetry was part and parcel of the Chinese literati identity. Some imagistic lyrics by Chan monks have little or no religious content at all and are indistinguishable from lyrics by the literati.

The poems of Hanshan and like poets were outside the mainstream, certainly in the Tang, and to a lesser extent in the Song and later dynasties.[141] However, we are not traditional readers or critics, and are not bound by their poetic tastes! There is no doubting the energy and life in these poems, as generations of modern readers will attest. Further, the vernacular style is an asset in translation, as alphabetic languages do not feature a significant divide between spoken and written forms as does Chinese, and a personal and colloquial "voice" in poetry is prized. Yet I hope that readers will also appreciate the many imagistic lyrics translated here, for the mainstream secular poetic forms and approaches, with "Chan code" additions, do better reflect the Chan views of language and the world. The explanation of "poetry of the selfless realm" provided previously applies to Chan poetry in general, but Chan imagistic lyrics in particular.

NOTE ON THE TRANSLATIONS

My object in compiling this anthology has been twofold: to present accurate and readable translations of representative Chan poems (the majority of which have not been translated before) and to provide full context for their interpretation, because apparent simplicity belies a complex ideology and approach to language. The Chan poetic code was a relatively stable and distinct form of communication; thus interpretation of a particular poem can be aided immensely by comparative analysis. The poetic code carries over into encounter dialogues, which are now recognized as literary products. It follows that the approach used to interpret Chan poems could fruitfully be used to illuminate these dialogues. Poetry was not just an ancillary Chan practice, it was central.

The annotations to the poems in the following anthology section, as well as introductions to the monk-poets, are arranged at the back of the book according to the poem numbers, rather than inserted as endnotes and indicated by superscript numbers within the texts. This is to allow readers to experience the poems unmediated, and form their own interpretations. Then they may turn to the detailed information at the back for more nuanced context. The poet introductions and notes are presented only as starting points for approaching the poems and are not intended to be standard or comprehensive explanations. Many key images and ideas recur in multiple poems; in such cases, a note is provided at first occurrence. The general index will serve as a finding aid.

Chinese *shi* poetry is unfailingly regular, and many of the translations mimic the original four-line or eight-line forms. English/American poetry is not regular in the same ways, and readers unfamiliar with Chinese poetry may find such consistency monotonous in a long anthology, particularly since the range of themes and styles in Chan poetry is relatively narrow. Further, to always use line length as the criterion for dividing a text may obscure subtler rhythms and patterns that are intrinsic to the original poem's integrity. Thus I have aimed for variety in the translations as much as possible. Poetry in English does not often rhyme these days, but Chinese classical poetry always does. Translation anthologies that consistently present Chinese poetry in loose, informal "free verse" provide an inaccurate impression of the original works. A "middle way" has been adopted for this book. Some poems are presented in rhyme, or even doggerel if a highly "vernacular" style is present in the original. The majority of translations are in free verse, but I have endeavored to distinguish them by linguistic style: a "talky," informal quality is suitable for some vernacular poems, while imagistic poems call for more austere, elegant, and structured language. Chinese lines have frequently been broken into two or three in translation, to make for better scanning in English. There is a rationale for this. As mentioned previously, Chinese poetic lines contain caesurae — minor pauses between words. The pentasyllabic line naturally breaks into a 2/3 rhythm; the heptasyllabic line breaks into 4/3 and can further be subdivided into 2/2/3. Poets use the lines in various ways, sometimes employing continuous syntax, other times juxtaposing discrete images. Whether to translate a heptsayllabic line, say, into a single line of English, or two or three, depends on the specific case. Finally, there are internal structures built into various Chinese poetic forms that should be reflected in some way in translations. Parallelism translates fairly well, but larger patterns also should be taken into account, like the functional difference among couplets in a *lüshi,* rhyme schemes, or the tonal prosodic alternation present in *jinti shi.* These deep structures give a poem a sense of completeness and integrity to the Chinese reader. Although a specific structure may not be easily translatable, often it is possible to create a structure in English that fulfills the same purpose. For example, in numerous translations regular patterns of line lengths are employed to reflect all but the next-to-last line of the original, where the pattern is varied. This practice is on the principle that a rhythmic pattern, then a break in the pattern, and finally a return to it is an effective way to create closure. Repetition alone does not do this, for it imparts the expectation that the pattern will continue indefinitely.

NOTES

1. On the lyric sense in the Chinese arts, see Kao, "Chinese Lyric Aesthetics."
2. Foulk, "Myth, Ritual, and Monastic Practice," esp. 220–221.
3. On this topic, see Wright, "The Discourse of Awakening"; and Faure, *Chan Insights and Oversights,* 195–242.
4. McRae, "Encounter Dialogue," esp. 339–330.
5. McRae, *Seeing Through Zen,* 78. See also Berling, "Bringing the Buddha down to Earth"; and Yanagida, "The 'Recorded Sayings' Texts."
6. From his *Shimen Wenzi Chan* (Literary Chan of Shimen), ch. 25; cited in Zhou Yukai, *Chanzong yu shige,* 54.
7. For example, the first chapter of *Daodejing* [The Way and Its Power] begins, "The Dao that can be spoken is not the eternal Dao." Confucius shows his impatience with language in *Analects* 17: "Heaven does not speak; yet the four seasons run their course thereby, the hundred creatures, each after its kind, are born thereby. Heaven does no speaking!" Translation from Waley, *The Analects,* 214.
8. Liu, *Language — Paradox — Poetics,* 56.
9. Translation from Watson, *Chuang Tzu,* 302. In contrast to the traditional Chinese position, some modern philosophers and critics see the metaphoricity of language as an insurmountable obstacle to a "correct" reading of a literary text, due to the variable and arbitrary nature of signifiers and their referents; for a comparison of traditional Chinese and modern views, see Tang, "Literary Interpretation."
10. A few Buddhist nuns and other women of the Tang dynasty appear in Chan sources, and there is evidence of large numbers of nuns in the Song, yet only a small number of their poems are extant; see Hsieh, "Images of Women"; and Levering, "Miao-tao and Her Teacher Ta-hui." A greater number of poems by eminent Ming and Qing dynasty nuns

are extant; see Grant, "Through the Empty Gate" and *Eminent Nuns*. Grant's *Daughters of Emptiness* is an anthology of poems by Buddhist nuns from all periods.

11.   For an overview, see Williams and Tribe, *Buddhist Thought*.

12.   Williams, *Mahāyāna Buddhism*, 4. This section closely follows Williams's comprehensive synthesis.

13.   Williams, *Mahāyāna Buddhism*, 9.

14.   On original and early Buddhism, see Conze, *Buddhist Thought in India*, 31–116; and Williams and Tribe, *Buddhist Thought*, 1–95.

15.   Williams, *Mahāyāna Buddhism*, 3.

16.   Williams, *Mahāyāna Buddhism*, 14–15.

17.   Conze, *Buddhist Thought in India*, 69–79.

18.   Conze, *Buddhist Thought in India*, 34–79.

19.   Williams, *Mahāyāna Buddhism*, 16–20.

20.   Williams, *Mahāyāna Buddhism*, 19–20.

21.   Williams, *Mahāyāna Buddhism*, 49–54, 185–214.

22.   This four-phase scheme follows Conze, *Prajñāpāramitā Literature*; cited by Williams, *Mahāyāna Buddhism*, 41.

23.   In China, the *Platform Sūtra of the Sixth Patriarch* defined it as "arriving at the other shore"; McRae, *Platform Sutra*, 42.

24.   Williams, *Mahāyāna Buddhism*, 42–49.

25.   Williams, *Mahāyāna Buddhism*, 62.

26.   Conze, "Ontology," 127.

27.   Conze, "Ontology," 126.

28.   Williams, *Mahāyāna Buddhism*, 55–76; quote 69.

29.   Conze, *Buddhist Thought in India*, 238–249; quote 249.

30.   Williams, *Mahāyāna Buddhism*, 77–85; quote 85.

31.   Williams, *Mahāyāna Buddhism*, 86–93.

32.   Williams, *Mahāyāna Buddhism*, 96–102.

33.   Williams, *Mahāyāna Buddhism*, 96–192; quote 101.

34.   Conze, *Buddhist Thought in India*, 233.

35.   Williams, *Mahāyāna Buddhism*, 167–184.

36.   Conze, *Buddhist Thought in India*, 229. See also Williams, *Mahāyāna Buddhism*, 120–127.

37.   Williams, *Mahāyāna Buddhism*, 121.

38.   Gómez, "Selected Verses," lxxxi; quoted in Williams, *Mahāyāna Buddhism*, 121.

39.   Williams, *Mahāyāna Buddhism*, 122–123.

40.   On the sinicization of Buddhism, see Ch'en, *Chinese Transformation*; and Zürcher, *Buddhist Conquest*.

41.   Hakeda, *Awakening of Faith*, 5; see also note 4, 107. On the importance of the text in East Asian Buddhism, see also Williams, *Mahāyāna Buddhism*, 109–112.

42. Hakeda, *Awakening of Faith*, 28. Subsequent quotes in this section marked with page numbers are from this source.

43. The *locus classicus* for the term is the *Sūtra on the Perfection of Wisdom Spoken by Mañjuśri*, wherein it says that it means to take the *dharmadhātu* as an object [in meditation]; see Faure "One-Practice Samādhi," 100. For the range of meditation practices in early Chinese Buddhism, see Donner, "Sudden and Gradual"; Stevenson, "Four Kinds of Samādhi"; and Sponberg, "Meditation."

44. Donner, "Sudden and Gradual," 212. See also Hakeda, *Awakening of Faith*, 100–102.

45. Williams, *Mahāyāna Buddhism*, 111–112.

46. See also Hershock, *Chan Buddhism*.

47. McRae, *Seeing Through Zen*, 3.

48. McRae, *Seeing Through Zen*, 1–11; quote 8.

49. McRae, *Seeing Through Zen*, 7–11. A comparison of early Chan texts reveals that the basic lineage changed repeatedly before settling into its standard form in the *Transmission of the Lamp of the Jingde Period* (compiled 1004). Differences and additions in subsequent anthologies in the Song and later dynasties suggest that lineage remained fluid as individuals and groups vied for inclusion. See Yampolsky, *Platform Sutra*, 1–57; Foulk, "Myth, Ritual, and Monastic Practice."

50. McRae, *Seeing Through Zen*, 13.

51. For example, it is difficult to reconcile the Japanese legend that long years of meditation caused Bodhidharma's arms and legs to wither and fall off (represented in the popular Daruma-san roly-poly dolls) with the Chinese legend that he founded the Shaolin style of *gongfu* martial arts!

52. McRae, *Seeing Through Zen*, 13, 15–17, 22–28.

53. McRae, *Seeing Through Zen*, 28–31.

54. McRae, *Seeing Through Zen*, 32–33; quote 33. On the Bodhidharma legacy, see also McRae, *Northern School*.

55. Bielefeldt, *Dōgen's Manuals*, 1. A short, clear survey of Japanese scholarship on Early Chan is found in Yampolsky, "New Japanese Studies." See also Zeuschner, "Selected Bibliography"; and Heine, "A Critical Survey."

56. McRae, *Seeing Through Zen*, 17–18, 33–36. See also Chappell, "Fourth Ch'an Patriarch."

57. McRae, *Seeing Through Zen*, 36–44; quote 40. See also Chappell, "Fourth Ch'an Patriarch"; McRae, *Northern School*; and Faure, *Will to Orthodoxy*.

58. McRae, *Seeing Through Zen*, 45–53; quote 49. See also McRae, *Northern School*; and Faure, *Will to Orthodoxy*.

59. See Lai, "Tao-sheng's Theory"; and Bielefeldt, *Dōgen's Manuals*, 78–106.

60. Williams, *Mahāyāna Buddhism*, 134–136.

61. Gómez, "Purifying Gold," 78–79.

62. McRae, *Seeing Through Zen*, 54–56; quoted phrases 54.

63. One recent collection is wholly devoted to the gradual/sudden controversy; see Gregory, ed., *Sudden and Gradual*. See also McRae, *Northern School*; and Faure, *Will to Orthodoxy* and *Rhetoric of Immediacy*.

64. Gómez, "Purifying Gold," 79–86.

65. On this topic, see Zeuschner, "The Concept of *li nien*."

66. Yanagida, "Sudden Awakening," 19.

67. For example, the *Treatise of the Five Upāya* directly addresses any potential charge of quietism, relegating to the path of the arhat those who become "attached to immobility and abolish the six awarenesses to experience the *nirvāṇa* of emptiness and quietude"; see Faure, *Will to Orthodoxy*, 43–44.

68. For complete translations, see Yampolsky, *Platform Sutra*; and McRae, *Platform Sutra*.

69. Oxhead Mountain near modern Nanjing in Jiangsu was the major center of the school, thus the name. For a study of its history and thought, see McRae, "Ox-head School."

70. McRae, *Seeing Through Zen*, 56–69.

71. McRae, *Platform Sutra*, 46. Subsequent quotes in this section marked with page numbers are from this source.

72. McRae, *Seeing Through Zen*, 40–44.

73. See Faure, "One-Practice Samādhi"; quote 110. The term in the *Platform Sutra* is the same as *yixing sanmei* in the *Awakening of Faith*, yet the interpretation differs.

74. Though the absolutist position on sudden/gradual enlightenment became Chan orthodoxy, moderate thinkers like Guifeng Zongmi (780–841) described a range of intermediate approaches and called for a harmony of scholastic teachings with Chan practice; see Gregory, "Sudden Enlightenment Followed by Gradual Cultivation," *Inquiry Into the Origin of Humanity*, and *Tsung-mi*. Similar balance is seen in Song Chan; see Gimello, "Mārga and Culture." Faure, *Rhetoric of Immediacy*, demonstrates that there was always a wide gap between Chan rhetoric and behavior.

75. The Dunhuang text has two versions of Huineng's poem, both of which differ slightly from this, the standard version.

76. McRae, *Seeing Through Zen*, 60–65. See also Demiéville, "Mirror of the Mind"; Gómez, "Purifying Gold," 71–96; McRae, "Ox-head School" and *Northern School*.

77. From *The Discourse Records of Layman Pang* (Pang Jushi yulu), ch. 1, X69n1336, 131a.

78. McRae, *Seeing Through Zen*, 74–100; *Northern School*, 91–97. See also Berling, "Bringing the Buddha down to Earth"; Yanagida, "The 'Recorded Sayings' Texts"; and Jin, *Hongzhou School*.

79. McRae, *Seeing Through Zen*, 113.

80. Foulk, "Myth, Ritual, and Monastic Practice," 150, 153; see also Faure, *Chan Insights and Oversights*, 129–154.

81. Faure, *Chan Insights and Oversights*, 148.

82. Seven such texts were produced between 952 and 1252, and others followed in the dynasties after the Song.

83. McRae, *Seeing Through Zen*, 107–118; Weinstein, *Buddhism Under the T'ang*.

84. See Yanagida, "Li-tai fa-pao chi."

85. Lai, "Sinitic Mandalas."

86. Buswell, "The 'Short-cut' Approach," 338–343.

87. This is the so-called "naturalist heresy"; see Faure, *Rhetoric of Immediacy*, 59–63; *Chan Insights and Oversights*, 264–266.

88. See Kieschnick, *The Eminent Monk*.

89. The patronage of the elite was a key factor underlying Chan success in the Song. On this topic, see Welter, *Monks, Rulers, and Literati*.

90. See Weidner, ed., *Cultural Intersections*.

91. Foulk, "Myth, Ritual, and Monastic Practice," 147–151, quote 149; Huang, "Elite and Clergy."

92. Foulk, "Myth, Ritual, and Monastic Practice," 150.

93. See Yifa, *Buddhist Monastic Codes*; and Collcutt, "Early Ch'an Monastic Rule." For descriptions of the physical layout and organization of Chinese monasteries, see Foulk, "Myth, Ritual, and Monastic Practice"; Hammond, "Beijing's Zhihua Monastery"; and PripMøller, *Chinese Buddhist Monasteries*. The Chinese hierarchized system of imperially sponsored monasteries, called the Five Mountains and Ten Temples, also became a model for Japanese Buddhism.

94. Faure, *Rhetoric of Immediacy*.

95. T47n1998, 886, from *Dahui Pujue chanshi yulu*, ch. 17.

96. Schlütter, "Silent Illumination"; Buswell, "The 'Short-cut' Approach"; McRae, *Seeing Through Zen*, 126–133.

97. Bielefeldt, *Dōgen's Manuals*, 102.

98. Bielefeldt, *Dōgen's Manuals*, 100.

99. Bielefeldt, *Dōgen's Manuals*, 100.

100. Schlütter, "Silent Illumination," 112. See also McRae, *Seeing Through Zen*, 133–138.

101. Schlütter, "Silent Illumination," 116–126; quote 119. Schlütter, *How Zen Became Zen*, is a comprehensive analysis of the Song controversy.

102. Bielefeldt, *Dōgen's Manuals*, 99.

103. Bielefeldt, "Ch'ang-lu Tsung-tse's *Tso-Ch'an I*," 129. There are significant differences between Cao-Dong and Sōtō approaches to meditation; see Bielefeldt, *Dōgen's Manuals*.

104. For an extended discussion of the pitfalls encountered when Chinese Chan is viewed through Japanese Zen or Western stereotypes, see Faure, *Chan Insights and Oversights*.

105. Iriya, "Chinese Poetry and Zen," 60–61; Zhou Yukai, *Chanzong yu shige*, 26–33.

106. Like the "Song Confirming the Way" attributed to Yongjia Xuanjue (665–713) in the *Record of the Transmission of the Lamp Composed in the Jingde Period*; for a translation, see Lu, *Ch'an and Zen Teaching*, vol. 3, 103–145. See also Lu's versions of the forty transmission *gāthās* of the buddhas and patriarchs, vol. 2, 25–53.

107. Text from Zhou Yukai, *Chanzong yu shige,* 129.

108. *QTS,* 23: 815.9179, 816.9185, 816.9195.

109. Nielson, "Chiao-jan," 22.

110. For a translation and analysis of Yan Yu's poetry criticism, see Owen, *Readings,* 391–420.

111. See Zhou Yukai, *Chanzong yu shige,* 128–146; Lynn, "Yan Yu and the Later Tradition" and "Examination of the Ch'an-Poetry Analogy."

112. *QTS* 23: 816.9187.

113. Translated in Tu, "Some Aspects of the *Jen-chien tz'u-hua,*" 27.

114. Good introductions to Chinese poetry are Liu, *Art of Chinese Poetry;* Cheng, *Chinese Poetic Writing;* and Cai, *How to Read Chinese Poetry.* Kao and Mei, "Syntax, Diction, and Imagery" and "Meaning, Metaphor, and Allusion" provide more detailed explanations of poetic language.

115. For example, Ye Mengde (1077–1148) writes, "In recent times many priests have taken up the study of poetry, yet all lack a spirit of detached understanding; they for the most part gather up the phrases other writers have discarded and model their own poems after them. Though they still manage a style of their own of sorts, their diction is notoriously vulgar. People say their verse 'savors of sour bean-paste'"; quoted in Iriya, "Chinese Poetry and Zen," 64. See also Zhou Yukai, *Chanzong yu shige,* 45–53.

116. Frye, *Anatomy of Criticism,* esp. 71–128.

117. See Frankel, *Flowering Plum.*

118. Buswell, "The 'Short-cut' Approach," 334.

119. Buswell, *Korean Approach to Zen,* 164; see also "The 'Short-cut' Approach," 335.

120. Faure, *Chan Insights and Oversights,* 162; see also his general discussion of space and place, 155–174.

121. McRae, *Platform Sutra,* 66.

122. Buswell, "The 'Short-cut' Approach," 335; and *Korean Approach to Zen,* 164.

123. From *Mohe banruo boluomi jing* 1, T8n223, 217; and *Da Zhidu lun* 6, T25n1509, 102. Translations from Schmidt, *Yang Wan-li,* 79.

124. From *Jingde Chuandeng lu* 7, T51n2076, 253

125. Forms related to musical tunes are significant exceptions.

126. Chang, "Description of Landscapes," 109.

127. Frodsham, "Chinese Nature Poetry," 72. See also his *Murmuring Stream.*

128. *QTS* 4: 126.1274–1275.

129. Gao, *Tang Song shi juyao,* 750.

130. On this topic vis-à-vis Western poetry, see Herrnstein-Smith, *Poetic Closure.*

131. Watson, *Chuang Tzu,* 36.

132. From *Da Niepan jing* 39, T12n374, 597; translated in Henricks, *Poetry of Han-shan,* 224.

133. Pulleyblank, "Linguistic Evidence"; see also Chi-yu Wu, "A Study of Han-shan."

134. Examples include Waley, "27 Poems by Han-shan"; Snyder, "Cold Mountain Poems" and *Riprap*; Watson, *Cold Mountain*; Henricks, *Poetry of Han-shan*; Red Pine, *Collected Songs of Cold Mountain*; and Hobson, *Poems of Hanshan*. Japanese translations include Iriya, *Kanzan*; and Iritani and Matsumura, *Kanzan shi*. Hanshan poems are often featured in Chan/Zen poetry anthologies, such as Stryk and Ikemoto, *Crane's Bill* and *Let the Spring Breeze Enter*; Red Pine and O'Connor, *Clouds Should Know Me by Now*; Seaton and Maloney, *Drifting Boat*; and Hamill and Seaton, *Poetry of Zen*.

135. For a comprehensive chronological list of modern Chinese studies of Chan poetry through 2001, see Wu Yansheng, *Chanzong shige jingjie*. Wu has been particularly influential in Chan poetry studies in China, while Tu Sung-po (Du Songbo) has been very active in Taiwan. There has also been a surge in the number of Chinese anthologies of Chan poetry in recent years, though many are of mixed quality. Some of the interest appears to have been sparked by Hanshan's enormous popularity in the West. In this connection we might cite Sun Ch'i's (Sun Qi) 1974 book, which carries the engaging title *Hanshan yu xipi* (Hanshan and the Hippies)!

136. The terms are borrowed from Zhou Yukai, *Chanzong yu shige*, 40.

137. Chinese text from Zhou Yukai, *Chanzong yu shige*, 41.

138. See Mair, "Script and Word." Chan "encounter dialogues" are a particularly good example. As they are presented as records of oral communication, the vernacular is used consistently.

139. *QTS* 24: 842.9507.

140. Frye, *Anatomy of Criticism*, 271; see also 4–5. This is Frye's restatement of John Stuart Mill, who wrote in "What is Poetry?" (1833), "Eloquence is heard, poetry is overheard. Eloquence supposes an audience; the peculiarity of poetry appears to us to lie in the poet's utter unconsciousness of a listener." See Mill, *Essays on Poetry*, 12.

141. When the great literatus Ji Yun (1724–1805), general editor of the massive *Complete Books of the Four Treasuries*, offered an assessment of monk-poets of the Tang, he did not even mention Hanshan: "There were many Tang monks who wrote poetry. In quality none can surpass Jiaoran, Qiji, and Guanxiu. However, Jiaoran is a bit weak, and Guanxiu is a bit common. Qiji must be considered the best." These three poets wrote imagistic lyrics, as their works conform to contemporary ideas about the nature of poetry, while still addressing Chan content. From Ji Yun's preface to a thirteenth-century anthology, *Tangseng hongxiu ji*, in *Sibu congkan*, vol. 1356.

Poems

Tang Dynasty (618–907)

AND Five Dynasties (907–960)

1 |

He's always been with me,
    but I don't know his name;
We just follow fate together
    and go on like this, that's all.
From olden days till now
    even sages have not seen —
How could the common crowd in a muddled age
    hope to understand?

從來共住不知名。任運相將祇麼行。自古上賢猶不識。造次凡流豈可明。
— SHITOU XIQIAN 石頭希遷 (700-790)

2 | THE GRASS HUT SONG

I built a hut of grass—
It has no jewels or treasure;
After lunch, I think I'll take a little nap.
When new, the grass thatch looked fresh;
Now it's old, and more grass patches up the holes.

The dweller in the hut
Has always been here,
Not in the center, not inside, not outside.
Where people of the world would dwell, I will not dwell;
What people of the world would love, I do not love.

This hut is small,
But contains the world;
The old man in the tiny room has come to understand.
Great bodhisattvas believe without a doubt,
But when lesser beings hear it, they think it strange.

You ask:
Is this hut falling down?
Whether it falls or not, the original master is here.
Not south, north, east, or west—
To have a firm foundation is the most important thing.

Beneath green pines,
Within bright windows,
Jade palaces and red mansions cannot compare.
Head muffled in my cassock, ten thousand things stop;
The mountain monk is then aware of nothing.

Why live in this hut?
No need to explain;
I'm not talking up prayer mats to sell you.
Shine the reflections back, and return home;
Open to the divine root, and never turn away.

Meet patriarchs and teachers,
Take their lessons to heart;
Weave thatch to build a hut, and never leave again.
Spend a lifetime just following change,
And then wave your hand and go without regret.

A thousand words,
Ten thousand explanations;
I just want to tell you not to be ignorant.
If you wish to meet the deathless one within the hut,
He's no different from this skin bag here and now.

草庵歌

吾結草庵無寶貝。飯了從容圖睡快。成時初見茆草新。破後還將茆草蓋。
住庵人、鎮常在。不屬中間與内外。世人住處我不住。世人愛處我不愛。
庵雖小、含法界。方丈老人相體解。上乘菩薩信無疑。中下聞之必生怪。
問此庵、壞不壞。壞與不壞主元在。不居南北與東西。基上堅牢以為最。
青松下、明窗内。玉殿朱樓未為對。衲帔幪頭萬事休。此時山僧都不會。
住此庵、休作解。誰誇鋪席圖人買。迴光返照便歸來。廓達靈根非向背。
遇祖師、親訓誨。結草為庵莫生退。百年拋卻任縱橫。擺手便行且無罪。
千種言、萬般解。只要教君長不昧。欲識庵中不死人。豈離而今遮皮袋。
— SHITOU XIQIAN 石頭希遷 (700-790)

3 |

My mind is like the autumn moon,
As fresh and pure as a jade pond.
But nothing really compares with it —
Tell me, how can I explain?

吾心似秋月。碧潭清皎潔。無物堪比倫。教我如何說。
— HANSHAN 寒山 (TANG DYNASTY)

4 |

Water clear in the jade stream;
Moonlight white over Cold Mountain.
Through wordless knowing, my spirit shines;
I watch the void, and the world becomes calm.

碧潤泉水清。寒山月華白。默知神自明。觀空境逾寂。
—HANSHAN 寒山 (TANG DYNASTY)

5 |

My home lies below green cliffs,
In a yard full of weeds I never mow.
New vines hang down, tangled and coiled;
Old stones stand up, lofty and sheer.
Mountain fruits—the monkeys grab them;
Fish in the pool—caught in white egrets' beaks.
Immortal books, just one or two,
I read beneath a tree

mumble, mumble

家住綠巖下。庭蕪更不芟。新藤垂繚繞。古石豎巉巖。
山果獼猴摘。池魚白鷺銜。仙書一兩卷。樹下讀喃喃。
—HANSHAN 寒山 (TANG DYNASTY)

6 |

Were you a fool in a past incarnation?
You won't now be reaching illumination.
Do you suffer, these days, from want and strife?
It's all due to doings in some past life.
If, in this life, you don't make a change,
Then, in the next life, it will all be the same.
There's no boat, on this shore nor the other;
Vast, vast—it's hard to cross over.

生前大愚癡。不為今日悟。今日如許貧。總是前生作。
今生又不修。來生還如故。兩岸各無船。渺渺難濟渡。
—HANSHAN 寒山 (TANG DYNASTY)

7 |

my joy is the Everyday Way,
by misty vines, in caves of stone.

wild feelings—I've let them loose!
I drift along in the company of clouds.

there's a road that doesn't reach the world;
there's no-mind—how can one ascend?

on a stone couch I sit alone at night;
the round moon rises on Cold Mountain.

自樂平生道。煙蘿石洞間。野情多放曠。長伴白雲閒。
有路不通世。無心孰可攀。石床孤夜坐。圓月上寒山。
—HANSHAN 寒山 (TANG DYNASTY)

8 |

there's a chamber in my home,
and not one thing is in it.
pure, clean, stately in emptiness,
shining, glittering, as bright as day.
vegetable fare supports my paltry body;
a leather-lined coat covers my illusory substance.
let a thousand sages appear before you—
I have the True Buddha!

余家有一窟。窟中無一物。淨潔空堂堂。光華明日日。
蔬食養微軀。布裘遮幻質。任你千聖現。我有天真佛。
—HANSHAN 寒山 (TANG DYNASTY)

9 |

when recluses slip this human world,
most go to sleep in the mountains.

green vines are sparse but unyielding;
emerald streams murmur without cease.

high they soar in peaceful joy;
vast their thoughts, so pure and unhurried.

avoiding all stain of worldly things,
their hearts as tranquil as white lotus.

隱士遁人間。多向山中眠。青蘿疏麓麓。碧澗響聯聯。
騰騰且安樂。悠悠自清閒。免有染世事。心靜如白蓮。
— HANSHAN 寒山 (TANG DYNASTY)

10 |

Even monkeys can be taught;
Why do people lack the zeal?
When the Lead Cart's in a ditch,
Shouldn't Back Cart turn its wheels?
If you don't see that this is true,
An evil death may come to you.
Carry on, you'll be a yakṣa;
Change, and be a bodhisattva!

獼猴尚教得。人何不憤發。前車既落阬。後車須改轍。
若也不知此。恐君惡合殺。此來是夜叉。變即成菩薩。
— SHIDE 拾得 (TANG DYNASTY)

11 |

no going
no coming
at root transparent

not inside
nor outside
but in the center

a pure crystal
without flaw

brightness reaches out
beyond man and heaven

無去無來本湛然。不居內外及中間。一顆水精絕瑕翳。光明透滿出人天。
—SHIDE 拾得 (TANG DYNASTY)

12 |

The old buddha road is overgrown;
Fools reach it, but still are lost.

Since old karma is heavy,
They can never know the way.

To understand nirvāṇa's rule,
Strip your mind bare.

After bitter study in many lives,
You'll see the Master of Paradise.

古佛路凄凄。愚人到卻迷。只緣前業重。所以不能知。
欲識無為理。心中不掛絲。生生勤苦學。必定睹天師。
—SHIDE 拾得 (TANG DYNASTY)

13 |

a steep mountain path — long, far;
a treacherous pass — ten thousand rods high.

by Stone Bridge, covered in green moss,
flying white clouds are sometimes seen.

waterfalls float like silk;
the moon's image falls on a shining pond.

I climb even higher, to the summit of Hua Peak,
and wait for the lone crane to come.

　　迢迢山徑峻。萬仞險隘危。石橋莓苔綠。時見白雲飛。
　　瀑布懸如練。月影落潭暉。更登華頂上。猶待孤鶴期。
　　— SHIDE 拾得 (TANG DYNASTY)

14 | WRITTEN ON THE WALL

At root there is not a single thing,
And no dust that can be brushed away.
If you can understand to this point,
No need to sit straight-backed!

　　壁上詩

　　本來無一物。亦無塵可拂。若能了達此。不用坐兀兀。
　　— FENGGAN 豐干 (TANG DYNASTY)

15 |

I saw the man die,
And my guts were hot like fire.
It's not that I cared about the man —
I was scared I'd be next.

我見那漢死。肚裏熱似火。不是惜那漢。恐畏還到我。
— WANG FANZHI 王梵志 (CA. SEVENTH CENTURY)

16 |

I drowned in the Three Evil Ways,
Was carried off by Demons of Ignorance.
In startled dread, my body suddenly died;
Suddenly: lackeys of Fate's Judge held me thrall.
They bound me behind, and cudgeled me forward
Across the No-Hope River.
They dragged me face down before the court,
And flailed me all over to make me stand.

On the seventh day after my death,
My sentence was set: Tortured Ghost.
Oxhead demons impaled me with steel forks;
Hell's minions stabbed me with knives.
Smashed in a mortar and ground in a mill,
Over and over I lived and died.
In torment I lost my mind,
With no way to see my home.

My wife is now another man's wife;
My son heeds a second father.
The servant waits on the brand-new bridegroom;
The maid follows the second-time bride.
My team of horses wears golden saddles
With carved stirrups and silver traces,
But the horn bow has no master to pull it,
And a treasured sword is thrown in the dirt.

After the hundred days of mourning are over,
Your family forgets all about you.
Money and goods—other people get them;
From of old it's a common tale.
Those who come before scrimp and save,
Those who come after have no shame.

Thus it is that the goods-hoarding slave
Meets his poor and miserable death.

> 沉淪三惡道。負持愚癡鬼。荒忙身卒死。即屬伺命使。
> 反縛棒驅走。先渡奈河水。倒拽至廳前。枷棒遍身起。
> 死經一七日。刑名受罪鬼。牛頭鐵叉杈。獄卒把刀掇。
> 碓擣磑磨身。覆生還覆死。撩亂失精神。無由見家裏。
> 妻是他人妻。兒被後翁使。奴事新郎君。婢逐後娘子。
> 馴馬被金鞍。鏤鐙銀鞦轡。角弓無主張。寶劍拋著地。
> 設卻百日齋。渾家忘卻你。錢財他人用。古來尋常事。
> 前人多貯積。後人無慚愧。此是守財奴。不免貧窮死。
> —WANG FANZHI 王梵志 (CA. SEVENTH CENTURY)

17 |

Living beings are blockheads
Dwelling forever in lightless holes.
In their hearts, only deceit and lies;
In their mouths, fake prayers to Buddha.

> 眾生頭兀兀。常住無明窟。心裏唯欺謾。口中佯念佛。
> —WANG FANZHI 王梵志 (CA. SEVENTH CENTURY)

18 |

I have a word to say:
Stop thinking, and forget causation.
Clever talk won't get it,
Only mind transmission.

> 吾有一言。絕慮忘緣。巧說不得。只用心傳。
> —WANG FANZHI 王梵志 (CA. SEVENTH CENTURY)

19 |

The melancholy of worldly things
Can't match the hills and mountains,

Where green pines hide the sun
And jasper streams flow long.
Mountain clouds are my tent,
The night moon is my fishing hook;
I sleep beneath wisteria,
My pillow a block of stone.
I don't look up to the Son of Heaven—
Why should I envy lords and kings?
Life and death with no worries;
What sadness could there be?

世事悠悠。不如山丘。青松蔽日。碧澗長流。山雲當幕。夜月為鉤。
臥藤蘿下。塊石枕頭。不朝天子。豈羨王侯。生死無慮。更復何憂。
— WANG FANZHI 王梵志 (CA. SEVENTH CENTURY)

20 | OLD RIVERMAN

Quiet is the home of the old riverman;
River birds fly in and out the door.
Arising early
    he goes off fishing;
In deep night
    the moon lights the way home.
Wild rice ripens
    under fragrant dew;
Floating heart grows plump
    in warm mist.
Light-spirited and free, beyond all dust,
He wears a straw raincoat in a tiny boat.

谿叟

谿叟居處靜。谿鳥入門飛。早起釣魚去。夜深乘月歸。
露香蔬米熟。煙煖荇絲肥。瀟灑塵埃外。扁舟一草衣。
— JINGYUN 景雲 (CA. 715-770)

21 | NEW WELLSPRING AT YIFENG TEMPLE

A new spring wells up;
Light clouds shine through.

Gently, it drops to a lotus pond;
Lines of moss slowly sink from view.

Its simplicity unites my empty thoughts;
Its purity greater than other streams.

On any night of clear moonlight
I hear it rippling in my dreams.

宜豐新泉

泉源新湧出。洞澈映纖雲。稍落芙蓉沼。初淹苔蘚文。
素將空意合。淨與眾流分。每到清宵月。泠泠夢裏聞。
—LINGYI 靈一 (728-762)

22 | WRITTEN AT A MONASTERY

A placid moon leads me across Tiger Stream;
Vines and lichens trail from snowy pines.
Countless green mountains, my journey almost done;
In a deep place of white clouds, so many old monks.

題僧院

虎溪閒月引相過。帶雪松枝挂薜蘿。無限青山行欲盡。白雲深處老僧多。
—LINGYI 靈一 (728-762)

23 | DRINKING TEA AT GREEN MOUNTAIN POND WITH LAYMAN YUAN

A rustic spring, a little fire,
amid white clouds;

We sit and drink fragrant tea,
admiring this mountain.

Below the cliff our boat is tied,
but we can't bear to leave;

Flowing water in a green stream
murmurs at dusk.

與元居士青山潭飲茶

野泉煙水白雲間。坐飲香茶愛此山。巖下維舟不忍去。青溪流水暮潺潺。
—LINGYI 靈一 (728-762)

24 | WRITTEN AT EASTERN HERMITAGE

the road twists and turns
to the monk's Chan cell;

clear forest shade
opens to the sun.

cold bamboo shadows
encroach upon the pathway stones;

autumn wind sounds
reach the sūtra-chanting terrace.

calm clouds, untethered,
grow and shrink as they will;

tame birds, without motive,
come and go as they please.

best of all,
we discuss mysteries before a sliver sun,

heedless of the night bell
urging our return.

題東蘭若

上人禪室路裵回。萬木清陰向日開。寒竹影侵行遶石。秋風聲入誦經臺。
閒雲不繫從舒卷。狎鳥無機任往來。更惜片陽談妙理。歸時莫帶暝鍾催。
— LINGYI 靈一 (728-762)

25 | CLOUDS ON THE STREAM

Stretching and curling to what purpose?
Twining around the stream and belting the void above.
You have form, but are not an encumbered thing;
Following the wind, leaving no trace behind.
Don't blame me for always pursuing you:
Floating without roots, you're just like me.

溪雲

舒卷意何窮。縈流復帶空。有形不累物。無跡去隨風。
莫怪長相逐。飄然與我同。
— JIAORAN 皎然 (730-799)

26 | LODGING ON AN AUTUMN NIGHT
AT BROKEN MOUNTAIN TEMPLE

falling leaves in the autumn wind
cover the empty mountain;

a sputtering lamp in an ancient temple
on a cliff of stone.

the passersby of former days
have all gone away;

chill clouds each night
fly back alone.

秋晚宿破山寺

秋風落葉滿空山。古寺殘燈石壁間。昔日經行人去盡。寒雲夜夜自飛還。
— JIAORAN 皎然 (730-799)

27 | SENDING OFF MONK WEILIANG
ON HIS RETURN TO DONGTING LAKE

this lake,
always famed among people;

for love of distant floating clouds,
you return alone.

a lone moon in an empty sky
reveals the mind ground;

boundless waters —
mountains in a mirror.

送維諒上人歸洞庭

從來湖上勝人間。遠愛浮雲獨自還。孤月空天見心地。寥寥一水鏡中山。
— JIAORAN 皎然 (730-799)

28 | ACCOMPANYING VICE CENSOR-IN-CHIEF LU ON A LEISURELY RAMBLE TO A MOUNTAIN TEMPLE

A rustic temple
beyond the human realm;

Leaving the boat,
we climb to the distant peak.

The forest thins,
revealing the bright moon;

In countless ravines,
we calmly hear the bell.

Holding candles
brightens the jade hills;

Touching water
shakes the reflections.

How can we hope
to remain together?

Beyond the dust
we will meet again.

陪盧中丞閒遊山寺

野寺出人境。捨舟登遠峰。林開明見月。萬壑靜聞鐘。
擁燭明山翠。交麾動水容。如何股肱守。塵外得相逢。
—JIAORAN 皎然 (730-799)

29 | EARLY AUTUMN IN TONGLU, WISHING TO RETURN HOME; SENT TO MONK DAOYAN

Autumn comes early on the Tong River;
I miss the days on my old mountain.

quiet nights, wind rang the bell;
no people, bamboo swept the courtyard.

gibbons came to touch the clear water;
birds flew down to peck the cold pears.

I should be about my task—
The homeward heart has its time.

早秋桐廬思歸示道諺上人

桐江秋信早。憶在故山時。靜夜風鳴磬。無人竹掃墀。
猿來觸淨水。鳥下啄寒梨。可即關吾事。歸心自有期。
— JIAORAN 皎然 (730-799)

30 | FLOATING ALONE ON WEST STREAM

How can I send feelings of the Dao?
In a plain skiff on the broad stream.

True Nature loves the soaring crane;
The Nameless longs for wild mountains.

Passing through cold, a lush grove of bamboo;
Entering quiet, scattered clouds at leisure.

Floating, floating, who is my companion?
Only the moon responds, and returns home with me.

西溪獨泛

道情何所寄。素舸漫流間。真性憐高鶴。無名羨野山。
經寒叢竹秀。入靜片雲閒。泛泛誰為侶。唯應共月還。
— JIAORAN 皎然 (7 3 0 - 7 9 9)

31 | CASE REVIEWER TANG HOSTS CHAN MASTER JUE AT HENGSHUI PAVILION

Friends in the mountains, meetings few;
On a bright morning we gather at the river hall.

snow clears: jade needles on the pine trees;
mist warms: green tendrils of healing herbs.

silently we face a crane from Immortal Isle;
leisurely we read books from ancient temples.

Cherish the one who knocks at the barrier —
Ultimate Truth in a profound mind.

湯評事衡水亭會覺禪師

山侶相逢少。清晨會水亭。雪晴松葉翠。煙暖藥苗青。
靜對滄洲鶴。閑看古寺經。應憐叩關子。了義共心冥。
— JIAORAN 皎然 (7 3 0 - 7 9 9)

32 | HEARING THE BELL

At the ancient temple on Cold Mountain,
A distant bell rises on a strong wind.
The sounds linger, the moonlit trees stir;
The echoes fade, the frosted sky empties.
Ringing through the long night
In the mind realm of a Chan monk.

聞鐘

古寺寒山上。遠鐘揚好風。聲餘月樹動。響盡霜天空。
永夜一禪子。泠然心境中。
— JIAORAN 皎然 (730-799)

33 | INSTRUCTING MAHĀYĀNA MONKS IN MY CELL SOUTH OF THE LAKE

The nirvāṇa shore I haven't found
For vain love of a boat unbound.
Thoughts that East Mount clouds convey
At year's end: still far, far away.

湖南蘭若示大乘諸公

未到無為岸。空憐不繫舟。東山白雲意。歲晚尚悠悠。
— JIAORAN 皎然 (730-799)

34 | MEETING RAIN AT A BUDDHIST TEMPLE

still, still that Empty Gate
draining my body;

mild, mild the stream rain
washing travelers' dust away.

I lie down and face white clouds,
and this feeling remains;

let others have their yellow birds
drunk with fragrant spring.

精舍遇雨

空門寂寂淡吾身。溪雨微微洗客塵。臥向白雲情未盡。任他黃鳥醉芳春。

—QINGJIANG 清江 (FL. 766-804)

35 |

From a round mirror as bright as day,
Wisdom shines out without obstruction.
In Sanskrit, it's pāramitā;
In the language of Tang, infinite meaning.
Those who speak of it speak of marklessness;
Those who realize it leave words behind.
As soon as you mention the peerless Way,
You help others, and also help yourself.
If you can enter into this truth,
Without moving, you'll reach the buddha land.
The phenomenal world is but a trifle —
It's better to stretch out your legs and sleep.

圓鏡朗如日。涌出無礙智。梵語波羅蜜。唐言無量義。
說者說無相。離者離文字。但說無上道。利他還自利。
若能入理行。不動到如地。緣事常區區。不如展腳睡。

—PANG YUN 龐蘊 (LAYMAN PANG) (?-815)

36 |

Kill the guardians of the body;
When all are dead, you will dwell in peace.
If you can understand this point,
Then iron boats will float upon the water.

護身須是殺。殺盡始安居。會得個中意。鐵船水上浮。

—PANG YUN 龐蘊 (LAYMAN PANG) (?-815)

37 |

Sit straight-backed to seek the Buddha Dharma,
And the Dharma will move far away from you.
Abandon Dharma, and grasp it with no-mind,
And then it will be like coming home.
Through nonseeking escape the Three Realms;
To have thoughts is to be a fool.
If you seek the Buddha and search for transcendence—
You're no master!

端坐求如法。如法轉相違。拋法無心取。始自卻來歸。
無求出三界。有念則成癡。求佛覓解脫。不是丈夫兒。
—PANG YUN 龐蘊 (LAYMAN PANG) (?-815)

38 |

In the mountains I lost my mind,
Followed my nature, and let my words soar.
The words I speak are of the empty void,
Where there are no snakes or rats.
Have mind, and passion waves will rise;
No mind, and it's the Pure Land.
The Pure Land gives birth to True Buddha,
And Buddha transmits Buddha words.
The Buddha can save all living beings;
Living beings are the mother of Buddha.

山中失卻心。任運騰騰語。語即說空空。空中無蛇鼠。
有心波浪起。無心是净土。净土生真佛。佛還傳佛語。
佛能度眾生。眾生是佛母。
—PANG YUN 龐蘊 (LAYMAN PANG) (?-815)

39 |

A pondful of lotus:

    I'll never lack for clothes.

Acres of pine flowers:

    more than enough to eat.

But worldly men have found this dwelling—

Once more I move my hut

        deeper

        into

        mountains

一池荷葉衣無盡。數畝松花食有餘。剛被世人知住處。又移茅屋入深居。

—DAMEI FACHANG　大梅法常 (752-839)

40 | BEES AT THE WINDOW

The door is open,

    but you won't go out;

Smacking against the window—

    such foolishness!

A hundred years of stabbing at old paper;

When will you poke your heads through?

窗蜂

空門不肯出。投窗也大癡。百年鑽故紙。何日出頭時。

—GULING SHENZAN　古靈神贊 (FL. NINTH CENTURY)

41 | LOOKING FOR A RECLUSE BUT NOT FINDING HIM

I asked a boy beneath a pine tree;

He said, "Master has gone to pick herbs

Right here on this mountain . . ."

Clouds thick, whereabouts unknown.

尋隱者不遇

松下問童子。言師採藥去。只在此山中。雲深不知處。
— JIA DAO 賈島 (BUDDHIST NAME WUBEN 無本) (779-843)

42 | QUATRAIN

In the ocean deep is a moon as bright
And round as the wheel in the sky.
If I could have an inch of its light,
I'd buy a thousand miles of spring.

絕句

海底有明月。圓於天上輪。得之一寸光。可買千里春。
— JIA DAO 賈島 (BUDDHIST NAME WUBEN 無本) (779-843)

43 | LODGING AFTER RAIN ON
    ADJUTANT LIU'S POND

Blue Stream: an autumn rush of jade;
Water here clear as it rises.

Reed sounds join the rain;
Lotus fragrance circles my lamp.

Above the bank, an ancient Qin road;
Facing the hall, a ruined Han tomb.

Quietly imagine the source of the spring
Falling down hidden cliffs, how many?

雨後宿劉司馬池上

藍溪秋漱玉。此地漲清澄。蘆葦聲兼雨。芰荷香遶燈。
岸頭秦古道。亭面漢荒陵。靜想泉根本。幽崖落幾層。
— JIA DAO 賈島 (BUDDHIST NAME WUBEN 無本) (779-843)

44 | DRIFTING ON SOUTH STREAM WITH DIRECTOR HAN OF THE BUREAU OF APPOINTMENTS

We leave late from the pondside
    and drift into the stream,
Hearing the autumn rush of a stone spring
    in the dark night below.
Above the magnolia boat
    and the mountain men:
Moonlight on the ford,
    clouds scatter to and fro.

和韓吏部泛南溪

溪裏晚從池岸出。石泉秋急夜深聞。木蘭船共山人上。月映渡頭零落雲。
— JIA DAO 賈島 (BUDDHIST NAME WUBEN 無本) (779-843)

45 | TRAVELING TO A MOUNTAIN TEMPLE

A thousand-peak road
winds to an end;

This temple in the trees—
did it once have a name?

Step by step
enter the mountain shadows;

From room to room
hear the sound of water.

For many years
men's traces gone;

Lingering brightness
clear on icy rocks.

I could find a dwelling here,

And in peace and leisure
pass this life away.

遊山寺

千峰路盤盡。林寺昔何名。步步入山影。房房聞水聲。
多年人跡斷。殘照石陰清。自可求居止。安閒過此生。
—WUKE 無可 (CA. 780-845)

46 | SENT TO MONK YUAN AT QINGLONG TEMPLE

I slow my steps,
and enter cold bamboo;

Quiet meditation:
clepsydra sounds pass by.

From a tall pine,
the last cone falls;

In the deep well,
ice traces grow.

Chimes come to an end;
branches move in the wind;

Lamps are hung;
the room is bright in snow.

When will you summon me for a visit?

By moonlight I'll climb
to your mountain temple.

寄青龍寺原上人

斂屨入寒竹。安禪過漏聲。高杉殘子落。深井凍痕生。
罷磬風枝動。懸燈雪屋明。何當招我宿。乘月上方行。
—WUKE 無可 (CA. 780-845)

47 | CHRYSANTHEMUMS

By the east fence, after quake and fall,
Delicate beauty is roused by the cold.

Pressed by rain, alarmed by desolation,
After enduring frost, suddenly you bloom.

Rustic fragrance fills travelers' sleeves;
Palace buds float in imperial cups.

Spring orchid cannot compare:
Butterflies drift in from afar.

菊

東籬搖落後。密豔被寒催。夾雨驚新拆。經霜忽盡開。
野香盈客袖。禁蕊泛天杯。不共春蘭並。悠揚遠蝶來。
—WUKE 無可 (CA. 780-845)

48 | SENDING OFF A MONK

Within the four seas, no ties to bind you;
Wandering is your heart's delight.

A hundred years —
    three cassocks;
Ten thousand miles —
    a single walking staff.

Night lessens the shadows
    of clear day;
Spring melts the traces
    of past snow.

Gone to a place deep in white clouds —
Who knows which peak is your home?

送僧

四海無拘繫。行心興自濃。百年三事衲。萬里一枝筇。
夜減當晴影。春消過雪蹤。白雲深處去。知宿在何峰。
— WUKE　無可 (CA. 780-845)

49 |

In the thirty years
    that I searched for the sword,
How often the fallen leaves
    sprouted anew on the branches!
But ever since I saw
    the blossoms of peach,
From then until now —
    not one doubt.

三十年來尋劍客。幾回落葉又抽枝。自從一見桃花後。直至如今更不疑。
— LINGYUN ZHIQIN　靈雲志勤 (FL. NINTH CENTURY)

50 |

No searching for him outside,
Lest he move far, far away from me.
Now that I go my way alone,
I meet him everywhere!
Now he is exactly me,

But I am not now he!
Understanding should be this way,
To accord with True Suchness.

切忌從他覓。迢迢與我疏。我今獨自往。處處得逢渠。
渠今正是我。我今不是渠。應須恁麼會。方得契如如。
—DONGSHAN LIANGJIE 洞山良价 (807-869)

51 |

Green mountain is white cloud's father;
White cloud is green mountain's son.
All day white cloud stays close by;
Green mountain never knows.

青山白雲父。白雲青山兒。白雲終日倚。青山總不知。
—DONGSHAN LIANGJIE 洞山良价 (807-869)

52 | LIVING IN THE MOUNTAINS

I watch the empty yard at evening—
Mind to mind, the masters' truth is revealed.

Mist rises, separating summit colors;
Rain falls, muting sounds of the spring.

Gibbons cry lingeringly in distant trees;
Sunlight shines suddenly on serried cliffs.

A thought even more worth discussing:
New bamboo is sprouting beneath the trees!

山居八詠二

晚望虛庭物。心心見祖情。煙開分嶽色。雨霧減泉聲。
遠樹猿長嘯。層巖日乍明。更堪論的意。林下筍新生。
—CHANGDA 常達 (D. 874)

53 | LIVING IN THE MOUNTAINS

At an ancient temple, I lean on a balcony rail,
And hear the Wondrous Function rise.

In the empty courtyard, the pure color of moon;
As night advances, chime sounds move.

The water clock turns: cold watches ring faster;
Lamps sputter: cool flames die away.

The Primordial Void and the Ten Thousand Things
Are telling each other the Mysterious Secret.

山居八詠六

古寺憑欄危。時聞舉妙機。庭空月色淨。夜迴磬聲移。
漏轉寒更急。燈殘冷焰微。太虛同萬象。相謂話玄微。
—CHANGDA 常達 (D. 874)

54 | LIVING IN THE MOUNTAINS

From master to master, a single thought:
The long warm days of spring.

Sedge grass green under clearing frost;
Herbs fragrant in a gentle wind.

The moon full: the purity of thusness;
Flowers bloom: perfume of the bodhi tree.

In the courtyard, where orioles call,
I hear, at times, perfect words.

山居八詠八

祖祖唯心旨。春融日正長。霜輕莎草綠。風細藥苗香。
月滿真如淨。花開覺樹芳。庭前鶯囀處。時聽語圓常。
— CHANGDA 常達 (D. 874)

55 | LOOKING FOR THE MOUNTAIN MONK ZHENSHENG
BUT NOT FINDING HIM

A Chan hut beneath a pine;
Moss lush, paths indistinct.

Green mountains:
    seen at spring's end;
Flowing water:
    heard in deep night.

He's not sitting
    on a gaze-at-the-mind rock;
Perhaps he's followed
    roused-from-concentration clouds?

Monkeys and apes can't be asked where he is:
Cliffs and valleys alone in empty twilight.

尋山僧真勝上人不遇

松下禪栖所。苔滋徑莫分。青山春暮見。流水夜深聞。
不坐看心石。應隨出定雲。猿猱非可問。巖谷自空矄。
— QIBAI 栖白 (FL. 847-860)

56 |

In this world, I wander free,
A wild monk 'midst humanity.
Let them all laugh and call!
My spirit soars where'er I be.

宇内為閑客。人中作野僧。任從他笑我。隨處自騰騰。

—ZHANGZHOU LUOHAN HESHANG 漳州羅漢和尚 (FL. 860-874)

57 |

On top of a hundred-foot pole,
    a man unmoved;
Though he's entered somewhere,
    it's not real.
On top of a hundred-foot pole
    take a step forward;
Then: everywhere in the ten directions
    is your whole body.

百丈竿頭不動人。雖然得入未為真。百丈竿頭須進步。十方世界是全身。

—CHANGSHA JINGCEN 長沙景岑 (D. 868)

58 | FISHERMAN

Wind cruel, waves wild,
    but his body is at ease;

Head covered in frost and snow,
    his back to green mountains.

We meet, and I ask, "Where is your home?"

He turns and points to cottages
    among the flowering reeds.

漁者

風惡波狂身似閒。滿頭霜雪背青山。相逢略問家何在。回指蘆花滿舍間。

—GUANXIU 貫休 (832-912)

59 | MEETING AN OLD MONK IN DEEP MOUNTAINS

a cassock of coarse threads
　　a mind of moonlike kind;
a short mattock in his hand
　　to hew the sticks he finds.
by dark stones on the streamside
　　over fallen leaves he goes;
a few wisps of cloud
　　trail two brows of snow.

深山逢老僧

衲衣線粗心似月。自把短鋤鋤榾柮。青石溪邊踏葉行。數片雲隨兩眉雪。
—GUANXIU　貫休 (832-912)

60 | LIVING IN THE MOUNTAINS

The mind of the mind of the mind
　　is not past sound and sight;
In a stone room on a high peak
　　my hair hangs loose.
I raise bamboo, but never pull
　　shoots growing in the road;
I love pines, and leave the branches
　　that hinder other men's way.
Burning incense, reading books—
　　clouds rise from the steps;
Raising the curtain, dispelling thought—
　　the moon is on the pond.
So many old friends,
　　their hair all white,
I wonder
　　how they are today?

山居

心心心不住希夷。石屋巉岊白髮垂。惜竹不除當路筍。愛松留得礙人枝。
焚香開卷霞生砌。卷箔冥心月在池。多少故人頭盡白。不知今日又何之。
—GUANXIU 貫休 (832-912)

6l | HEARING THE NEW CICADAS; SENT TO GUIYONG

New cicadas
    call through the night,
Cheep, cheep
    on the stream's far bank.
The cuckoo
    adds voice to the din—
Can you hear it,
    my old friend?
I raise the blinds,
    and flowers shake the moon;
I close my eyes,
    and steps give rise to clouds.
In the end,
    we will fade away and go,
To the western mountain
    where phoenix and crane gather.

聞新蟬寄桂雍

新蟬終夜叫。喓喓隔溪瀆。杜宇仍相雜。故人聞不聞。
捲簾花動月。冥目砌生雲。終共謝時去。西山鸞鶴群。
—GUANXIU 貫休 (832-912)

62 | EVENING WATCH

At sunset, as blue river stills,
A fresh, slow lotus roundelay.

To find the place where flowers grow,
Follow the moon across the bay.

晚望

落日碧江靜。蓮唱清且閒。更尋花發處。借月過前灣。
—GUANXIU 貫休 (832-912)

63 | OLD FRONTIER SONG

Battlefield bones ground into dust
Fly into soldiers' eyes.
Yellow clouds turn suddenly black:
Wailing ghosts of war are forming ranks.
Evil winds howl on the great desert,
Bugles urgent, but we dare not go out!
Who will stand before the Son of Heaven
And sing *this* frontier fortress song?

古塞下曲

戰骨踐成塵。飛入征人目。黃雲忽變黑。戰鬼作陣哭。
陰風吼大漠。火號出不得。誰為天子前。唱此邊城曲。
—GUANXIU 貫休 (832-912)

64 | FISHING AT ZENG DEEP

Quiet scene, clear river—a peaceful time;
Red flag and painted boat shake the fishing cliff.

The mind reaches its time, like the passing of spring;
The sun sets, but must wait for the cranes to return.

Wind breaks up the colored clouds, revealing a mountain temple;
Boatmen sing "White Snow" as blossoms fly on the island.

I wish I were on that boat of immortals—
Jade waves splash up, wetting our grass robes.

釣罾潭

境靜江清無事時。紅旌畫鷁動漁磯。心期只是行春去。日暮還應待鶴歸。
風破綺霞山寺出。人歌白雪島花飛。自憐亦在仙舟上。玉浪翻翻濺草衣。
— GUANXIU　貫休 (832-912)

65 | NIGHT RAIN

The night rain soaks grass on the hill,
Where fresh wind blows in dead trees.
Slowly I chant an Indian sage's prayer—
Purer than jade, its clarity.

夜雨

夜雨山草溼。爽籟雜枯木。閒吟竺仙偈。清絕過于玉。
— GUANXIU　貫休 (832-912)

66 | STAYING OVERNIGHT AT THE YANLING FISHING TERRACE

Cold valley, ruined terrace,
Seven-mile Shoal;

Worthies still follow
the river's eastward flow.

A lone gibbon's cry
cracks moon in dark sky;

Gloom in pondside autumn trees
from a thousand years ago.

宿嚴陵釣臺

寒谷荒臺七里洲。賢人永逐水東流。獨猿叫斷青天月。千古冥冥潭樹秋。
—SHENYING 神穎 (FL. 860-873)

67 | STAYING AT DAOLIN TEMPLE;
SENT TO CHAN MASTER YUELU

Before the gate,
    a stone road crosses the central peak;
Tree shadows and stream sounds
    hang in an empty sky.
Search: you will not find—
    you'll labor high and low;
Walk: it's not there—
    you'll weary of east and west.
The roots of my beard
    all white as a lone cloud;
The traces of my mind
    all forgotten in a crescent moon.
I will long remember
    this high window on a summer day,
Old pine and green cypress
    in an afternoon wind.

道林寺居寄岳麓禪師二首一

門前石路徹中峰。樹影泉聲在半空。尋去未應勞上下。往來殊已倦西東。
髭根盡白孤雲並。心跡全忘片月同。長憶高窗夏天裏。古松青檜午時風。
—QIJI 齊己 (FL. 881)

68 | OLD PINE

Thunder and lightning don't dare to topple you;
Scales and wrinkles—power over ten thousand things.

Wood grubs die in your wasted joints;
Snakes coil in your rotten roots.

A shadow is cast, soaking a monk's meditation;
A sound carries, chilling a dream of cranes.

On any night of wind and rain,
Ghosts and spirits must be watching.

古松

雷電不敢伐。鱗皴勢萬端。蠹依枯節死。蛇入朽根盤。
影浸僧禪逕。聲吹鶴夢寒。尋常風雨夜。應有鬼神看。
— QIJI 齊己 (FL. 881)

69 | BOAT WINDOW

In a lonely boat, I lean on a quiet window;
Clear waves draw near and cool my face.

Raising my head, still there are obstructions;
Lowering my head, no obstacles at all.

A passing glimpse of shorebird green;
A breaking up of reflected sunset glow.

When will I reach the mountain temple,
And from a high hall see this river land?

船窗

孤舸憑幽窗。清波逼面涼。舉頭還有礙。低眼即無妨。
瞥過沙禽翠。斜分夕照光。何時到山寺。上閣看江鄉。
— QIJI 齊己 (FL. 881)

70 | CLOSE THE DOOR

No worries about outside matters,
I deaden my heart, and close the door alone.

No one comes to ask after me;
White day becomes yellow dusk again.

The lamp attracts shadows of flying moths;
The window melts traces of scattered snow.

Within my mind, brightness comes of itself—
A single line of the patriarchs' words.

閉門

外事休關念。灰心獨閉門。無人來問我。白日又黃昏。
燈集飛蛾影。窗銷迸雪痕。中心自明了。一句祖師言。
—QIJI 齊己 (FL. 881)

71 | WRITTEN AT A HERMITAGE IN ZHENZHOU

In the heart of the waves, a fine temple,
The far shore is in bloom!

No tall trees obstruct the eyes;
Before the door, only distant sands.

Travelers from the sea join our morning meals;
Fishermen's homes are reached by the evening bell.

Autumn waves calm in the stone cauldron;
After meditation, there is mountain tea.

題真州精舍

波心精舍好。那岸是繁華。礙目無高樹。當門即遠沙。
晨齋來海客。夜磬到漁家。石鼎秋濤靜。禪回有岳茶。
— QIJI 齊己 (FL. 881)

72 | WHITE LOTUS AT DONGLIN

A bodhisattva is born in Tuṣita Heaven;
An empty pond is filled with white lotus.
Autumn wind blows under a bright moon,
On fast days before the Portrait Hall.
Past color: the many flowers fall;
Rare fragrance: Baihe incense smolders.
Who understands that unsullied nature
Grows in a fertile mind ground?

題東林白蓮

大士生兜率。空池滿白蓮。秋風明月下。齋日影堂前。
色後群芳拆。香殊百和燃。誰知不染性。一片好心田。
— QIJI 齊己 (FL. 881)

73 | RAIN ON A SUMMER DAY; SENT TO A FRIEND
IN ADMINISTRATIVE SERVICE

A north wind blows down a summer rain;
Light bamboo rustles by the southern hall.

It's cool lying on my pillow of bean pods;
Lotus Peak enters my dreaming soul.

Raindrops scatter through the windows;
Rushing streams have left tracks in the yard.

This pure joy knows no bounds —
The clearing sky comes to say a word.

夏日雨中寄幕中知己

北風吹夏雨。和竹亞南軒。豆枕敧涼冷。蓮峰入夢魂。
窗多斜迸溼。庭遍瀑流痕。清興知無限。晴來示一言。
—QIJI 齊己 (FL. 881)

74 | AMUSING MYSELF

I know it's all a dream;
After awakening, what need to strive?

I die, and ascend the lonely peak;
Ashes fly as the fire burns out.

When clouds are gone, empty blue appears;
When the heavens are still, the moon flows by.

Save me from crowds of disciples
Like those that mourn at Stone Monk's grave!

自遣

了然知是夢。既覺更何求。死入孤峰去。灰飛一燼休。
雲無空碧在。天靜月華流。免有諸徒弟。時來弔石頭。
—QIJI 齊己 (FL. 881)

75 | FACING SNOW

delicate, dense:
    falling in silence
    from the jasper void.

whirling, swirling:
    dancing in harmony
    with the light wind.
the recluse chants and stares
    at the place he'll find the words:
they float in the window
    and drop down on his inkstone.

對雪

密密無聲墜碧空。霏霏有韻舞微風。幽人吟望搜辭處。飄入窗來落硯中。
—ZILAN 子蘭 (FL. 889-904)

76 | EVENING SCENE

Lotus in the pond fades and falls,
chrysanthemums bloom;

Leaning on a staff, chanting poems,
I climb to my grass room.

Evening clouds that filled my eyes
roll away with the wind;

From a cold trumpet at the tribunal hall —
a few long notes ascend.

晚景

池荷衰颯菊芬芳。策杖吟詩上草堂。滿目暮雲風卷盡。郡樓寒角數聲長。
—ZILAN 子蘭 (FL. 889-904)

77 | STAYING OVERNIGHT AT A MOUNTAIN TEMPLE
      AT QINGYUAN GORGE

A temple close to the rising road;
The jangle of belt stones is often heard.

Through reflection, we open the wisdom eye;
Homing birds rest in the heart of Chan.

Chimes meet the dawn on the Starry River;
My window joins the shade of summer trees.

Here I can sit quietly—
No need for forests and clouds.

宿清遠峽山寺

寺近朝天路。多聞玉佩音。鑒人開慧眼。歸鳥息禪心。
磬接星河曙。窗連夏木深。此中能宴坐。何必在雲林。
—SHANGYAN 尚顏 (LATE NINTH CENTURY)

78 | HERDBOY

The ox is caught, and freely you ride;
Light rain flies in the spring wind.
In green mountains and green grass,
One flute and one straw raincape.
The sun rises, and you go out singing;
The moon bright, and clapping hands, you return.
How could anyone be like you?
Not "real" and not "not real."

牧童

牛得自由騎。春風細雨飛。青山青草裏。一笛一蓑衣。
日出唱歌去。月明撫掌歸。何人得似爾。無是亦無非。
—QICHAN 棲蟾 (FL. LATE NINTH CENTURY)

79 | ROADS

South, north, east, and west they go,
Limitless dust for ten thousand ages.
At pass and river, no ending place;
In wind and snow, traveling men.
Over towering heights, the mountains reach Shu;
Across great plains, the land enters Qin.
You who restlessly seek fame and profit—
This coming and going, when will it cease?

路

南北東西去。茫茫萬古塵。關河無盡處。風雪有行人。
險極山通蜀。平多地入秦。營營名利者。來往豈辭頻。
—XUANBAO 玄寶 (TANG DYNASTY: NO DATES)

80 | OLD PLUM TREE

Tortured by fire
   harassed by wind
      roots drowned by water;
Frost cracks you
   snow shrivels you
      old moss leaves tracks.
But east wind submits
   to neither chill nor heat:
Again comes clear fragrance
   as the soul returns.

古梅

火虐風饕水漬根。霜皴雪皺古苔痕。東風未肯隨寒暑。又藁清香與返魂。
—ANONYMOUS MONK 無名釋 (TANG DYNASTY)

81 | DEATH GĀTHĀ

My road lies beyond the blue sky,
Where white clouds roam as they please.
A rootless tree grows in the universe —
Yellow leaves are cast back by the breeze.

遺偈

我路碧空外。白雲無處閑。世有無根樹。黃葉風送還。
— SHUSHAN KUANGREN 疏山匡仁 (FL. LATE NINTH TO EARLY
TENTH CENTURIES)

82 | PEONIES

Dazzling peony,
    beloved of spring,
Half-reclines on the red balustrade
    and waits to bloom.

Under heaven, no flower can compare;
Among men, only nobles are fitting company.

Stealing fragrance: black ants creep
    slanting through the leaves;
Espying blossoms: golden bees hang
    inverted from the stems.

A mind awakened to Chan will not be moved,
But the youth of Wuling may be driven mad.

牧丹

三春堪惜牧丹奇。半依朱欄欲綻時。天下更無花盛此。人間偏得貴相宜。
偷香黑蟻斜穿葉。覷蕊黃蜂倒挂枝。除卻解禪心不動。算應狂殺五陵兒。
— LINGQUAN GUIREN 靈泉歸仁 (FL. TENTH CENTURY)

83 | SENT TO AN ELDER MONK ON THE FAN RIVER

A face so thin
that cheekbones jut out;

A countenance covered
in wisps of hanging snow.

You sit on a rock,
and birds believe you're dead;

You go out the door,
and people call you fool.

The pond reflecting your body
reaches Chu in the south;

The cypress that drenches your shadow
grew in Sui times.

The planet Taibai
has crossed the summer sky;

Clear wind
cools your four limbs.

贈樊川長老

瘦顏顴骨見。滿面雪毫垂。坐石鳥疑死。出門人謂癡。
照身潭入楚。浸影檜生隋。太白曾經夏。清風涼四肢。
—KEZHI 可止 (859-934)

84 | WORDS OF CRITICISM

A gold fleck in the eye clouds vision;
A pearl in a robe is only dust on Dharma.

If you don't value your own spirit,
Who are buddhas and patriarchs to you?

褒貶句

金屑眼中翳。衣珠法上塵。己靈猶不重。佛祖為何人
—YUNMEN WENYAN 雲門文偃 (864-949)

85 | THE MIND SEAL

I ask you:
what is the "mind seal"?

Who would ever dare
to give it or receive it?

The tranquility of countless eons
is nothing other than this,

But call it the mind seal
and soon it's just empty talk.

You should know that truth
arises from the empty nature,

Like a lotus in the fire
of a red-hot brazier.

Don't just call out "no-mind"
and say it's the Dao:

Between the Dao and no-mind
there are still many barriers.

心印

問君心印作何顏。心印何人敢授傳。歷劫坦然無異色。呼為心印早虛言。
須知本自虛空性。將喻紅爐火裏蓮。莫謂無心云是道。無心猶隔一重關。
—TONG'AN CHANGCHA 同安常察 (D. 961)

86 | REACHING THE ROOT

You must not serve the Void King
while still on the road:

Lean on your staff,
and strive to reach home!

When clouds and waters block the way,
stay not there;

The hidden place in Snowy Mountains
cannot be forgotten.

Remembering past days,
my face like jade;

Sighing as I return,
my sidelocks like frost.

I reach home, and wave my hand—
but no one knows me,

And I have not a single thing to offer
in the ancestral hall.

達本

勿於中路事空王。策杖還須達本鄉。雲水隔時君莫住。雪山深處我非忘。
尋思去日顏如玉。嗟歎迴來鬢似霜。撒手到家人不識。更無一物獻尊堂。
—TONG'AN CHANGCHA 同安常察 (D. 961)

87 | RETURNING TO THE SOURCE

Return to the root, come back to the source —
still incomplete!

The origin is nowhere to dwell,
and nothing to call "home."

Pine paths, ten thousand years old,
are covered by deep snow;

Belts of peaks and hills
lie hidden in the clouds.

When both guest and host are silent,
perfect delusion;

When the ways of lord and vassal merge,
falsity within truth.

How to sing
a homecoming tune?

In bright moonlight before the hall
a dead tree is in bloom.

還源

返本還源事已差。本來無住不名家。萬年松逕雪深覆。一帶峰巒雲更遮。
賓主穆時全是妄。君臣合處正中邪。還鄉曲調如何唱。明月堂前枯樹華。
—TONG'AN CHANGCHA 同安常察 (D. 961)

88 | MOTIVATING POWER

The city of Nirvāṇa
is still far above you;

To reach it by road or path
there's no set time.

For a time you hang up a dirty robe,
and call it "Buddha,"

But set a jeweled emperor in place —
what name would be left for him?

The wooden man at midnight
pulls on his boots and leaves;

The stone girl at dawn
puts on her hat and returns.

In the jade pool of ten thousand ages,
the moon of the Empty Realm:

Over and over scoop it up,
and you will understand.

迴機

涅槃城裏尚猶危。陌路相逢沒定期。權挂垢衣云是佛。卻裝珍御復名誰。
木人夜半穿靴去。石女天明戴帽歸。萬古碧潭空界月。再三撈漉始應知。
—TONG'AN CHANGCHA 同安常察 (D. 961)

89 | ONE REALITY

In front of Deadwood Mountain,
so many forks in the road;

Arriving travelers stumble
and cannot go on.

White egrets standing in the snow
are not the same color;

The bright moon and rush blossoms
do not look alike.

When I know, know, know—
there's nothing that I know;

Where it's deep, deep, deep—
reject the deep place.

Give your all
in singing this song of mystery:

Is it merely a moonbeam
plucked out of space?

一色

枯木巖前差路多。行人到此盡蹉跎。鷺鷥立雪非同色。明月蘆華不似他。
了了了時無可了。玄玄玄處亦須訶。殷勤為唱玄中曲。空裏蟾光撮得麼。
—TONG'AN CHANGCHA 同安常察 (D. 961)

Song Dynasty (960–1279)

I've practiced measureless Chan,
    studied the boundless Way,
Looked through to the Dharma Body
    hidden in Dipper stars!
But I am old now,
    so broken and weak,
I see you,
    but I've no strength to speak.
Now only my hoe blade
    understands my mind:
Use it once more to tend pines
    up on Diamond Peak.

遺偈

參禪學道莫茫茫。問透法身北斗藏。余今老倒尪羸甚。見人無力得商量。
唯有钁頭知我意。栽松時復上金剛。
— DONGSHAN XIAOCONG 洞山曉聰 (D. 1030)

clouds merge after rain
in half-broken dawn;

surrounding peaks like a painting—
soaring spires of jade.

Subhūti never mastered
sitting in the mountains,

yet he brought heaven's blossoms
down to shake the earth.

　道貴如愚

雨過雲凝曉半開。數峰如畫碧崔嵬。空生不解巖中坐。惹得天花動地來。
—XUEDOU ZHONGXIAN 雪竇重顯 (980-1052)

92 |

wizened face
thin frame
a staff on which to lean—

surely it's Subhūti
stepped out from painted scene.

perceiving void
does not permit
leaving sound and sight:

it's like hearing a lone gibbon's cry
beneath the moon at night.

貌古形疏倚杖梨。分明畫出須菩提。解空不許離聲色。似聽孤猿月下啼。
—JINGTU WEIZHENG 淨土惟政 (986-1049)

93 | ENTERING THE CAPITAL BY BOAT

The Great River flows on without end;
When will we reach the imperial city?
If we are blessed with a cool, fair wind—
Stop paddling those oars!

入京舟中作

長江行不盡。帝里到何時。既得涼風便。休將櫓棹施。
—SHISHUANG CHUYUAN 石霜楚圓 (987-1040)

94 |

Quiet night:
a lone boat rides the wide waves;

Rush flowers on the banks
face the round moon.

Golden scales dive deep into a pool:

For nought will the old fisherman
ply his bamboo pole.

孤舟夜靜泛波瀾。兩岸蘆花對月圓。金麟自入深潭去。空使漁翁執釣竿。
—YUANJIAN FAYUAN 圓鑒法遠 (991-1067)

95 | DEATH GĀTHĀ

I had nothing when I came
    and have nothing as I go,

Like a floating cloud
    crossing the Great Void.

Abandoning this sack of bones and skin,

Is like frost and snow
   entering a red-hot brazier.

遺偈

來時無物去亦無。譬似浮雲過太虛。拋下一條皮袋骨。還如霜雪入洪爐。
—YUANJIAN FAYUAN 圓鑒法遠 (991-1067)

96 | LEAVING THE TEMPLE AND
       DEPARTING FROM MOUNT LU

For ten years a monk on Lu peak,
Today I leave the serried cliffs.

old friends see me off at the riverside;
my lonely crane boat ascends the waves.

the water flows, following the twisting bank;
the sail fills when the wind soars.

To stay or go makes no difference:
Chan monks have ended love and hate.

退院別廬山

十年廬嶽僧。一旦出巖層。舊友臨江別。孤舟帶鶴登。
水流隨岸曲。帆勢任風騰。去住本無著。禪家絕愛憎。
—HUANGLONG HUINAN 黃龍慧南 (1002-1069)

97 | INSTRUCTING CHAN DISCIPLES
AT A HIGH TERRACE ON NANYUE MOUNTAIN

To part the grass and see the wind
    and distinguish true from false,
You must first pluck out
    all the sand from your eyes.
Raise your heads,
    as if tasting Tianhuang's cake;
Empty your minds —
    it's hard to drink Zhaozhou's tea.
Without a word,
    Nanquan returned to his cell;
Lingyun wrote a poem
    when enlightened by peach blossoms.
Explain these to me
    from the beginning:
Let me see the true master
    of the Dharma forest.

南嶽高臺示禪者

撥草占風辨正邪。先須拈卻眼中沙。舉頭若味天皇餅。虛心難喫趙州茶。
南泉無語歸方丈。靈雲有頌悟桃花。從頭為我雌黃出。要見叢林正作家。
—HUANGLONG HUINAN 黃龍慧南 (1002-1069)

98 | PARTING FROM A MONK

when chrysanthemums are sweet
and grass turns bleak,

staves in hand by woodland side
of journeys south we speak.

I know your old mountain
has no gold or jade;

close your brushwood gate alone
and watch the sunset fade.

送僧

黃菊香時綠草衰。杖藜林際話南歸。也知舊岳無金石。獨掩柴門對落暉。
—FACHANG YIYU 法昌倚遇 (1005-1081)

99 | THE FISHERMAN GIVES UP FISHING

When sun shines on green mountains
    melting banks of snow,
A fisherman returns home,
    singing as he goes.
Let others who would chase the waves
    and on the ripples ride,
Take up their long fisher poles
    and watch the ocean tide.

漁人罷釣

日照青山積雪銷。漁人歸去自歌謠。從他逐浪隨波者。時把長竿望海潮。
—FACHANG YIYU 法昌倚遇 (1005-1081)

100 | READING THE *RECORD OF THE TRANSMISSION OF THE LAMP*

Throughout the ninety days of spring,
Roving bees vie for the finest flowers.
When fragrance is all carried to the hive,
To whom do withered petals fall?

讀傳燈錄

九十芳春日。游蜂競採花。香歸蜜房盡。殘葉落誰家。

—BAOJUE ZUXIN 寶覺祖心 (1025-1100)

101 | A NEWLY TRANSPLANTED SUNFLOWER

A lone root still shallow—
　　growth is slow;
One or two stems rise
　　in spring's tranquil glow.
With heart unchanged, it always
　　faces sunlight rays;
Pure fragrance as it was
　　in Shanglin garden days.

新徙葵花

孤根尚淺發生遲。澹泊春光一兩枝。不改寸心長向日。清香還在上林時。

—BAOJUE ZUXIN 寶覺祖心 (1025-1100)

102 | WHITE CLOUD MOUNTAIN ON A SUMMER DAY

Summer days are best in mountain temples;
The joy of rambling—must it ever end?

In a quiet court, long sweet grass;
By steep crags, broken clouds pass.

Cavern water flows, far beyond the portico;
Peak wind blows, strongly to our sitting mats.

Even better—on nights when stars are few,
The moon shines through wisteria and pine.

白雲夏日

夏日宜山寺。優游趣幾何。閑庭芳艸長。危嶺斷雲過。
洞水穿廊遠。岩風入座多。更當星少夜。月色透松蘿。
—BAIYUN SHOUDUAN 白雲守端 (1025-1072)

103 | SUMMER NIGHT

In a pine cottage I finish lonely meditations,
And raise the curtain to enjoy the evening cool.
A graceful moon leans on the green bamboo,
And wordlessly crosses the eastern wall.

夏夜

松室開孤定。褰帷納夜涼。嬋娟依翠竹。無語過東牆。
—MIAOZONG DAOQIAN 妙總道潛 (1043-1106?)

104 | BAMBOO SHOOTS

Cracking through lichens and moss,
Soon towering over a low fence.

Leaves may fall in wind and rain,
But roots stand winter's violence.

Perhaps a phoenix flute, a tune to play
Or a fishing pole—who can say?

If allowed to grow without frustration,
In time you'll see a dragon transformation.

新笋竹

迸破莓苔地。亭亭出短籬。籜隨風雨解。根有歲寒期。

鳳管終須奏。漁竿莫可窺。儼容常守節。定見化龍時。

—KAIFU DAONING 開福道寧 (1053-1113)

105 |

This year spring ends,
another year spring.

Wild grass and hill flowers
are always new.

Sunrise
is not caused
by temple bells and drums;

Moonlight
is not made
for walkers in the night.

一年春盡一年春。野草山花幾度新。天曉不因鍾鼓動。月明非為夜行人。

—YUN'GAI ZHIBEN 雲蓋智本 (1035-1107)

106 | SENDING OFF THE HONORABLE PALACE LIBRARY EDITOR TANG SONGMING ON HIS RETURN TO GUAN STREAM

crisscrossed shadows of cypress and pine,
a twisting, turning road;

returning through clouds,
the tap of your staff sounds cold.

the mountain moon seen every night
in the world of men,

looks different when seen
from rocks above the stream.

寄唐秘校送明長老歸灌溪

松檜交陰路屈盤。穿雲歸去錫聲寒。人間夜夜見山月。不似溪頭石上看。
—YUN'GAI ZHIBEN 雲蓋智本 (1035-1107)

107 | DEATH *GĀTHĀ*

Now at seventy-six,
My earthly ties are done.
In life, no love for heaven;
In death, no fear of hell.
I let go, and lie down
    beyond the Three Realms;
Soaring, soaring free —
    what shackles could there be?

遺偈

吾年七十六。世緣今已足。生不愛天堂。死不怕地獄。
撒手橫身三界外。騰騰任運何拘束。
—FURONG DAOKAI 芙蓉道楷 (1043-1118)

108 | LIVING IN THE MOUNTAINS

High passes of white clouds
    are not for me;
I let go,
    and return to my mountain.

incense from a jade censer
    curls and roils;
water in a stone brook
    burbles and splashes..

courtyard trees
    surrounded in mist;

window frames
    spattered by raindrops.

Walking or sitting still—
Always in tranquility.

山居

不戀白雲關。家山撒手還。玉爐香旖旎。石澗水潺湲。
庭樹煙籠合。窗軒雨灑斑。經行及坐臥。常在寂寥間。
—DANXIA ZICHUN 丹霞子淳 (1064-1117)

109 | LIVING IN THE MOUNTAINS

Fair hills and streams face my window;
Through the year, I come and go alone.

lazily watching white clouds
    rise on jasper peaks;
quietly hearing clear chimes
    fall in murmuring water.

sound enters beyond sound—
    it's easy to distinguish;
but void seems within void—
    it's hard to understand.

This thought cannot be captured;
Let it follow flowing water,
        down to the world of men.

山居

當軒唯有好溪山。卒歲無人共往還。閑看白雲生翠碧。靜聞清磬落潺湲。
聲將聲入分猶易。空以空藏見即難。此箇不能收拾得。任隨流水落人間。
—CHANGLING SHOUZHUO 長靈守卓 (1065-1123)

110 | AFTER HANSHAN

What kind of a thing is existence?
The Wondrous Function flows everywhere.

the spring light clears,
    mountain birds call;
the sun sets,
    clouds return to their caves.

the finger exists,
    and so does the horse;
the mind is not,
    and the Buddha also is not.

Whoever can merge "this" and "that" —
Take my hand, and enter the dark mystery.

擬寒山

有物是何物。周流泄妙機。春晴山鳥語。日暮洞雲歸。
指是馬還是。心非佛亦非。誰能同彼此。攜手入玄微。
— CHANGLING SHOUZHUO 長靈守卓 (1065–1123)

111 | INSTRUCTIONS FOR MY DISCIPLES

If learning the Way
is like guarding imperial walls,

Oppose the six thieves by day!
Be alert once night falls!

But the general of the central army
can issue orders:

Spear and shield shall not be raised
'til peace comes to our borders.

示徒

學道猶如守禁城。晝防六賊夜惺惺。中軍主將能行令。不動干戈治太平。

—XINGKONG MIAOPU 性空妙普 (1071-1142)

112 | DEATH *GĀTHĀ*

To die sitting or die standing,
Can't match death by water.
First, you save on firewood;
Second, no need to dig a hole.
I'll just wave my hand and go—
Joy like this can't be wrong.
Who is it who understands me?
Only the Boatman Monk.
High winds don't last a hundred thousand years;
Few now sing the fisherman's song.

遺偈

坐脫立亡。不若水葬。一省柴燒。二省開壙。撒手便行。不妨快暢。
誰是知音。船子和尚。高風難繼百千年。一曲漁歌少人唱。

—XINGKONG MIAOPU 性空妙普 (1071-1142)

113 | THE TERRACE OF SPREADING CLOUDS
ON MOUNT LINGYAN

Quiet sitting at the root of clouds,
    no wish to raise my head,
Much less do I have any words
    to teach a stream of monks!
Ten thousand forms ranged in the trees
    have clearly said:
Those of you with voices—
    why not hang them on the wall?

靈巖披雲臺

兀坐雲根懶舉頭。更無言句示禪流。森羅萬象分明說。有口何妨挂壁休。

—CISHOU HUAISHEN 慈受懷深 (1077-1132)

114 | WALKING SONG TO INSTRUCT MONKS AT ZIFU TEMPLE

Don't speak of other people's faults and strengths—
You'll talk this way, then that, and just bring disaster.
To close your mouth and hide your tongue
Is the best prescription for cultivation.

資福訓童行頌

莫說他人短與長。說來說去自招殃。若能閉口深藏舌。便是修身第一方。

—CISHOU HUAISHEN 慈受懷深 (1077-1132)

115 | WRITTEN AT KE PAVILION ON WEST LAKE AT HANGZHOU

I'm glad to see
your heart can brave the cold;

I shut the door
and all day face jade bamboo.

When meeting you,
those who lack Xiangyan's eyes.

See only: waving in the wind
and carrying the rain

題杭州西湖可堂

喜見君心有歲寒。閉門終日對琅玕。相逢不具香嚴眼。祇作敲風帶雨看。
—CISHOU HUAISHEN 慈受懷深 (1077-1132)

116 |

Raindrops wash the light pink of tender peach buds;
Breezes sway the pale green of delicate willow shoots.
Strange stones appear in the shadows of white clouds;
Old trees are fresh in the light of green waters.

雨洗淡紅桃蕚嫩。風搖淺碧柳絲輕。白雲影裏怪石露。綠水光中枯木清。
—BAOFENG WEIZHAO 寶峰惟照 (1084-1128)

117 | LEAVETAKING

When the bucket's bottom falls out,
   the great world is boundless;
Where life's root breaks,
   the jade pond is clear.
Take a pinch of snow from this red-hot brazier:
Scatter it among men
   as lanterns shining in the night.

贈別

桶底脫時大地闊。命根斷處碧潭清。好將一點紅爐雪。散作人間照夜燈。
—DAHUI ZONGGAO 大慧宗杲 (1089-1163)

118 | FOR LAYMAN LI

In dead meditation,
   I wash confusion from my breast;
Clear as dew,

a dot of empty light remains.
The dust of the world
    can become the Pure Land;
Every leaf and every blossom
    grows from the divine root.
No-mind
    is like clouds watering the earth;
Enlightenment
    is like moonlight destroying darkness.
Expansive or reductive, this or that —
    the method depends on me;
Each of us
    can reach the Dhāraṇī Gate.

與李居士

枯禪胸底洗餘紛。一點虛明湛若存。刹刹塵塵成淨土。華華葉葉發靈根。
無心頗肖雲為潤。有照渾如月破昏。舒卷縱橫俱在我。箇人真得總持門。
—HONGZHI ZHENGJUE 宏智正覺 (1091–1157)

119 | SENDING OFF MONK HUI UPRIVER
TO BUY HEMP AND RICE

Reed flowers under the bright moon,
    vast river waters;
Like a swift arrow, your sailing boat
    shatters the cold light.
When you arrive in Luling
    and pay the price of rice,
Then open your lips to speak —
    you'll be exactly right.

送慧禪人往上江糴麻米

蘆華明月水茫茫。激箭風舟破冷光。親到廬陵酬米價。那時開口便相當。
—HONGZHI ZHENGJUE 宏智正覺 (1091–1157)

Sunlight angles over Cloud Retreat,
the walls half red;

The frozen grove begins to warm;
birds call in the wind.

I've forgotten my body
in a vine-covered window;

Eyes closed amid incense fragrance,
a hundred worries are empty.

渤潭雲庵偶作

曦色雲庵半堵紅。霜林初暖鳥啼風。不知人在蘿窗裏。瞑目爐薰百慮空。
—HONGZHI ZHENGJUE 宏智正覺 (1091-1157)

121 | BEGGING SONG FOR THE BELL RINGER

When leaves fall,
    frost comes to the empty mountain;
From the tower at night,
    an occasional strike of the bell.
Following the wind,
    crossing the wooded hills,
Calling the moon
    to a vine-covered window.
The echo
    crosses the sky above the valleys;
The sound
    flies unhindered to the river.
Dreams recede
    as heaven wills the dawn;
Butterflies disappear,
    two by two.

禪人發心幹鐘乞頌

木落空山霜。夜樓時一撞。隨風度林嶺。喚月到蘿窗。
響應虛傳谷。聲飛不礙江。夢回天意曉。蝴蝶失雙雙。
— HONGZHI ZHENGJUE 宏智正覺 (1091-1157)

122 | RETURNING TO MY OLD HOME IN THE SOUTHERN HILLS

A rattan staff for company, I'm content to roam;
The past still holds me: I search for my old home.

dream thoughts of clouds and waters,
    my lonely mat held firm;
views of hills and forests
    through four empty windows.

an autumn robe unlined,
    hard rains caused alarm;
noon meals unsalted,
    but sweet with tender greens.

Old ways can surely help me reach my basic goal:
The Dao is like a nesting bird, or a fish in its pool.

還南麓舊居

枝藤結伴得游娛。懷習難寧尋舊居。雲水夢思孤榻穩。山林眼味四窗虛。
秋衣未絮怯繁雨。午飯無鹽甘軟蔬。老境端來償底志。道同巢鳥與淵魚。
— HONGZHI ZHENGJUE 宏智正覺 (1091-1157)

123 | DEATH GĀTHĀ

Dreams, illusions, flowers in the air
For sixty-seven years;
The white bird disappears in the mist,

Autumn waters merge with the sky.

遺偈

夢幻空花。六十七年。白鳥煙沒。秋水天連。
—HONGZHI ZHENGJUE 宏智正覺 (1091-1157)

124 | ATTAINMENT

strange crags on the summit,
　　slow, slow clouds;
the source of the stream,
　　murmuring water.
before climbers reach
　　the limit
　　of the mountain,
the eyes of most
　　are blocked
　　by green peaks.

頂有異峰雲冉冉。源無別派水泠泠。遊山未到山窮處。終被青山礙眼睛。
—BAIYANG FASHUN 白楊法順 (1076-1139)

125 |

My home is atop a lonely peak;
All year my gate is half closed.
I sigh that my body's grown old —
Pass on this life to sons and grandsons!

家住孤峰頂。長年半掩門。自嗟身已老。活計付兒孫。
—HUAYAN ZUJUE 華嚴祖覺 (1087-1150)

126 |

Leaving the woods behind me,
    I board the covered boat;
Heaven's net is vast, vast!
    There can be no escape.
But who believes from karma
    there is no hiding place?
Returning home, I'm not afraid
    to raise my voice out loud.

出林依舊入蓬蒿。天網恢恢不可逃。
誰信業緣無避處。歸來不怕語聲高。
—HUAYAN ZUJUE 華嚴祖覺 (1087-1150)

127 | LIVING IN THE MOUNTAINS

purple bracken reaches out,
    bamboo shoots break through;
willow catkins are all flown,
    green shadows merge.
This must be the word of the Western Master:
yellow orioles stop and twitter,
    swallows call in their nests.

山居

紫蕨伸拳筍破梢。楊華飛盡綠陰交。分明西祖單傳句。黃鸝留鳴燕語巢。
—BOTANG NANYA 柏堂南雅 (FL. TWELFTH CENTURY)

128 |

Water streams down the mountain,
    thoughtless;
Clouds return to high caves,
    mindless.

When men can match
    the clouds and water,
Iron trees will blossom,
    and everywhere will be spring.

流水下山非有意。片雲歸洞本無心。人生若得如雲水。鐵樹開花遍界春。
— CI'AN SHOUJING 此菴守淨 (FL. MID-TWELFTH CENTURY)

129 |

Roosters announce the dawn at dusk;
The sun shines bright at midnight.
The Snow Mountain Teacher is startled awake,
And opens wide his red eyes.

黃昏雞報曉。半夜日頭明。驚起雪師子。瞠開紅眼睛。
— CHICHAN YUANMIAO 癡禪元妙 (1111-1164)

130 | A PRIEST'S STAFF

Three feet of black rattan
    ready to the hand;
Here is no mercy,
    nor even a hairsbreadth.
Buddhas, demons, sinners, saints —
    kill them all:
The diamond eye of wisdom
    only then will be revealed.

拄杖

三尺烏藤本現成。箇中毫髮不容情。佛魔凡聖俱搥殺。方顯金剛正眼睛。
— CHICHAN YUANMIAO 癡禪元妙 (1111-1164)

131 |

Moonlight shines
　　on the mountain valley;

The sound of a spring
　　falls down a steep cliff.

Between
　　the shimmer of water
　　　　and
　　the color of mountains,

One stick of rotten, dead wood.

月色照山谷。泉聲落斷崖。水光山色裡。一塊爛枯柴。
— GONG'AN ZUZHU 公案祖珠 (FL. 1163-1190)

132 | REACHING THE SHORE

when the golden fish is caught,
the heart can rest;

sing out loud and long
row the boat home.

by a stand of green willows,
the sky fills with snow;

endless blowing brightness
reaches the shore.

登岸

既得金鱗心便休。長歌撥棹倚歸舟。綠楊隄畔漫天雪。無限風光到岸頭。
— MENG'AN GE 夢菴格 (FL. TWELFTH CENTURY)

Three months of spring glow,
    nowhere will it stay;
All at once from willow tips
    it scatters all away.
Sadly, the spring wind's face
    cannot e'er be seen,
But look! Dead red petals
    are flowing in the stream.

示徒

三月韶光沒處收。一時散在柳梢頭。可憐不見春風面。卻看殘紅逐水流。
—ZHIWENG 止翁 (CA. 1150-1230)

134 |

For years I've shaved my head
    and worn a black robe,
But my only *true* loves
    are poetry and wine!
When roused, I watch Maitreya
    gamboling in the void,
And when sleepy, I take naps
    on Vairocana's head.
With a wave of my hand,
    I can confound the Ten Sages;
Lowering my head,
    I won't even *look* at the Three Worthies.
Vast, vast the universe
    but no one understands me:
They just say a crazy monk
    is wandering 'round the marketplace.

削髮披緇已有年。只同詩酒是姻緣。閒看彌勒空中戲。困向毗盧頂上眠。
撒手便能欺十聖。低頭端不顧三賢。茫茫宇宙無人識。猶道顛僧遶市廛。
—JIDIAN DAOJI 濟顛道濟 (1150-1209)

What need for the lovely trees of Xiao and Xiang?
I only want West Lake to turn into wine!
I'll lay my body down by West Lake side,
When a wave comes along, I'll drink a mouthful.

何須林景勝瀟湘。只願西湖化為酒。
和身臥倒西湖邊。一浪來時吞一口。
— JIDIAN DAOJI 濟顛道濟 (1150–1209)

136 |

Peach blossoms over the bank,
    bright red brocade;
Willows beside the levee,
    light green silk.
In the distance,
    a white egret spies a fish:
The calm lake shatters
    in a dot of blue.

出岸桃花紅錦英。夾堤楊柳綠絲輕。
遙看白鷺窺魚處。衝破平湖一點青。
— JIDIAN DAOJI 濟顛道濟 (1150–1209)

137 | DEATH GĀTHĀ

Sixty years of disorder and confusion—
The east wall has knocked down the west wall.
Now I'm tidying up and coming home;
As before, blue of water meets blue of sky.

遺偈

六十年來狼藉。東壁打到西壁。
如今收拾歸來。依舊水連天碧。
— JIDIAN DAOJI　濟顛道濟（1150–1209）

138 | SENDING OFF A FRIEND

My home is on the heights
　　of Lu Mountain,
Where lone gibbons cry
　　and the full moon shines.
How could you go back
　　to that world below?
Forget the sounds of heartbreak
　　of years gone by.

贈別

家住匡廬最上層。孤猿啼處月華明。如今底事思歸去。莫記當年腸斷聲。
— ZHEWENG RUYAN　浙翁如琰（1151–1225）

139 |

When lutes have no strings,
　　listeners are few—

From olden days 'til now,
　　only Zhong Ziqi.

How often I've tried
　　to play a song of spring!

Full moon in the empty hall,
　　strumming fingers stop.

琴到無絃聽者稀。古今惟有一鍾期。幾回擬鼓陽春曲。月滿虛堂下指遲。
—LAIKE 癩可 (FL. TWELFTH CENTURY)

140 | RIVER LANTERN

ten thousand miles of misty waves
    join with the white autumn;
a silver lantern, glittering
    floats in midstream.
as soon as they have looked upon
    this brilliant spark,
the wave chasers, the ripple followers
    will never rest.

水燈

萬里煙波接素秋。銀缸耿耿泛中流。自從一點光明後。逐浪隨波未肯休。
—CHIJUE DAOCHONG 痴絕道沖 (1169-1250)

141 | THE LAZY WATER BUFFALO

He never walks the farm paths,
    neither west nor east;
For years he's feared
    a yoke might touch his shoulders.
Abandoning sweet, tender grass
    within the pasture,
By green willows along the bank
    he feeds on wind and mist.

懶牛

不經南陌與西阡。犁杷年來怕上肩。棄卻欄中肥嫩艸。綠楊堤畔飽風煙。
—WUMEN HUIKAI 無門慧開 (1183-1260)

142 | WONTONS

Anxiously you fold your arms
    across your big tummy,
And then you're doing somersaults
    in a pot of boiling water.
When your whole body has turned to mush,
    such a scrumptious fragrance!
Is there any Chan monk who wouldn't
    open up his mouth?

餛飩

寬著肚皮急叉手。鑊湯裡面翻筋斗。渾身糜爛轉馨香。那箇禪和不開口。
— WUMEN HUIKAI 無門慧開 (1183 - 1260)

143 | CASTING THE SEAL

Golden flowers and a dappled horse
    emblazoned on a robe;
How often he raised a whip
    beneath the bright moon!
Yet for nought he raced here and there
    in the Yellow River land—
From the beginning until now,
    not a mark of merit.

鑄印

袍著金花勒小驄。揚鞭幾度月明中。黃河界上空來往。直至而今未樹功。
— XUTANG ZHIYU 虛堂智愚 (1185 - 1269)

144 .| MELTING THE SEAL

He's worn out the soles of iron boots
    and lived on wind and frost;
At year's end he comes home
    and sleeps on a bed of stone.
A pair of eyes,
    black as night,
Half follow the cloud shadows
    that hang in the cold hall.

銷印

鐵鞋無底飽風霜。歲晚歸來臥石牀。一對眼睛烏律律。伴隨雲影掛寒堂。
—XUTANG ZHIYU 虛堂智愚 (1185-1269)

145 | HEARING THE SNOW

A cold, windless night,
    yet there is sound in the bamboo—
Whoosh, shoosh,
    coming through my pine window.
Hearing with the ear
    can't match hearing with the mind;
I put aside a half-rolled scroll
    in the lantern's light.

聽雪

寒夜無風竹有聲。踈踈密密透松櫩。耳聞不似心聞好。歇却燈前半卷經。
—XUTANG ZHIYU 虛堂智愚 (1185-1269)

146 | ASKING FOR A CAT

Tiger-faced cat!
    born in the temple,
    a golden promise will make him mine.

My home is cold—
    no thieving rats here;
I just want to see him:
        topsy-turvy
        climbing up a tree

求貓子

堂上新生虎面狸。千金許我不應移。家寒故是無偷鼠。要見翻身上樹時。
—XUTANG ZHIYU 虛堂智愚 (1185-1269)

147 | HOME OF THE GREAT TEACHER

Clifftop cassia—flowers bloom
and fragrance fills the hall;

Underneath the green sedge leaves,
cold cicadas call.

The gentleman lives here,
in a western forest glen;

Roosters crow and dogs bark—
it's sunset again.

超師房

巖桂花開滿院香。青莎葉底有鳴螿。人家只在西林住。雞犬聲中又夕陽。
—WUWEN DAOCAN 無文道燦 (1213-1271)

3 |

On the threshing floor, the roller turns once;
For the first time this life, my eyes suddenly open.
The cold palace of the moon has no lock or key—
Crush the skull and return home.

土木場中輥一回。平生己眼豁然開。廣寒宮殿無關鑰。撞破髑髏歸去來。
—WUWEN DAOCAN 無文道燦 (1213-1271)

149 |

My home is not so far away,
Just follow the road at your feet.
A red sun rises on the mountaintop;
Stone rams lie in the grass beneath.
Human life, this hundred-year span,
In a finger's snap has passed us by.
A brush gate without lock or key;
To and fro, white clouds fly.

吾家不甚遙。看取腳下路。紅日上山頭。石羊草裏臥。
人間一百年。彈指聲中過。柴門無鎖鑰。白雲自來去。
—HENGCHUAN XINGGONG 橫川行琪 (1222-1289)

150 | DEATH GĀTHĀ

Heaven has made this hole
To store my withered bones.
Bones rot and become earth,
And earth bears living things.
Grow a bottle gourd
To hang on Zhaozhou's wall.
Escape the Wheel forever:
Rise over the Buddhas of Three Ages.

遺偈

天生一穴。藏吾枯骨。骨朽成土。土能生物。結箇葫蘆。掛趙州壁。
永脫輪迴。超三世佛。
—HENGCHUAN XINGGONG 橫川行琪 (1222–1289)

151 | TO MY BARBER

Suddenly this year, my hair looks like silk,
And my companions all laugh at an old fool.
Yet sir, you needn't come so often to pluck and shave me,
For how many reach this white-headed age?

贈髮匠

年來頓覺髮如絲。多少傍人笑老癡。妙手不須頻摘剃。幾人得到白頭時。
—YUEJIAN WENMING 月澗文明 (1231–?)

152 | MEDITATION DEPORTMENT AT MOUNT TIANTONG

Walking:
　　Suddenly you slip, and fall down a hole;
　　　　So change direction,
　　While Hidden Pavilion collapses in laughter.

Standing:
　　Your body in distress, until it can take no more;
　　　　Who will know?
　　Tame gulls and nesting egrets.

Sitting:
　　Concentration breaks on your rush mat;
　　　　That sound in the pines
　　Is a light breeze passing.

Lying:
    Taibai Peak is a big pillow;
        Stretch out your legs
    And traverse the void.

天童四威儀

行　無端失腳墮深坑。轉得步。笑倒更幽亭。
住　一身貧到無貧處。有誰知。狎鷗并宿鷺。
坐　卻被蒲團先識破。松作聲。元是微風過。
臥　太白一峰枕頭大。伸雙腳。虛空俱踏破。
—YUEJIAN WENMING　月澗文明 (1231-?)

153 | PICKING TEA

Hand in hand, entering the thick wood,
Searching for the heart of the spring wind.
Feeling only the sharp spikes in their grasps,
Never noticing the mist wet on their robes.

摘茶

拚雙赤手入叢林。要覓春風一寸心。但覺爪牙歸掌握。不知煙霧濕衣襟。
—YUEJIAN WENMING　月澗文明 (1231-?)

154 | SKULL BENEATH A PINE

Skull in the grass,
    body in a dream,
Stop sense and feeling,
    and see what's really real.
On Cold Food Days,
    on Beimang graveyard roads,
Pine flowers in every tree
    carry the spring.

松下枯髏

草裡枯髏夢裡身。識情歷盡見全真。北邙寒食山前路。那樹松花不帶春。

—YUETANG ZUYIN 悅堂祖闍 (1234-1308)

155 | READING A RECORD OF MY TEACHER'S WORDS

A green flag west of the painted bridge,
　　a hanging wineshop sign;
Willow catkins blow about
　　and levees fill with rain.
Mistakenly, I take a draught
　　of thousand-day wine—
Bury me drunk in a lonely grave,
　　I'll not return again!

讀本師語錄

青旗斜出畫橋西。楊柳飛花水滿堤。一酌誤人千日酒。醉埋荒塚不思歸。

—YUNWAI YUNXIU 雲外雲岫 (1242-1324)

156 | WRITING OUT THE *DIAMOND SŪTRA* IN BLOOD

Climb the needle point
　　for merit to be won,
And words, two thousand years old,
　　unobstructed flow.
My ten fingers dripping
　　with the blood my mother gave me—
Dying red every leaf
　　in the Jetavana Garden.

血書金剛經

向一針鋒上策功。二千年遠話流通。淋漓十指孃生血。染得祇園葉葉紅。

—SONGYAN YONGXIU 松巖永秀 (FL. LATE THIRTEENTH CENTURY)

Yuan Dynasty (1279–1368)

AND Ming Dynasty (1368–1644)

SENDING OFF ATTENDANT JIN TO VISIT
HIS TEACHER

No shackles on this body,
    you come and go as you please;
Half a lifetime spent
    in journeys to famous mountains.
A smack beneath the ribs
    taught you about pain;
Three answers to the call
    and you passed through the gate.
The essentials and the mysteries,
    both perfectly complete;
No matter the stress or strain,
    you remain at ease.
When master and disciple meet,
    ask no questions!
Look at each other
    and smile.

次韻送金侍者省師

身世無拘任往還。半生行腳為名山。一拳肋下才知痛。三應聲中已透關。

要要玄玄並了了。勞勞役役與閒閒。師資會遇都休問。只合相看展笑顏。
—GULIN QINGMAO 古林清茂 (1262-1329)

158 | SWEEPING THE FLOOR

Sweep away old piles of trash,
But dust still covers the floor.
When you cast the handle from you:
Dharma flowers,
    five-petaled,
        blossom on the broom.

掃地

蕩盡從前垃圾堆。依然滿地是塵埃。等閒和柄都拋卻。五葉曇花帚上開。
—ZHONGFENG MINGBEN 中峰明本 (1263-1323)

159 | EMBRACING THE PURE LAND

Turbid water clears,
    a mind pearl brightens;
A wild heart is stilled,
    Buddha is complete.
All before my eyes
    are hometown roads;
No need for others
    to point the way back.

懷淨土詩

濁水盡清珠有力。亂心不動佛無機。眼前盡是家鄉路。不用逢人覓指歸。
—ZHONGFENG MINGBEN 中峰明本 (1263-1323)

160 | INSTRUCTIONS FOR CHAN MEDITATION

The best means to a mind at rest
Is a secret not for telling.
Who knows the moon in the pool begins
In the sky above the dwelling?

示安禪人

好個安心法。當陽妙不傳。誰知潭底月。元在屋頭天。
— WUJIAN XIANDU　無見先睹 (1265-1334)

161 | FOLLOWING THE RHYMES
OF CHAN MASTER YONGMING

Few can reach
　　the pure chill of clouds,
The awareness
　　that self and things return together.
Red of peach and white of pear
　　can help to find Pure Truth;
Swallow voices and oriole calls
　　reveal the Wondrous Function.
When rains flood the streams,
　　shadows of fish gather;
As clouds return to mountain caves,
　　sunlight dims.
Offer this piece of silence
　　to one who understands you:
Real is not real
　　and not is not-not.

和永明禪師韻

清冷雲中到者稀。廓然物我自同歸。桃紅李白資真諦。燕語鶯啼闡妙機。
新水漲溪魚影密。宿雲歸洞日光微。祇將一默酬知己。是不是兮非不非。
— WUJIAN XIANDU　無見先睹 (1265-1334)

162 | FOLLOWING THE RHYMES
OF CHAN MASTER YONGMING

Upon reaching home,
    forget the road back;
Before reaching home,
    the road seems so long!
Whenever I see a fallen flower
    carried away by the water,
I laugh and watch dead trees
    standing up to the sky.
On the fathomless Knowledge Sea,
    strange waves are stilled;
In a single heart field,
    rare shoots can grow.
Build a thatched hut,
    big enough to rest your knees;
Empty windows
    won't block morning in the mountains.

和永明禪師韻

到家舊路須忘卻。未到家時路覺遙。每見落花隨逝水。笑看枯木上凌霄。
千尋學海空奇浪。一片心田長異苗。搆得茅菴可容膝。虛窗不礙四山朝。
—WUJIAN XIANDU 無見先睹 (1265–1334)

163 | FOLLOWING THE RHYMES
OF CHAN MASTER YONGMING

Quietly sitting on a brushwood bed,
    I break all bonds;
Everything before me
    merges in the True Function.
On its own,
    moss wraps around a fragrant tree;
From time to time,
    pine dew drips on a robe of faded colors.

Sweet spring in a stone fissure,
the taste of tea perfect;
Thin soil at the root of clouds,
bracken shoots frail.
Pair by pair,
white eagles disappear in the mist;
A lone woodsman's song
bids farewell to the setting sun.

和永明禪師韻

默坐柴床絕所依。眼前物物契真機。莓苔自裹生香樹。松露時沾壞色衣。
石鏬泉甘茶味足。雲根上淺蕨苗微。雙雙白鷺衝煙去。一曲樵歌送落暉。
— WUJIAN XIANDU　無見先睹 (1265-1334)

164 | SENDING OFF TEMPLE LIBRARIAN SUI BACK TO LINGYIN

Buddhas and patriarchs
shattered the gate of mystery;
Ten thousand words, a thousand sūtras—
explaining was not easy.
Before moving their tongues
they spat out sweet dew;
The moon on White Lotus Peak
shines coldly upon men.

送遂藏主歸靈隱

從來佛祖碎玄關。萬論千經下口難。未動舌頭俱吐露。白蓮峰月照人寒。
— CHUSHI FANQI　楚石梵琦 (1296-1370)

165 | AUTUMN NIGHT IN A MOUNTAIN TOWER

Moonlight as white as day;
Pine shadows as many as clouds.
In the empty window,
 a mountain about to fall;
As the lantern flickers,
 the night divides in two.
Reflections in the river
 reveal the heavens;
Sounds of the spring
 are heard beyond the trees.
Sitting alone in this small tower,
With whom can I speak of this beauty?

山樓秋夜

月色白如畫。松陰多似雲。窗虛山欲墮。燈炧夜初分。
河影中天見。泉聲隔樹聞。小樓成獨坐。此景與誰論。
—YU'AN ZHIJI 愚菴智及 (1311-1378)

166 | MISCELLANEOUS WORDS ON
LIVING IN THE MOUNTAINS

I remember:
 walking the Su Embankment,
 crossing the Six Bridges,
 my silk cap floating off with the wind.
My head was covered
 in snow of lake and hills;
The glaring sun has failed so far
 to melt it off again.

山居雜言

憶在蘇堤過六橋。小番羅帽被風飄。滿頭帶得湖山雪。幾度驕陽曬不消。
—TIANRU WEIZE 天如惟則 (D. 1354)

167 | SENDING OFF YU XIAOLIN,
A MONK FROM MY HOMETOWN

If the folks at home ask when I'll return,
Say that for now I'm going back to the mountains.
A rush mat in a half-sized room,
By the Wusong River, among the Nine Peaks.

送鄉僧昱曉林

鄉人問我幾時還。向道如今又入山。一箇蒲團半間屋。吳松江上九峰間。
—TIANRU WEIZE 天如惟則 (D. 1354)

168 | WINTER

Head muffled in my cassock,
red-hot fire in the hearth;

Snow cold—
sadly I hear the highland temple bell.

I open the door in wonder,
for the mountain is now a sea!

Ten thousand silver waves
reveal one peak.

一峰雲外菴和韻四景

衲被蒙頭宿火紅。雪寒愁聽上方鐘。開門忽怪山為海。萬疊銀濤露一峰。
—TIANRU WEIZE 天如惟則 (D. 1354)

169 | INSTRUCTIONS FOR MY FRIENDS

Desolate trees atop the wall;
Dying grass beneath the wall.
How long can lush growth last,
Ere again it withered falls?
Life has no roots or source;
Experience is a mix of ugly and fine.
Ever since I fell to earth,
Countless worries have daily been mine.
Transformation silently creeps on;
My face and temples—suddenly I'm old.
Why is it, in our hundred-year spans,
So little joy is ours to hold?
Look at men since ancient time—
How many understood the mind?

示友人

蕭蕭墙頭樹。靡靡墙下草。繁茂曾幾何。已復見枯槁。
人生無根源。身世雜醜好。自從墮地來。萬念日紛擾。
運化潛消磨。容鬢不知老。如何百年間。樂意常自少。
君看古來人。心事誰獨了。
—TIANRU WEIZE 天如惟則 (D. 1354)

170 | FUNERAL POEM

Rain falls: the tears of heaven;
Thunder rolls: laments of the earth.
From the west, all of the buddhas
Surge forward, by chariot and horse.

雨落天垂淚。雷鳴地舉哀。西天諸佛子。同送馬如來。
—JITAN ZONGLE 季潭宗泐 (1318-1391)

171 | RHYMING WITH OLD PATRIARCH GUIYUAN'S MOUNTAIN SONG

Courtyard trees in bright colors;
Rare birds sing sweet songs.
All merges in a single thought;
Distinctions are completely gone.
At leisure I often sit apart;
My poem done, I chant aloud.
Dark, dark—the Pine Gate road;
Far, far—the thick white clouds.

追和歸源老祖山謳

庭樹有佳色。珍禽多好音。渾然一片境。了無差別心。
閑來常獨坐。詩成還自吟。窅窅松門路。迢迢白雲深。
—DAI'AN PUZHUANG 呆菴普莊 (1347–1403)

172 | SENDING OFF ATTENDANT YAO

Seekers of Dao must learn to be idiots;
    come, enter my Idiot's Hut!
Once the Idiot teaches you to be idiots,
    your mouths won't be able to speak.
No speaking, no hearing,
    no gain and no loss.
You'll shake your heads, and everywhere wander;
    lean on your staffs, and carry the sun.
Just laugh at old Xianglin,
    his paper robe as black as lacquer!
Three times three isn't nine,
    but nine times nine is eighty-one.

送要侍者

道人要學呆。來入呆菴室。呆菴教汝呆。有口說不出。
不說亦不聞。無得亦無失。掉頭遊諸方。拄杖挑紅日。
笑他老香林。紙襖黑如漆。三三不是九。九九八十一。
—DAI'AN PUZHUANG 呆菴普莊 (1347-1403)

173 | CROSSING CAO STREAM

I walk through endless vistas of empty green,
Until the winding Cao blocks the temple road.
You ask what message comes from south of the peaks?
In the sound of water, white birds on green mountains.

踏來空翠幾千重。曲折曹溪鎖梵宮。欲問嶺南傳底事。青山白鳥水聲中。
—ZIBO ZHENKE 紫柏真可 (1543-1603)

174 | SENDING OFF CHAN MONK GAO BACK TO CIHUA

A leaf boat floats
    on an endless sea;
Misty waters vast and vague,
    the ford is hard to find.
Go back to your mountain,
    fulfill your life's goal;
A secluded place of flowers
    where birds call the spring.

送誥禪人歸慈化

杯浮一葉森無垠。煙水茫茫苦問津。歸去家山生意滿。百花深處鳥啼春。
—HANSHAN DEQING 憨山德清 (1546-1623)

175 | LIVING IN THE MOUNTAINS

Clouds break over the land, spring light stirs;
A faint scent of plum blossom, whence does it come?
I lean on my staff to look for the secret valley,
While one branch hangs low over the eastern wall.

山居

雲開四野動春光。何處梅花送暗香。曳杖欲尋幽谷去。一枝斜倚在東牆。
—HANSHAN DEQING 憨山德清 (1546-1623)

176 | NIGHT DEPARTURE ON LING RIVER

As wild water twists and turns,
An empty boat floats where it will.

Watching the moon, the color brightens;
Hearing the river, the sound slowly stills.

Floating clouds are beyond my body;
White hair frames my mirrored face.

Don't say I've tarried too long:
Ahead lies my old mountain place.

夜發凌江

虛舟隨所適。一水絕間關。月色看逾好。江聲聽轉閒。
浮雲身外事。白髮鏡中顏。莫謂漂零久。前途即故山。
—HANSHAN DEQING 憨山德清 (1546-1623)

177 | LIVING IN THE MOUNTAINS

My hut is no bigger than a ladle,
But within, I do as I please.

Colored clouds
    rise from doors and casements;
The moon and stars
    are suspended on the porch.

Thoughts end:
    my mind becomes tranquil;
Dust dissolves:
    the world is just thus.

The southern wind reaches my sitting mat,
Rustling through six empty windows.

山居

斗大一菴居。其中任卷舒。雲霞生戶牖。星月挂庭除。
念息心愈寂。塵消境自如。南熏時入座。颯颯六窗虛。
—HANSHAN DEQING 憨山德清 (1546-1623)

178 | SITTING AT NIGHT, ENJOYING THE COOL

I love the colors of a clearing night,
And in autumn, the birth of the bracing air.
Leaves in the wood
    heavy after rain;
Clouds on the peak
    light in the wind.
In quiet contemplation,
    I see there is no me;
Through strict practice,
    I've tired of having a name.
I sit and watch the moon in emptiness,
Intently facing the solitary light.

夜坐納涼

夜色喜新晴。迎秋爽氣生。雨餘林葉重。風度嶺雲輕。
靜慮觀無我。藏修厭有名。坐看空界月。歷歷對孤明。
— HANSHAN DEQING 憨山德清 (1546-1623)

179 | DEATH *GĀTHĀ* (#1)

A simple robe clothed my body
    in the land within the seas,
But now at last I've come back—
    to Sumeru Peak.
Raising my head beyond the heavens,
    I open wisdom eyes,
And, gazing down,
    behold winds in the ten directions.

遺偈

野衲橫身四海中。端然迴出須彌峰。舉頭天外豁惺眼。府視十方世界風。
— MIYUN YUANWU 密雲圓悟 (1566-1642)

180 | DEATH *GĀTHĀ* (#2)

Over the ten directions I stretch out
    and sleep at my ease;
Why give a care about paradise,
    east, west, south, or north?
I am the sole master of the universe;
    my whole body is revealed.
If anyone should come to ask after me,
    they'll just get my big fist.

遺偈

十方世界恣橫眠。那管東西南北天。唯我獨尊全體現。人來問着只粗拳。
—MIYUN YUANWU 密雲圓悟 (1566-1642)

181 | SEEING PLUM BLOSSOMS AT DRUM MOUNTAIN FOR THE FIRST TIME

After a thousand miles of rugged road,
I no longer love this old body.
My footsteps: utterly without strength;
Before my eyes: only clouds.
I've seen many birds come home to roost,
But met few people to ask about the ford.
Don't blame plum blossoms for laughing at me—
I stumble along, through yet another spring.

初入鼓山見梅花偶成

崎嶇千里道。不惜老來身。腳下渾無力。眼前惟有雲。
多逢投宿鳥。罕見問津人。莫怪梅花笑。蹉跎又一春。
—WUYI YUANLAI 無異元來 (1575-1630)

182 | THOUGHTS ON CLIMBING DRINKWATER RIDGE

Misty steps like scales of fish,
My staff in hand, I stride ahead.
Water jets from a dragon's mouth;
Pines grow in a cracked stone bed.
Ancient trees hide wondrous birds;
Serried hills: jade screens outspread.

In *dhyāna* thought, ageless retreat,
Fame and gain are matters slight.
I see this is no idler's place;

The Way, in a flash, brings such delight.
To further know Bodhidharma's will:
The sky is clear; the far stream bright.

登喝水巖有感

雲磴如鱗砌。扶筇縱步行。水從龍口出。松倚石痕生。
古樹藏嘉羽。層山疊翠屏。禪那千古寄。名利一身輕。
豁爾非遊境。翛然樂道情。更窮西祖意。天朗遠川明。
—WUYI YUANLAI 無異元來 (1575-1630)

183 | LIVING IN THE MOUNTAINS

I alone love steep cliffsides;
way up high I choose to live.

dense clouds hide my little room;
thick trees protect the low walls.

lush cassia can beckon the recluse,
but tranquil orchid always blooms alone.

thinking back on the past,
it seems like madness now.

山居

獨喜重巒峻。卜居在上方。雲深埋小屋。樹密護低墻。
叢桂堪招隱。幽蘭每自芳。回思前日事。深似失頭狂。
—YONGJUE YUANXIAN 永覺元賢 (1578-1657)

184 | CELEBRATING THE COMPLETION OF DISCORDLESS
HERMITAGE ON AN EARLY SPRING DAY

when willow eyes open,
    and face the cold birds,
a new Chan cottage
    is raised in green hills.

how many travelers
    will find my quiet valley?
trails of smoke from tea fires
    drift out of the level grove.

within the room
    time has no winter or summer;
beyond the door
    let the world have its past and present.

I give thanks:
    my dream of the dusty world is over;
with dirty head and muddy face,
    I sleep in thick clouds.

初春日慶無諍居落成

初開柳眼對霜禽。新搆禪房倚翠岑。客屐幾能來僻谷。茶煙每自出平林。
室中日月無寒暑。門外江山任古今。長揖世間塵夢絕。灰頭土面臥雲深。
—YONGJUE YUANXIAN 永覺元賢 (1578-1657)

185 | SMALL POND

An idle half acre in front of the window
Is cleared for a small square pond.
As clouds pass, for a time they leave reflections;
When the moon comes, it brings a temporary light.
Flowers are watered, and spring gains in color;

Inkstones are washed, and leave fragrance behind.
Only in the pond's water
Can I quietly forget myself.

小塘

窗前閒半畝。開作小方塘。雲過暫留影。月來時有光。
灌花春借色。洗硯墨流香。唯有塘中水。澹然卻自忘。
—YONGJUE YUANXIAN 永覺元賢 (1578-1657)

186 | LYING MEDITATION

In deep mountains, a lotus clock drips;
A roomful of wind is gentle and cool.
On my seven-foot rope bed
With arms bent, I sleep with the clouds.
Existence and void are mixed up;
Saints and sinners are cast away.
Don't say there are no things at all:
A bright mirror floats alone in the sky.

臥

山深蓮漏永。一室風俏然。繩床方七尺。曲肱伴雲眠。
有無渾不計。凡聖亦都捐。莫謂全無物。孤明一鏡懸。
—YONGJUE YUANXIAN 永覺元賢 (1578-1657)

187 | IN PRAISE OF THE WOODEN FISH

A shape
    that heaven never gave;
A substance
    culled from orange trees.
You wear scales
    but never touch the water;

Rhythm flows
    from where a heart would be.
At the prompting
    of master and monk,
You can mark the beat
    of Sanskrit song.
You spend your time
    with bell and chime—
Could any fisherman
    dare do you wrong?

詠魚鼓

成象非天育。擄材取鄧林。披鱗未涉水。流韻出無心。
權秉師僧令。能和梵唄音。祇同鐘磬侶。漁父豈相侵。
—YONGJUE YUANXIAN 永覺元賢 (1578–1657)

188 | TRAVELING TO WHITE-WATER MOUNTAIN MONASTERY

Rising at dawn, I pass the southern gate,
My traveling cloak chill as iron.

The green pine road, long, long!
Cold clouds merge, slowly, slowly!

Piled-up crags, each lofty and steep;
Mountains so sheer the road seems to end.

Where a small bridge crosses a deep ravine,
I stop to cut a cloud-climbing staff.

High peaks pierce the emerald void;
Among them is a shrine to the Lord of Law.

Each gate is more and more secluded;
The old monk has brows like snow.

Barefoot in his haste, he invites the guest in;
Roaring with laughter, he plays the host.

From a stone fissure he draws fresh water,
And brews "sparrow-tongue" tea in a bronze bowl.

The small room overlooks a steep cliff;
We open the window and await the bright moon.

A pine wind blows, cooling our ears;
The sound of running water is never-ending.

He asks about the flower held in Buddha's hand,
But I cannot answer even a single word.

He then begs me to write a new poem,
And like water from a dike, it pours forth.

Don't say this is Chan of the written word—
Perhaps it will disappear like sweet dew.

遊白水山剎

晨起出南郊。征衣冷如鐵。迢迢青松道。冉冉寒雲結。
疊嶺每崔嵬。山窮路欲絕。小橋架危壑。思理緣雲策。
崎嶇穿翠微。中有法王闕。重門亦窈窕。僧老眉如雪。
迎賓解倒屣。軒渠笑相接。石隙取新泉。銅瓶烹雀舌。
小樓瞰絕崖。開窗待明月。松風吹凍耳。濤聲未曾歇。
問我拈華旨。一字不能說。乞我寫新詩。便似隄頭決。
莫道文字禪。恐是甘露滅。
—YONGJUE YUANXIAN 永覺元賢 (1578-1657)

189 | MY SEVENTIETH BIRTHDAY

I've reached my seventieth year,
Eyes dark and teeth few.
Legs lame, it's hard to walk about;

Wind and snow cover my bald head.
Reviewing my long life,
Time has passed
      like a
      bad
      dream

But . . .
A thousand ages are only a moment's thought;
Mulberry groves might rise from the sea —
    it doesn't matter.
In the ten directions, all is shadow,
Mirrored reflections of no substance.
Even the *bodhi* is not real,
Much less the myriad vulgar things!

A hundred worries all disappear
When at leisure I read old Buddhist books.
In deep night,
   I recline on my bench alone;
The moon's light
      floods
      the outer
      porch

七旬誕日

行年今七十。眼暗齒亦疏。躐躇難舉步。風雪滿頭顱。
閱世良已久。机夢歷居諸。千古止一念。滄桑不用歔。
十界同影事。鏡體本皆無。菩提尚非實。況彼俗之餘。
百慮俱消盡。閒披古佛書。夜深獨隱几。明月滿庭除。
—YONGJUE YUANXIAN 永覺元賢 (1578-1657)

190 | LODGING ON NORTH MOUNTAIN;
     PRESENTED TO ABBOT WEI

Old cloud-topped pines
    rustle in clear waves of wind;
Above a twisting, turning brook,
    a solitary hut.
Spring doesn't heed
    a bamboo gate shut tight;
Wildly singing mountain birds
    stamp on the flower stems.

宿北山贈唯山主

載雲松老響晴濤。數轉谿灣見把茅。
深閉竹籬春不管。亂啼山鳥踏花稍。
—SANYI MINGYU 三宜明盂 (1599-1665)

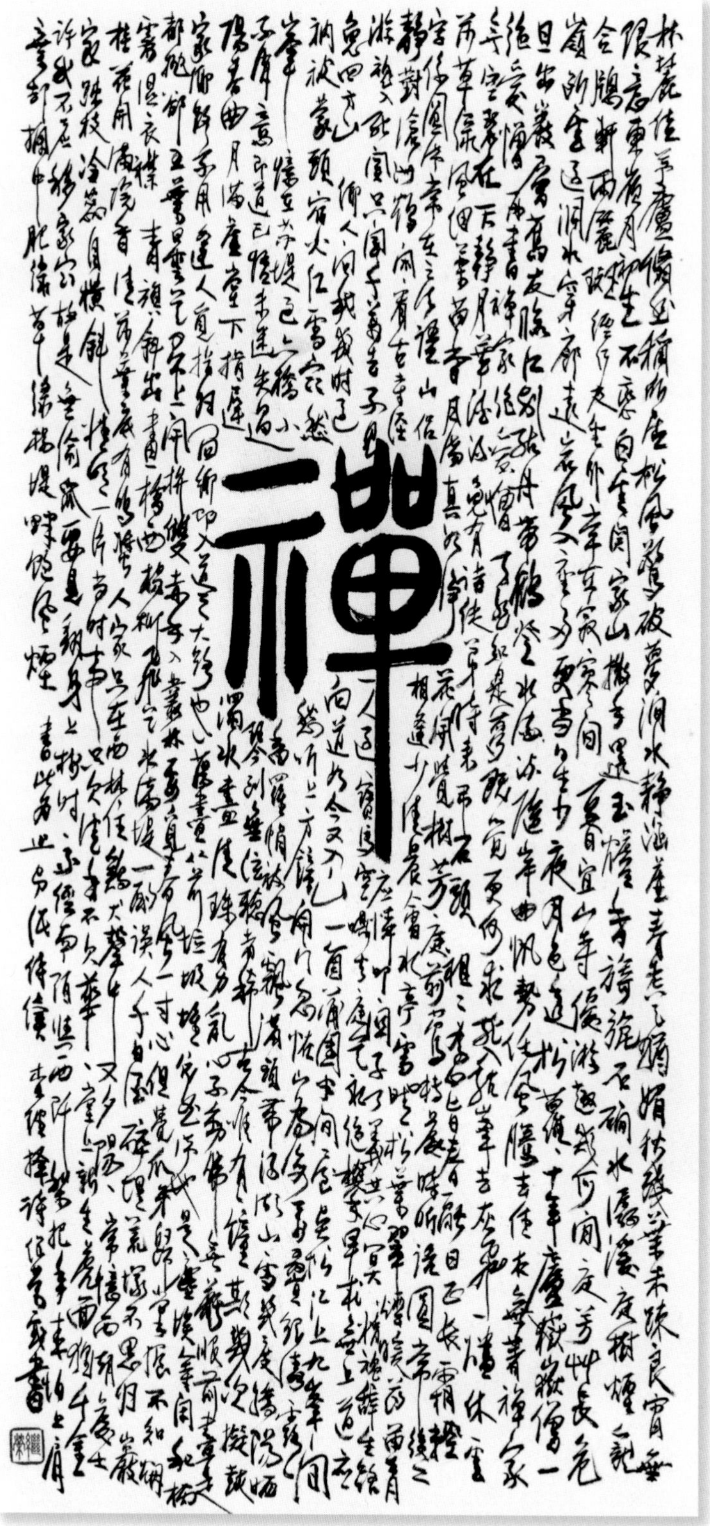
禪

孤根當隙發重遲 澶泊春光一兩枝 不改寸心

長向日清 香還在上林寺

寶覺祖心句

求貓子

堂弟新生虎面貍

千金許我不令移

家寒故是無爭寵

要見翻身上樹時

Introductions to the Poets and Explanatory Notes

*Introductions to the poets are marked with an asterisk. The source material is primarily the transmission-of-the-lamp anthologies, so the influence of mythmaking is very apparent. Moreover, poem attributions to some major masters are suspect. Monks abandoned their birth names when they took their vows. A monk's name is generally four characters: the first two are usually the name of the mountain or temple with which he was most associated, and the last two are his name in religion. The most influential masters often became known by the name of their mountain or temple alone. Often there is also a cognomen (*zi*) and/or a sobriquet (*hao*); the former is a fairly formal alternate name, while the latter, lighter in tone, can be a studio name, pen name, or even a popular nickname. Finally, a monk who enjoyed imperial favor might gain one or more honorific titles, bestowed either during his lifetime or posthumously.

Notes to the texts are marked in italics. Besides providing definitions of terms and contextualizing information, the notes include some suggestions for interpretation. These should be taken only as starting points for approaching the poems, rather than as standard or comprehensive explanations. Chinese characters for transliterated terms are in the glossary.

SOURCES ARE LISTED IN THE ENDNOTES.
POETIC FORMS OF ORIGINAL TEXTS ARE CITED IN THE ENDNOTES.

Tang Dynasty (618–907) and Five Dynasties (907–960)

1. Shitou Xiqian, *Untitled*[1]

    *Shitou Xiqian (700–790) and Mazu Daoyi (709–788) are credited by tradition as the two most influential Chan masters in the second generation after the Sixth Patriarch Huineng. Shitou was from Gaoyao in Duanzhou (in Guangdong); his family name was Chen. The anthologies describe him as a sensitive child who rescued many cows from death in local ritual sacrifices. He was said to have been an informal student of the Sixth Patriarch, and after Huineng's death, the disciple and Dharma heir of Qingyuan Xingsi (?–740) in Jiangxi. In the early years of the Tianbao reign (742–756), he moved to Nansi Temple at Mount Heng (in Hunan) and remained there for the rest of his life. To the east of the temple was a stone ledge. He built a hermitage on it and began calling himself Shitou Heshang (Stone Monk). He taught sixty-three disciples.[2] In modern times, a Japanese dentist recovered a mummy from a ruined Chinese monastery in Hunan. He claimed the mummy was Shitou's and took it to Japan. It remains today in Sōjiji Temple in Yokohama.[3]

    He's always been with me — the buddha nature, *tathāgatagarbha*.

2. Shitou Xiqian, *The Grass Hut Song*[4]

    Grass hut (cao'an, caotang) — euphemism for the domicile of a recluse. The *Platform Sūtra* notes, "Good friends, the physical body is a house, but you can't take refuge in it."[5]

    The old man in the tiny room (fangzhang laoren) — *fangzhang* means "ten square feet," and alludes to the tiny size of the sickroom in which the layman Vimalakīrti isolated himself while teaching the doctrine of emptiness to Buddha's disciples, as related in the *Vimalakīrtinirdeśa sūtra.* The term was used to refer to the room of the abbot in a Chinese Buddhist monastery.

Bodhisattva (pusa)—advanced beings who vow to attain enlightenment to save all those suffering in *saṃsāra.* One who has accomplished the bodhisattva practice is a buddha.

Shine the reflections back (huiguang fanzhao)—the term in general use refers to the glow of colored light in the sky at sunset. Chan Buddhists use it to suggest that through meditation on the emptiness of *dharmas* the practitioner gains *prajñā,* and the light of this wisdom reveals the buddha nature within.

divine root (linggen)—the buddha nature, *tathāgatagarbha.* In the "mind field" (xintian), enlightenment grows from the root.

skin bag (pidai)—the body. Also "sack of bones and skin" (pidaigu), "stinking sack of skin" (chou pidai), or "worn-out sack" (binang).

3.   Hanshan, *Untitled*[6]

*Hanshan (Cold Mountain) was a legendary Tang dynasty recluse on Mount Tiantai (in Tiantai, Zhejiang). There is no compelling evidence that such a person ever existed, yet the tales and texts associated with his name have had an enormous impact on East Asian cultures. The prototypical carefree Buddhist vagabond, Hanshan was said to frequent Guoqing Temple on Mount Tiantai, often in company with two other eccentric recluses, Shide and Fenggan. When Prefect Lü Qiuyin asked for Buddhist teachers on Mount Tiantai, Master Fenggan (who was considered an incarnation of Amitābha) directed him to Hanshan and Shide. The prefect sought the two out in the temple kitchen to pay his respects, and unconsciously bowed to them. The two eccentrics just laughed at him and hand in hand walked out the temple gate, saying, "Fenggan talks too much! Talks too much! If you didn't recognize Amitābha, what good will it do to bow to us?" When the prefect offered presents of clothing and medicine, Hanshan just yelled out, "Thief! Go away, thief!" He slipped into a fissure in the rock, which then sealed itself, leaving no trace. Hanshan was sometimes considered an incarnation of Mañjuśrī, the Bodhisattva of Wisdom. The Tang dynasty *Gleanings of Immortal Biographies* describes him as a recluse of the Dali period (766–780), yet also claims that a mysterious stranger who visited a Daoist adept in the year 872 was the selfsame Hanshan, made immortal through Daoist meditation techniques! The collection that bears Hanshan's name is not linguistically or stylistically uniform, and it has been suggested that the more than three hundred poems in it were composed at different times and by different people.[7] Viewed as a whole, the collection is characterized by simple, near-colloquial language and didactic, admonitory purpose. Hanshan is also associated with Cold Mountain

Temple atop Mount Han (near Suzhou, Jiangsu); local tradition has it that the temple was given this name because Hanshan and Shide lived there during the Zhenguan reign period (627–649).[8]

For an explication of this poem, see the introduction.

4. Hanshan, *Untitled*[9]

wordless knowing (mozhi) — enlightenment comes completely and spontaneously from within, in a process that is inexplicable and unteachable.

watch the void (guankong) — a deliberate meditative exercise aimed at realizing the illusory nature of reality.

world — the text uses the word *jing* (Skt. *viṣaya*), or "realm." See the introduction.

5. Hanshan, *Untitled*[10]

fruits and fish — the attainment of enlightenment was very often couched in physical metaphors of harvest or capture. Also metaphorically significant here are the fruits as culmination of a natural process and the fish as denizens of a mountain spring — the pure source of a stream.

monkeys — the monkey or gibbon as representation for the human mind goes back in China at least to the early fifth century. In Chan poetry these animals convey two quite distinct types of mind, depending on context. First, they reflect the insatiable curiosity of the uncultivated mind wholly immersed in the world of causation. *Nirvāṇa Sūtra* 29 says,

> The heart and nature of sentient beings is like that of the monkey. The nature of the monkey is that he rejects one thing and holds on to another. The heart and nature of sentient beings is also like this. They hold on to and are attached to the *dharmas* of form, sound, smell, taste, and touch without any temporary stop.[11]

This idea is described in the phrase, "Monkeys search for the moon in the water" (*mihou tan shuiyue*). The *Mahāsāṅghika Vinaya* tells of a band of 500 monkeys who see the moon's reflection at the bottom of a well. In order to rescue the moon, the monkey king grasps a tree branch and a chain of monkeys forms, each grasping the tail of the one before. The branch breaks, and all the monkeys fall into the well.[12] Second, monkeys suggest the Original Mind, or buddha mind, spontaneous and free of time and space. Thus they carry "ancient mirrors" in the following anecdote featuring Xuefeng Yicun (822–908): "While the master and monks were on the way to the temple farm to perform daily labor, they encountered a group of monkeys. The master said, 'These animals all carry ancient mirrors on their backs, but they've come to steal the rice from my stalks!'"[13]

white egrets—in Daoist usage the egret or crane or heron represents the sage, or the Dao itself. The source is probably the sixth century B.C.E. legend of Wangzi Qiao, an immortal known for soaring on the back of a crane above sacred Mount Song. In Chan discourse, the egret/crane/heron refers to the enlightened mind. The pairing of monkey and bird became a common polarity, conveying the harmonious integration of activity (*dong*) and stillness (*jing*). Jiashan Shanhui (805–881) was asked, "What is the *viṣaya* of Jiashan?" (i.e., his level of understanding of true reality). The master answered, "Holding its young, the gibbon returns behind the green mountain/A flower in its beak, the bird descends before the blue cliff."[14]

6. Hanshan, *Untitled*[15]

a fool—ignorance (*chi*, Skt. *moha*) is one of the "three poisons" (*sandu*) that obstructs Buddhist attainment; the other two are desire and anger. The "three poisons" are sometimes described as "poisonous snakes" (*dushe*) or "poisonous dragons" (*dulong*).

There's no boat—the *[Larger] Boundless Life Sūtra*, one of the three most important Pure Land school texts, notes: "When the mind's eye sees the Truth, you can cross to the other shore."[16] A similar statement is made in the *Nirvāṇa Sūtra.*[17] Buddha says in the *Diamond Sūtra*, "Monks, you should know that the Dharma I teach is like a raft. Even the Dharma should be abandoned; how much more so the Not-Dharma?"[18] Crossing rivers or streams, and related images like fords, boats, and rafts became frequent Buddhist metaphors for the process of enlightenment; all are related to the idea of bodies of water as the mind. Here, the crucial idea is that there is no boat; in Chan Buddhism, there is nothing on which to rely—nothing you can use as a "vehicle" to salvation.

This shore nor the other—"this shore" refers to *saṃsāra* and "the other" to *nirvāṇa*.

7. Hanshan, *Untitled*[19]

Everyday Way (pingsheng dao)—the idea that the everyday acts of an enlightened person will naturally harmonize with the buddha mind, and that the route to enlightenment is through everyday acts. Equivalent to "everyday mind" (*pingchang xin*), the term ascribed to Mazu Daoyi and Nanquan Puyuan (748–834).[20]

no-mind (wuxin)—the boundless mind without intentional thought, enlightenment.

8.   Hanshan, *Untitled*[21]

chamber (ku)—literally "cave," and if the legend that Hanshan lived in a cave on Mount Tiantai is relevant, the word may mean that here (though that would suggest there is a cave inside a cave!). Yet more generally a *chanku* is a meditation cell, and by extension a monastery.

leather-lined coat (buqiu)—a cotton cloth coat with a hide or fur lining. In literary texts, this simple garment is almost *de rigueur* for mountain recluses.

True Buddha (tianzhen fo)—another name for the *dharmakāya*, the Dharma body of the Buddha, the Absolute, Suchness (Skt. *bhūtatathatā*).

9.   Hanshan, *Untitled*[22]

white lotus—the lotus is a favored symbol in Buddhist texts. The Buddha is often depicted or described as holding a lotus flower, and he and the various Buddhist deities sit or stand on pedestals of lotus. The *Flower Garland Sūtra* describes the universe itself as an infinitely large lotus flower. One explanation of the association is that the pure blossoms arise from the muck at the bottom of still water, analogous to Buddha's attainment of *nirvāṇa* while dwelling in *saṃsāra*. Hence the lotus became a symbol for the buddha nature in everyone. The white lotus (*bailian*; Skt. *puṇḍarīka*) is a metaphor for the inner mind; it had a specific Chinese association with the Pure Land (Lotus) school.

10.   Shide, *Untitled*[23]

*Shide (Foundling) (Tang dynasty) is as popular as but no more historical than Hanshan. According to legend, he was so called because as a child he was found on the road by Master Fenggan of Guoqing Temple on Mount Tiantai (in Tiantai, Zhejiang). He was set to work overseeing the lamps and incense in the refectory, but then one day he climbed up on the altar, sat down cross-legged, and began to snack on the offerings, while loudly cursing the solemn Buddha image. The angry monks drove Shide out, and he was demoted to cooking and washing dishes. He saved the kitchen scraps for the times his friend Hanshan would come down from his cave hermitage. Shide once noticed that birds were eating the offerings left for the tutelary deity of the monastery. He then beat the deity's image, saying, "You can't even protect your food. How could you protect the monastery?" That night, the god appeared in the dreams of all of the monks in the temple, saying, "Shide has beaten me!" The next morning, when the monks saw the whip marks on the image and found they had all had the same dream, they realized Shide was no ordinary man. Shide eventually left with Hanshan; to where, no one knows. He is sometimes considered an incarnation of Samantabhadra, the Bodhisattva of Great Vows. More than fifty poems are collected under Shide's name; the style is similar to that of the Hanshan corpus.[24]

carts (che) — carts and wheels have several distinct Buddhist meanings. The "turning wheel" (Ch. *lunhui*) is the round of rebirth, *saṃsāra*. The goal of Buddhists would seem to be to stop the wheel, or to escape from it. However, other usages are more positive. Mahāyāna itself is the "Great Vehicle" (*dasheng*) to salvation, and Buddha turns the "Wheel of Dharma" (*falun*). Carts also represent the "expedient means" used by Buddha and the other enlightened to encourage living beings of lesser understanding to progress on the spiritual path. These are the three carts from the parable of the burning house in the *Lotus Sūtra*: a wealthy man returns home to find the house in flames while all his sons remain inside, oblivious of the danger. The man entices his sons out by promising them rides on goat carts, deer carts, and ox carts, whereupon they discover only a single great cart in which to ride — the "one vehicle" that represents the bodhisattva path.[25] Wheels are also sometimes metaphors for the higher levels of attainment, as their turning (*zhuan*) carries the practitioner to a "place of transformation" or "turning place" (*zhuanchu*). It says in *Transmission* 2, "Following the ten thousand *viṣaya*, the mind turns/And at the turning point truly can find peace."[26] The commentary to *Blue Cliff* 37 says, "If you can speak of the place without speech or go to the place that cannot be traveled to, then this can be called the place of turning the body."[27] The commentary to *Blue Cliff Record* 79, concerning Chan Master Touzi Datong (845–914), includes these lines: "A man of old once said, 'At the turning place of the Function Wheel, the practitioner remains lost.' Touzi's Function Wheel, however, turns round and round, completely without obstruction."[28]

evil death — there are three moral qualities in Buddhism: evil, good, and neutral. Deeds that have strong character, either good or bad, affect the stream of our present life and may produce a result in a future life — this is the functioning of karma. Evil karma can fix your next transfiguration; as such it is often referred to as "evil place" (*echu*) or "evil road" (*edao*). The evil destinies are three: to go to hell, to become a hungry ghost, and to be reborn as an animal.

Yakṣa (yecha) — a broad class of nature spirits in Indian mythology. Some are benevolent; others (as here) are demons who harm human beings.

11. Shide, *Untitled*[29]

a pure crystal — here, the buddha nature inherent in the human mind. Rock crystal (Skt. *sphaṭikā*; Ch. *shuijing*) is one of the Seven Jewels (Skt. *sapta ratna*; Ch. *qibao*). The *[Larger] Boundless Life Sūtra* describes the Pure Land paradise of Sukhāvāti as adorned with sparkling trees made of the Seven Jewels, which make sweet sounds when moved by the wind. They surround ponds of lotus, from which spring rays of light containing myriad buddhas to teach the Dharma.[30] Shide's focus is the transparency and reflectivity of crystal. His poem alludes directly to the *Pratyutpanna samādhi sūtra* (Concentration That Perceives the Buddhas of the Present), a very early Indian Mahāyāna text. In it Buddha explains that pure mirrors, crystals, oil, and water all perfectly reflect what is before them, yet "The reflections do not arise from within, nor do they enter from without." Just so the mind may think of Buddha, who "comes from nowhere" and "departs for nowhere." Yet even this "Buddha" is a mind creation. The truth is that the mind itself is buddha mind, and the mind without thoughts is *nirvāṇa*.[31] An image similar to the crystal is the drop of water. In *Treasury of the True Dharma Eye*, the Japanese master Dōgen (1200–1253) wrote that "incalculable buddha lands are realized even within a single drop of water," and further that "in the thorough study of the flowing or the not-flowing of a single [drop of] water, the entirety of the ten thousand things is instantly realized."[32] Fayan Wenyi meant this when he referred to "one drop of water from the Cao Stream source" (*Caoyuan yidi shui*), as Cao Stream is where the Sixth Patriarch Huineng taught.[33]

man and heaven—two of the Six Common Realms (*liudao* or *liuqu*) where a sentient being can be reborn: the worlds of hell, hungry ghosts, animals, *asuras* (demons), humans, and heavenly beings. Add to these the Four Sacred Realms of *śrāvakas* (the hearers—*arhans/arhats*), *pratyekabuddhas* (the self-enlightened), bodhisattvas, and buddhas to make Ten Realms (*shijie, shi fajie*) altogether.

12. Shide, *Untitled*[34]

Nirvāṇa's *rule*—Chinese Buddhists often employed Daoist terminology, with some change of meaning. The term here is literally "nonaction" (*wuwei*), and originally referred to the Daoist idea that the sage achieves everything by doing nothing that is contrary to Dao, the universal force. To Buddhists it refers to that which is "uncreated" and "unconditioned" and so is a frequent alternate term for *nirvāṇa*.

Strip your mind bare—literally "wear no threads in your mind." The reference is to the euphemism "wear not a single thread" (*yisi bugua* or *cunsi bugua*), which means "totally naked." In Buddhist contexts the phrase describes the mind completely free of delusions, as the word "threads" (*si*) is a homonym pun for "thoughts" or "worries."

many lives (shengsheng)—rebirth, *saṃsāra*. The *Śūraṃgama sūtra* says, "Life and then death, and death and then life, life after life and death after death, like a great turning wheel of fire that never ends."[35]

Master of Paradise—the term is likely short for "Master of Heaven and Man" (*tianren shi*) (Skt. Śāstā Devamanuṣyānām), an epithet for a buddha.[36]

13. Shide, *Untitled*[37]

Stone Bridge—a well-known site on Mount Tiantai. There are two streams that fall down cliffs and pass beneath the bridge. A story related by the Japanese pilgrim Jōjin (1011–1091) is that only "pure" monks may cross Stone Bridge. Legend has it that five hundred *luohan* (or *aluohan*—the Chinese transliteration for Skt. *arhan/arhat*) dwell nearby.[38] To Chinese Mahāyānists, *luohan* are beings who delay *nirvāṇa* while serving as "protectors of the Dharma" until the coming of Maitreya (*Mile fo*), the bodhisattva who is destined to become the Buddha of the Future.

Waterfalls (pubu)—the waterfall image presents some difficulty of interpretation. On the one hand, poets drew on the long tradition of Daoist-inspired landscape poetry and associated the waterfall with qualities of transparency/purity, natural dynamism, and proximity to the source of a stream. On the other, the "rushing torrent" (*puliu*) is the metaphor Cittamātra writer Vasubhandu used to describe the substratum consciousness in its *saṃsāric* aspect, the torrent that must be stilled for worries and aggravations (*fannao*; Skt. *kleśa*) to disperse and enlightenment to occur. The images of a waterfall and a rushing torrent *seem* distinct. Yet in some classical usage *puliu* is used incontrovertibly to mean waterfall, as in a poem by Cen Shen (715–770), "From the cliff hangs a suspended torrent;/ Brilliant white in space."[39] How to interpret the image in a Chinese Buddhist poem depends on context.

Hua Peak—the highest point around Mount Tiantai.

14. Fenggan, *Written on the Wall*[40]

*Fenggan (Tang dynasty) was the third of the legendary trio of eccentric recluses on Mount Tiantai, which included Hanshan and Shide. He was traditionally believed to have been a monk at Guoqing Temple, where he enjoyed pounding the rice. His face and appearance were surpassingly ugly: his hair was cut level with his eyebrows and shoulders, and he covered himself with a tattered, hide-lined cotton robe. Whenever anyone asked him about Buddhism, he would only say, "Anytime." His comings and goings were always sudden, and none could predict them. When he had leisure, he would often ride a tiger in and out the temple gates while loudly singing a song, terrifying the other monks. When Prefect Lü Qiuyin came to visit Guoqing Temple, he found that Fenggan had already died. When he entered Fenggan's old room, he found only tiger tracks. Fenggan was sometimes considered an incarnation of Amitābha, the Buddha of Boundless Light who rules the Pure Land paradise. Two poems are attributed to him.[41]

This poem is a variation on those attributed to Huineng and Shenxiu in the East Mountain poetry competition; see the introduction.

15. Wang Fanzhi, *Untitled*[42]

*Wang Fanzhi (Wang the Brahmacārin) (Tang dynasty) is the name associated with more than three hundred Tang dynasty proselytizing poems in a vernacular style, most of which are extant today solely due to the chance discovery in the early twentieth century of manuscripts sealed for a thousand years in the Dunhuang Buddhist caves in Gansu. As with Hanshan, Wang Fanzhi's historicity is very much an open question. The following intriguing story is as close as we come to a biography:

> Wang Fanzhi was from Liyang in Weizhou. Fifteen li east of the city of Liyang lived Wang Dezu. During the time of Emperor Wen of Sui (r. 589–601), a crabapple tree at Wang's home developed a burl as large as a bushel measure. After three years Dezu saw that it had rotted, so he cut into its bark. Therein he found an infant boy, whom he nurtured and raised. When the boy reached the age of seven, he could talk, and said, "Who gave birth to me? And what is my name?" Dezu told him the complete story. The boy then named himself Linmu Fantian [Brahma deva of the Tree]. Later this was changed to Fanzhi [Brahmacārin]. He said, "The Wang family raised me; I can be surnamed Wang." Fanzhi wrote poetry to instruct people, and it was exceedingly profound.

Fanzhi is not properly a name at all, but is rather a Chinese rendering of the Sanskrit term for a lay Buddhist celibate. Most researchers now believe that the collection was by a variety of hands in the early Tang period, and that the poems were used for instruction in Buddhist temples and monasteries. Mention of the Wang Fanzhi poems in a variety of Tang and Song dynasty sources, as well as a Heian period (784–897) reference in Japan, attests to their widespread popularity. Yet after the Song they were forgotten, until their unexpected reappearance at Dunhuang.[43]

16. Wang Fanzhi, *Untitled*[44]

Fate's Judge—Wang's poem includes a description of the Buddhist hells that closely matches that in other sources: Fate's Judge is the deity who decides the punishment your karma deserves; the No-Hope River, sometimes portrayed as running with blood, is the Chinese River Styx, the boundary dividing the hells from the world of the living; even the demons and particular punishments Wang describes have long textual histories. The most comprehensive—and terrifying—description is in the *Kṣitigarbha Sūtra*.[45] Punishment in the hells is temporary: evil karma is gradually erased through suffering, making rebirth possible.

seventh day—in popular Chinese Buddhist funeral observance, a prayer service was held on the seventh day after a death, and another every seven days until forty-nine days had passed, to assist the soul in gaining rebirth.

17. Wang Fanzhi, *Untitled*[46]

lightless holes (wuming ku)—equivalent to ignorance. "Darkness without illumination" (Ch. *wuming*, Skt. *avidya*) refers to the misperception of things as they really are, which is common to unenlightened people and is the basis of all their delusions and affliction.

18. Wang Fanzhi, *Untitled*[47]

mind transmission (xinchuan)—the direct mind-to-mind transmission from master to disciple.

19. Wang Fanzhi, *Untitled*[48]

20 Jingyun, *Old Riverman*[49]

*Jingyun was an accomplished poet and cursive-style calligrapher who was a contemporary of the poet Cen Shen (715–770). Three of his poems remain extant. Two poems by Cen provide additional key information. The first is "Together with Han Zun, I Pay a Visit to Monk Jingyun Hui to the East of Yanshi":

> In the shadow of the mountain, the old monk explains the Laṅkāvatāra,
> As homeward Yiyang travelers pass in the distance.
> Mist thick and grass wet from last night's rain;
> After rain, an autumn wind crosses the Grand Canal.
> On this empty mountain at close of day, dusty affairs are few;
> On the wide plain in the distance, travelers seem so small.
> By Ministers Shallows, the evening bell;
> Over Outrider Ford, one returning bird.

The geographical details allow us to pinpoint Jingyun's temple residence most likely on Mount Song (in Dengfeng, Henan). Another of Cen Shen's poems is "Crossing the Pass, I Stop by Huayue Temple on the Way to Visit Fahua Monk

Yun." Huayue Temple is better known as Songyue Temple, and was located on the middle of the three peaks that make up Mount Song. Fahua Temple was another name for Fawang Temple at the same location. Thus Monk Yun—almost certainly Jingyun—was associated with Fawang Temple on Mount Song when Cen Shen visited. Mount Song was where Bodhidharma had carried out his "wall-gazing" two centuries earlier.[50]

Wild rice (zizania latifolia)—an edible plant that grows in standing water.

Floating heart (nymphoides peltalum)—an edible form of water lily, with fringed leaves about four inches across and fringed yellow flowers about one inch across.

beyond all dust—"dust" (chen'ai) refers to defilements or afflictions that obscure the pure mind. By extension, it is the world of *saṃsāra*.

21. Lingyi, *New Wellspring at Yifeng Temple*[51]
*Lingyi (728–762) was from Guangling (Yangzhou, Jiangsu); his secular surname was Wu. Already at the age of nine he shunned corruption and resolved to become a monk. He came from a wealthy family, but when he shaved his head and became a monk at age twenty, he distributed his property to the orphans in his clan, taking with him only a cassock and staff. He became a disciple in the line of the eminent Tang monk Fali, who was a specialist in the *Vinaya* (monastic disciplinary rules). He first settled at Nan Xuanliu Temple on Mount Kuaiji (near Shaoxing, Zhejiang). Later he was abbot of several temples, including Yifeng Temple in Yuhang (Yuhang, Zhejiang). This temple faced a beautiful mountain scene, and Lingyi happily wandered alone. It was said his disciples benefited from his instruction "like good fields receiving spring rain." A *Discourse on the Dharma Nature* is attributed to him. Lingyi was a "friend beyond the dust" of secular poets Zhu Fang, Zhang Ji, Huangfu Zeng, and others. When he died, his friend Guanxiu (832–912) wrote, "A great branch in the Chan forest has broken/A roofbeam of the Dharma house has collapsed." More than forty poems attributed to him are extant.[52]

The event this poem describes is recorded in his entry in *Eminent Monks*. The temple was on high ground and originally had no wellspring. One day water suddenly and spontaneously came bubbling up, covering the courtyard.

22. Lingyi, *Written at a Monastery*[53]
Tiger Stream—the course of this stream ran in front of Donglin Temple on Mount Lu (near Jiujiang, Jiangxi). The stream figures in a legend about the monk Huiyuan (334–416), who founded the temple in 386. Huiyuan had made a vow never to cross the stream. One day, after a convivial (but certainly apocryphal!)

conversation with the poet Tao Qian (365–427) and the Daoist Master Lu Xiu-jing (406–477), the monk was seeing off his guests when without realizing it, he crossed the stream. A tiger thereupon roared. When Huiyuan first came to Mount Lu, he gathered around him 123 monks and laymen to study Buddhism and to swear to a life of purity before the image of Amitābha. Besides building the temple, the group grew white lotus as their symbol of purity; thus they were called the Lotus Society, also known as the White Lotus Society. This was the precursor to the Pure Land (Lotus) sect of Buddhism. According to the *Record of Mount Lu,* the water needed to fill the lotus pond magically gushed out of the nearby Dragon Spring when Huiyuan hit the ground with his staff.[54]

Vines and lichens—creeping fig (*ficus pumila*) and beard lichen (*usnea longis-sima*), which together are associated with hermits. The *locus classicus* is the "Moun-tain Spirit" poem of the "Nine Songs" of the *Songs of Chu* anthology (ca. third century B.C.E. to second century C.E.): "There is a man, on the mountainside/His coat is of creeping fig, and his belt of bearded lichen."

23. Lingyi, *Drinking Tea at Green Mountain Pond with Layman Yuan*[55]
Layman (jushi; *Skt.* grhapati *or* upāsaka*)*—one who cultivates the Buddhist way while remaining at home.

Tea—tea drinking was particularly associated with Chan and Zen. A legend (apparently of Japanese origin) states that Bodhidharma was once disgusted with himself for falling asleep while meditating, so he cut off his eyelids and cast them on the ground. They took root and became tea plants. It was believed that tea was good for the health and increased mental sharpness—a great boon to monks, who did not eat after midday and spent much of their time in meditation.

24   Lingyi, *Written at Eastern Hermitage*[56]
Cold bamboo—bamboo, pine, and plum comprise the "three friends of winter" (*suihan sanyou*), and in literature and art are frequent metaphors for one who maintains moral principles even in adversity. Bamboo and pine are evergreens, and the plum tree flowers before winter has passed. All three appear commonly in both secular and religious poetry. A monk asked Dayang Jingxuan (943–1027), "What is the *viṣaya* of Dayang?" The master answered, "The lone crane and the old gibbon call in the echoing valley;/Thin pines and cold bamboo hold the green mist."[57]

25. Jiaoran, *Clouds on the Stream*[58]
*Jiaoran (730–799), *zi* Qingshu, whose secular name was Xie Zhou, was born in Changcheng (Huzhou, Zhejiang) on the western shore of Lake Tai. He became

a monk at Lingyin Temple near West Lake in Hangzhou (Hangzhou, Zhejiang) and traveled widely throughout his life, studying with most major contemporary masters. His first teacher of note was *Vinaya* Master Shouzhi (d. 771). Jiaoran became a dominant figure on the literary scene in eighth-century China, known for his poetry, literary criticism, and conversation. He settled at Miaoxi Monastery on Mount Zhu, just south of Lake Tai, where he built a small dwelling that he named The Retreat at East Stream. Among his close friends and neighbors were Lu Yu (d. ca. 804), author of the *Classic of Tea,* and fellow monk-poet Lingche (746–816). Another frequent companion was the master calligrapher Yan Zhenqing (709–785), who was for a time the local prefect. Jiaoran also exchanged poems with the major Tang poet Wei Yingwu (737–ca. 792). Late in life he was invited by the court to submit his collected works to the imperial library. Several hundred of Jiaoran's poems are extant. His three works of criticism are the best contemporary description of the High Tang poetic style, in which the expression of emotion/ideas was contained within scenic description (the so-called "fusion of feeling and scene"). He also was the first to apply Chan terminology and concepts to poetic writing. Many of his poems reflect his active engagement with the secular world and desire for literary fame, while others affirm the detachment of the Chan practitioner. He clearly recognized the conflict, for in about 785 he gave up writing altogether to devote himself to Chan contemplation. However, within two or three years he was writing again.[59]

Clouds—an apt metaphor for the footloose and spontaneous quality of monks' lives; a related euphemism is "cloud and water monks" (*yunshui seng*). However, in other contexts the tendency of clouds to obscure the light or hide the path may be foremost, suggesting ignorance. The image is thus an excellent example of the variable nature of Chan metaphors.

26. Jiaoran, *Lodging on an Autumn Night at Broken Mountain Temple*[60]
Broken Mountain Temple—also called Xingfu Temple, on Mount Lu (in Changshu, Jiangsu).

lamp—Jiaoran's image of a solitary lamp glowing in a temple window recalls the Daoist exhortation to empty the mind in *Zhuangzi* 4, "Look into that closed room, the empty chamber where brightness is born! Fortune and blessing gather where there is stillness,"[61] and prefigures the Chan metaphor of "a single lamp within the room" (*shi'nei yizhan deng*) for the realization of the buddha nature within one's mind, as used, for example, in *Blue Cliff* 17. An analogous phrase, appearing in *Blue Cliff* 96, is "the True Buddha sits within the room" (*zhenfo wuli zuo*).

27. Jiaoran, *Sending off Monk Weiliang on His Return to Dongting Lake*[62]
    Dongting Lake — in south central China (in Hunan Province).
    mind ground (xindi) — the central metaphor relating Buddhism to the cultivation of growing things. The Dunhuang version of the *Platform Sūtra* includes the poem, "If correct flowers bloom in the mind ground,/Five blossoms flower from the stem./Together practice the *prajñā* wisdom;/In the future this will be the enlightenment of the Buddha."[63]
    mountains in a mirror — reflections point to the illusory nature of reality and the truth of *śūnyatā*. *Blue Cliff* 38 includes the line, "A picture of mountains in a mirror of water/Birds cannot fly across."

28. Jiaoran, *Accompanying Vice Censor-in-chief Lu on a Leisurely Ramble to a Mountain Temple*[64]
    Holding candles — the image recalls the phrase "holding candles to wander in the night" (bingzhu yeyou), attributed to Cao Pi (187–226), Emperor Wen of Wei. The implication is that life is short, so should be lived to the fullest.

29. Jiaoran, *Early Autumn in Tonglu, Wishing to Return Home; Sent to Monk Daoyan*[65]
    Tonglu — Tonglu, Zhejiang.

30. Jiaoran, *Floating Alone on West Stream*[66]
    Dao — the use of this term was not limited to the Daoists; Buddhists used it to refer to the path to enlightenment, and Confucians to the way of the sage.
    True Nature (zhenxing) — a Buddhist term with a Daoist origin. In Daoism, it is one's original nature as endowed by heaven. *Zhuangzi* 9 includes the line, "To munch grass, drink from the stream, lift up their feet and gallop — this is the true nature of horses."[67] In Chan it is the buddha nature within every living being. The *Platform Sūtra* says, "The instant you see into your own nature — this is the True [Buddha]."[68]
    Nameless (wuming) — also originally a Daoist term, meaning that which was before the creation of heaven and earth. Laozi wrote, "It was from the Nameless that Heaven and Earth sprang;/The named is but the mother that rears the ten thousand creatures, each after its kind."[69] In Chan, names and language are obstacles to enlightenment, because they are forms of discrimination. *Records of Linji* states, "Sūtras and commentaries take the three types of body [the Dharma Body, the Enjoyment Body, and the Transformation Body of Buddha] as the ultimate principles, but mountain monks see this as incorrect — the three types of body are names and language, and are three types of dependence."[70]

31   Jiaoran, *Case Reviewer Tang Hosts Chan Master Jue at Hengshui Pavilion*[71]
      Hengshui—a river in Pingxiang, Hebei.

> *Immortal Isle*—Cangzhou, a legendary land where immortal recluses dwell.

> *knocks at the barrier* (kouguan)—the words usually refer to imminent enlightenment; to cross the barrier is to reach truth. *Blue Cliff* 12 records, "Xuedou easily goes to where the barriers are broken and the hinges are smashed to reveal a little something to let you see."[72] Here, Jiaoran simultaneously praises Chan Master Jue for his Buddhist attainment and tells us that the guest is knocking at the gate of the pavilion.

> *Ultimate Truth* (liaoyi)—perfect enlightenment. The term is also used to describe teaching methods that lead directly to "pure truth," bypassing expedients and "conventional truth."

32.   Jiaoran, *Hearing the Bell*[73]
      Enlightenment triggered by simple sensory experience is frequently recorded in Chan texts. The master Xiangyan Zhixian (fl. ninth century) was so affected when he heard the sound of a tile shard hitting a piece of bamboo. Deshan Xuanjian (782–865) gained illumination when a candle was blown out and he was suddenly surrounded by darkness. Lingyun Zhiqin (fl. ninth century) was enlightened when he beheld the blossoming of peach flowers. The master's sudden shout was a frequent catalyst, as it was for Baizhang Huaihai (720–814); he remarked that Mazu's shout left him deaf for three days.

33.   Jiaoran, *Instructing Mahāyāna Monks in My Cell South of the Lake*[74]
      a boat unbound—Jiaoran's life without attachments, which he admits is still a failure. What he should do is abandon the boat to reach the other shore.

> *Thoughts that East Mount clouds convey*—an allusion to the teachings of the Fourth and Fifth Patriarchs, Daoxin and Hongren. See the introduction.

34.   Qingjiang, *Meeting Rain at a Buddhist Temple*[75]
      *Qingjiang was from Kuaiji (Shaoxing, Zhejiang). He was active from the Dali (766–780) to Zhenyuan (785–805) reign periods and was associated with Bianjue Temple in Xiangzhou (Xiangyang, Hubei). Against his parent's wishes he became a monk, studying under *Vinaya* masters Tanyi (d. 772) and Shouzhi (d. 771). His elders said of him, "This is a thousand-*li* colt of the Buddhist Gate." However, he did not get along well with people, owing to an arrogant and irritable temper. For minor reasons he argued with Tanyi and left the priesthood. He subsequently traveled widely, visiting *Vinaya* communities. He castigated himself: "I've traveled over half the empire, but there is no one like my first teacher." He

then returned to Tanyi and begged to be readmitted. Qingjiang also studied Chan and met on two occasions with National Teacher Nanyang Huizhong (d. 775), who "secretly transmitted the essentials of mind" to him; Qingjiang thus gained "total understanding of the mysterious principles." Known for his literary ability, in his day he was as well known as Jiaoran. More than twenty of his poems are extant.[76]

Empty Gate (kongmen)—a term for Buddhism, with focus on its emptiness doctrine.

draining my body (dan wushen)—the word *dan* literally means light, thin, or pale; the verbal use here suggests placidity or serenity of mind. Such Chan use of the word eventually led to its broader use in literary studies: in the Song period the "even and pale" (*pingdan*) was a much sought-after poetic quality.[77]

35. Pang Yun (Layman Pang), *Untitled*[78]

*Pang Yun (?–815), *zi* Daoxuan, popularly known as Pang Jushi (Layman Pang), is one of the most popular Tang Chan figures. Although details of his life are scarce and hard to verify, he is more definitely a historical personage than Hanshan or Wang Fanzhi. His discourse records are extant (in various recensions), and his dialogues with more than twenty Tang monks are included in the transmission-of-the-lamp literature. Layman Pang was from either Hengyang (in present Hunan) or Xiangyang (in Hubei); he certainly spent much of his life in Xiangyang, and died there. Some sources say his father was a magistrate in Hengyang. It is recorded that he devoted himself to Buddhism starting in his middle age, when he was already a householder with a wife and two children. He did not take up religion by half measures: the story goes that he loaded all his valuable possessions on a boat and then threw them into the waters of Lake Dongting to avoid the distraction of attachments. He gave up his house to be the site of a temple, while he and his daughter Lingzhao lived humbly and sold bamboo ladles in the market to make ends meet. The figures with whom Layman Pang associated were all disciples of either Shitou or Mazu, so it is no surprise that the approximately two hundred verses attributed to him appear firmly grounded in the tenets of the Hongzhou school.[79]

pāramitā—see the introduction.

marklessness—to lack the "three marks," to see the world in terms of emptiness; see the introduction.

36. Pang Yun (Layman Pang), *Untitled*[80]

guardians of the body (hushen)—the buddhas, deities, and even the Buddhist Dharma, to which believers address prayers for protection and help (*hushen jiachi*). Pang Yun says that faith in the power of prayer is a form of dependence that must be eradicated on the path to enlightenment.

37. Pang Yun (Layman Pang), *Untitled*[81]
Three Realms (Skt. triloka; Ch. sanjie*)*—the series of three "worlds" that the Buddhist experiences on the path to enlightenment: the Desire Realm (Skt. *kāmadhātu; Ch. yujie*), the Form Realm (Skt. *rūpadhātu; Ch. sejie*), and the Nonform Realm (Skt. *arūpadhātu; Ch. wusejie*).

38. Pang Yun (Layman Pang), *Untitled*[82]
snakes/rats—the physical world and time, based on an allusion to the short *Parable Sūtra*, a Tang dynasty text. To escape an evil elephant, a man suspends himself in a well by clinging to a root. Yet above him are two rats chewing on the root, while below four poisonous snakes await his fall. The text explains that the elephant is impermanence, the rats are day and night, and the snakes are the four elements—earth, water, fire, and wind.[83]

Pure Land (Jingtu)—Chan reinterprets the Pure Land as a metaphor for the enlightened mind. The *Platform Sūtra* notes, "It is only that the mind should be pure—then it is the Western [Paradise] of the self-nature!"[84]

39. Damei Fachang, *Untitled*[85]
*Damei Fachang (752–839) was from Xiangyang (in Hubei); his secular surname was Zheng. As a boy he became a Buddhist novice at Yuquan Temple on Mount Yuquan (in Dangyang, Hubei), where his amazing memory for the sūtra literature was noted. At twenty he was ordained a monk at Longxing Temple, and his interest turned to Chan. He joined the community of Mazu Daoyi (709–788). When he first met with the master, he asked, "What is the Buddha?" Mazu answered, "The mind is the Buddha (*jixin shifo,* or *jixin jifo*)." Fachang was immediately enlightened. This exchange became the basis for *Gateless Pass* 30. Fachang left Mazu and after a period of reclusion at Mount Tiantai, moved to Mount Damei (Great Plum Mountain) (in Yinxian, Zhejiang). He built a hermitage and lived there for almost forty years. When a visiting monk told him that Mazu had changed his Buddha-Dharma and now taught "not mind, not Buddha" (*feixin feifo*), Fachang said, "That old man just causes trouble for people, and there will never be an end! Let him have his 'not mind, not Buddha,' I'll just stick to 'the mind is the Buddha.'" The monk returned and told this to Mazu, who said, "The plum is ripe!" Fachang's hermitage became the nucleus for Husheng Temple, founded in 836. When he died three years later, he left sixty-nine disciples.[86]

At least one source attributes this poem to Longshan Yinshan (fl. late eighth to early ninth century), another disciple of Mazu who became a hermit. After an exchange with Dongshan Liangjie (807–869) and Sengmi (fl. early ninth century), Yinshan chanted the poem, then burned down his hut and retreated deeper into the mountains.[87]

40. Guling Shenzan, *Bees at the Window*[88]

*Guling Shenzan (fl. ninth century) was a disciple of Baizhang Huaihai (720–814). He had received his early training at Dazhong Temple on Mount Guling in Fuzhou (in Fujian) before leaving to seek out Huaihai. When he returned to Mount Guling, his original teacher asked him whether he had gained anything while away. He said no, and was set to work. One day his teacher was reading sūtras by a window, while a bee was buzzing against the windowpane. Shenzan intoned this poem in comment, which convinced his teacher of his spiritual progress. Shenzan was thereupon asked to teach the Dharma to the assembly, and he later became abbot for several years. When he was about to die, he shaved, bathed, rang the bell, and said to the community, "Do you understand the soundless *samādhi*?" The monks said no, and the master said, "Listen carefully, and think of nothing else." All the monks cocked their heads and listened intently, whereupon the master passed away.[89]

The door is open — a pun. The text has "empty gate," which is a euphemism for Buddhism.

old paper — windowpanes were made of oiled paper instead of glass in traditional China. Guling uses the image to counsel against reliance on the sūtra literature.

41. Jia Dao, *Looking for a Recluse but Not Finding Him*[90]

*Jia Dao (779–843), *zi* Langxian, *hao* Jieshi, was from Fanyang (Zhuoxian, Hebei — near modern-day Beijing). His introspective, sometimes melancholy poetry, with its delicate observations of the natural world, combined with scattered information about his difficult and poverty-stricken life, created for him the romantic reputation of a poets' poet. As a result, it is hard to tell where facts about him end and legends begin. We do know that he was from a poor family and was a monk only in the early part of his life, until about 810. His name in religion was Wuben (Rootless). One story has it that he moved to the "eastern capital" of Luoyang (Luoyang, Henan), where he was unhappy to find that local regulations forbade monks to leave their temples after noon. He wrote a poem about his frustration, which attracted the attention of the famed literatus Han Yu (768–824).

Some sources say it was Han who persuaded Jia Dao to return to secular life. In any case, it is certain that he became an important member of Han's literary circle, which also included Meng Jiao (751–814) and Zhang Ji (776–ca. 829). He repeatedly tried to pass the metropolitan civil service examinations, without success. During the reign of Emperor Wenzong (r. 827–841) he was slandered and banished to the south. Toward the end of his life, he held minor administrative posts in the area around Suizhou (Suining, Sichuan). In 840 he was transferred to Puzhou, just north of Suizhou, and in 843 promoted to Administrator of Revenue—his first position of real authority; however, he died before he could take the post. At his death, it was said, he owned only "a sick donkey and an old lute." When the news reached Wuke, Jia Dao's cousin and himself a Buddhist priest, in grief he wrote,

> All day I've drowned in sadness for you;
> Jieshi, you were so lofty and alone.
> Your poetic name will linger through the ages
> Yet as exile you passed through this life.
> Did you revise the poems you wrote in Shu?
> And now, only the slapdash funeral rites of Ba.
> By a dark gate I read your old scrolls;
> I wish to see you, but never will again.

Jia Dao maintained close relationships with "poet-monks" (*shiseng*) and other Buddhists throughout his life; many of his several hundred extant poems contain Buddhist resonances.[91]

There is a long tradition of "Looking for XX but not finding him" (*xun XX buyu*) poems in China; the subgenre has both Daoist and Buddhist associations. Typically, the recluse/sage/monk lives high atop a mountain; the poet's climb upward signifies a quest for spiritual attainment. Frequently the failure to find the master indicates a failure of the quest, as here: the clouds (of ignorance?) obscure the master's whereabouts. Occasionally poems in the subgenre are more complex: while the avowed goal of finding the master is not attained, the dynamic landscape itself subtly reveals his presence.

42. Jia Dao, *Quatrain*[92]

43. Jia Dao, *Lodging After Rain on Adjutant Liu's Pond*[93]
      Blue Stream—Lanqi in Lantian (Lantian, Shanxi).

Reeds — according to legend, First Patriarch Bodhidharma crossed the Yangtze on a reed; thus reeds/rushes are frequently associated with the Chan school, as in the phrase "Bodhidharma's reed" (*luye Damo*).

44. Jia Dao, *Drifting on South Stream with Director Han of the Bureau of Appointments* [94]
Director Han — the famous poet and essayist Han Yu (768–824), Jia Dao's close friend, who late in his career was Director of the Bureau of Appointments in the Ministry of Personnel.

the ford — the place where one "crosses to the other shore," both literally and metaphorically.

45. Wuke, *Traveling to a Mountain Temple* [95]
*Wuke, from Fanyang (Zhuoxian, Hebei), was Jia Dao's paternal cousin. He resided at Tianxian Temple. A poem by Jia Dao places his "grass hut" on Mount Song (in Dengfeng, Henan). Wuke was as well known a poet as his cousin. About one hundred of his poems are extant. [96]

46. Wuke, *Sent to Monk Yuan at Qinglong Temple* [97]
Qinglong Temple — in Jishan, Shanxi.

clepsydra — the Chinese water clock, which measured time by means of a steady drip of water into a container. One told the time by checking the water level on a scale of marks. A "lotus water clock" was purportedly invented by Huiyao, a disciple of White Lotus Society founder Huiyuan (334–416) on Mount Lu (near Jiujiang, Jiangxi). In the pond he planted a lotus of twelve leaves. As water ran from one leaf to the next, the twelve Chinese watches (two hours each) could be measured. [98]

mountain temple — the text uses the euphemism *shangfang*, which literally means highlands. By extension, the term can refer to an abbot.

47. Wuke, *Chrysanthemums* [99]
east fence — an allusion to the nature poet Tao Qian's (365–427) "Drinking Wine" poems. Tao grew chrysanthemums beneath his eastern fence; his Daoist-inspired poems describe the contentment and freedom that come when one follows one's own nature. The flowers become an emblem of this kind of life.

quake and fall — the withering of other plants and flowers. The chrysanthemum continues to bloom in the autumn, when many other plants have already faded. Thus it became a common poetic metaphor for longevity and vigorous old age.

Palace buds float in imperial cups—chrysanthemum was added to wine or made into tea, as a long-life tonic.

Butterflies—a symbol of the unreality and uncertainty of the world, based on the Daoist philosopher Zhuangzi's butterfly dream. In *Zhuangzi* 2, he wasn't sure if he had dreamed he was a butterfly or he was a butterfly dreaming he was Zhuangzi.

48. Wuke, *Sending off a Monk*[100]

four seas (sihai)—early Chinese conceived of four seas, one in each of the cardinal directions. "Within the four seas" means all over the empire.

three cassocks (sanshi na)—Chan monks wore robes of three kinds, with five, seven, or nine pieces of cloth sewn together, depending on the occasion.

49. Lingyun Zhiqin, *Untitled*[101]

*Lingyun Zhiqin (fl. ninth century) was from Changxi in Fuzhou (Xiapu, Fujian). He was a disciple of Guishan Lingyou (771–853) (one source has Changqing Da'an [793–883]), and as abbot taught at Mount Lingyun in Fuzhou and Mount Dagui in Tanzhou (in Hunan). When Zhiqin first arrived at Mount Dagui, he was inspired by the teachings of Guishan. Day and night he labored to understand, until his exhausted state of body and mind resembled that of one who is mourning his parents' deaths. All to no avail—but then suddenly he was enlightened when he saw the blossoming peach in spring; he joyfully wrote this poem as evidence. Upon reading it, Guishan Lingyou verified Zhiqin's enlightenment and bestowed the Dharma seal. Master Zhiqin is featured in a dozen short Chan exchanges. For example:

> A monk asked, "After such long battles in the desert, why has merit not been won?" The master replied, "The ruler has declared peace on the three frontiers;/Why bother to build a Great Wall of ten thousand miles?"

In other words, enlightenment will not be achieved through battle with the passions, but rather by focus on the buddha nature (the ruler) within.[102]

searched for the sword—a fruitless search for enlightenment. The allusion is to a story from the *Spring and Autumn Annals* (third century B.C.E.) about a man from Chu who inadvertently dropped his sword off a boat into a river. He then marked the side of the boat so that he would be able to find the sword again, and of course he never could. When his disciples blithely parroted Mazu Daoyi's (709–788) "the mind is the Buddha" dictum, Dongsi Ruhui (744–823) scolded them, "The mind is not the Buddha;/Knowledge is not the Way./The sword was long lost,/Before you marked the boat!"[103] The tie between swords and Buddhism is perhaps the image of "the precious sword of the Diamond King" (*Jin'gang wang baojian*), which is the sword of wisdom that cuts off delusion.

blossoms of peach—the image has deep cultural associations that underpin Lingyun Zhiqin's experience. Tao Qian's (365–427) famous prose work, "The Peach Blossom Spring," describes a lost fisherman who suddenly encounters a grove of flowering peach trees and discovers through it a route to a utopian world. Tao was responding to earlier otherworldly associations. Peaches—the fruit this time—represent immortality. The Queen Mother of the West, an ancient divinity eventually incorporated in the Daoist pantheon, is said to care for an orchard of peach trees at her palace on Mount Kunlun. The fruit ripens once every three thousand years, and a single bite will make one immortal. The God of Longevity also carries a peach.

doubt (yi)—Chinese Chan monks expected cultivation to be a struggle, characterized by great anxiety, even to the point of desperation. In fact, such "doubt" about who one really is, about the nature of the self, sometimes referred to as "a ball of doubt" (*yituan*), was considered a necessary precursor to enlightenment. In an acclaimed text by Gaofeng Yuanmiao (1238–1295) called *The Essentials of Chan*, three indispensable features of Chan practice are summarized: a great root of faith (*daxin'gen*), a great tenacity of purpose (*dafenzhi*), and a great feeling of doubt (*dayiqing*).[104]

50. Dongshan Liangjie, *Untitled*[105]

*Dongshan Liangjie (807–869), who together with his disciple Caoshan Benji (840–901) was retroactively credited with establishing the Cao-Dong school of Chan (the Japanese Sōtō Zen), was from Zhuji in Kuaiji (Zhuji, Zhejiang); his secular surname was Yu. He entered the Buddhist life while still a child, studying Chan with Lingmo (747–818) at Mount Wuxie in Wuzhou (in Zhejiang); he was formally ordained a monk at the age of twenty at Mount Song (in Dengfeng, Henan). After a period of wandering, and lively meetings with Chan masters such as Nanquan Puyuan (748–845) and Guishan Lingyou (771–853), he began studies with Yunyan Tansheng (782–841) at Mount Yunyan in Tanzhou (in Hunan). One day, when Liangjie was taking leave of his teacher, Tansheng said, "You must be very careful, as you've taken on this thing." Liangjie did not understand, but later, when he was crossing a stream, he saw his reflection in the water and was suddenly enlightened. He returned to the mountain and became Tansheng's disciple. Liangjie's career began in earnest after the Buddhist persecution of 845, when he became abbot of a temple at Mount Xinfeng in Ruizhou (in Gao'an, Jiangxi), but he passed most of the latter part of his life teaching at the nearby Puli Monastery on Mount Dong (in Xinchang, Jiangxi). He died in 869. The Tang court posthumously granted him the title Great Master of Original Enlightenment (Wuben Dashi). In 1985, on a hillside at Mount Dong, a small, eroded memorial stūpa was declared by Japanese Sōtō experts to be Liangjie's original resting place.[106]

Liangjie wrote this poem to describe his enlightenment.

51. Dongshan Liangjie, *Untitled*[107]

This simple poem is best understood as presenting the relationship between the absolute and the phenomenal, or *nirvāṇa* and *saṃsāra*. The absolute gives existence to the phenomenal, just as mountain caves are the birthplace of clouds in Chinese tradition. The phenomenal obscures the absolute, as mountains are hidden by clouds. Yet at the same time, the phenomenal reveals the absolute, as the shape of clouds shows the mountain beneath. Liangjie's discourse records include the following exchange:

> A monk asked, "What does 'Green mountain is white cloud's father' mean?" The master replied, "That which is not luxuriant." The monk continued, "Then what does 'White cloud is green mountain's son' mean?" The master answered, "That which does not discriminate between east and west." The monk asked, "What does 'All day white cloud stays close by' mean?" The master said, "Unable to leave." The monk asked, "What does 'Green mountain never knows' mean?" The master said, "Not seeing anything."[108]

Compare Lingyun Zhiqin's (fl. ninth century) words, found in *Transmission* 11: "Question: 'How can one obtain release from life, old age, sickness, and death?' The master answered, 'Green mountain never moves/White clouds come and go on their own.'"[109]

52. Changda, *Living in the Mountains*[110]

*Changda (d. 874), *zi* Wenju, had the secular surname Gu. He became a monk at Mount Dafu in Heyang (Mengxian, Henan). He undertook Buddhist *Vinaya* training, as well as study of Daoist texts, and was also a master of calligraphy in the Wang Xizhi (321–379) and Wang Xianzhi (344–386) styles. In his early years he traveled widely, studying Chan with famous masters. When the Buddhist persecution of 845 occurred, he escaped to the mountains and lived as a recluse at Poshan (Broken Mountain) Temple on Mount Lu (in Changshu, Jiangsu). After Buddhism was returned to favor, Changda gained a great reputation for "a purity akin to that of the white heron." However, he would not allow popularity to compromise his principles. He taught 51 disciples and in 872 was asked to give public lectures on the Dharma, but when aristocrats and literati came to his door, he refused to meet them. One sunny morning he assembled his followers in the courtyard, clasped his hands together, and made his final good-byes. He then lay down and stopped eating, and on the seventh day passed away. His memorial stūpa was erected 300 paces southeast of the temple. Eight "Living in the Mountains" poems are attributed to him.[111]

Mind to mind (xinxin) — mind-to-mind transmission, from teacher to student. Here, the landscape around him is the teacher — thus suggesting "the insentient expounding the Dharma" (*wuqing shuofa*). As Dongshan Liangjie (807–869) said, "How strange!/How strange!/Who could imagine the insentient could expound the Dharma?/Use your ears to hear and it's hard to understand./But listen with your eyes, and then will you know."[112]

53.   Changda, *Living in the Mountains*[113]
Wondrous Function (miaoji) — *ji* is literally "mechanism" or "functioning"; the ancient etymological dictionary *Shuowen jiezi* (second century C.E.) suggests the character originally described the trigger mechanism of a crossbow — thus implicitly a tremendous store of potential energy waiting to be unleashed. An alternate etymology has *ji* as the mechanism on a door that allows it to open. In Chan, *ji* is used in various senses and combinations. The present poem uses the word in a broad sense, to refer to the cosmos as a system with its own mysterious motivating power (Buddha). Analogously, this "mechanism" or "functioning" is used to describe the human mind: *ji* is the potentiality or power to receive the Dharma and realize the buddha nature within.

Primordial Void (taixu) — originally a Daoist term for the primordial ether out of which the cosmos is made, and for the great mysterious principle of Dao. As a Buddhist term, it refers to emptiness.

Ten Thousand Things (wanxiang) — the physical world of causation.

Mysterious Secret (xuanwei) — the absolute truth (of Buddha). *Xuan* (dark, mysterious) is another word/concept shared with the Daoists: Laozi describes the Dao as "the 'Darker than any Mystery,'/The Doorway whence issued all Secret Essences."[114] In Chan, the term refers to the absolute realm, which is beyond language.

54.   Changda, *Living in the Mountains*[115]
thusness (zhenru) — the "truth as it is," *bhūtatathatā,* the perfect and unchanging truth beyond phenomena, the buddha nature.

bodhi tree (jueshu) — literally, the tree of enlightenment; the pippala under which the Buddha attained enlightenment, also called *bodhidruma.*

55. Qibai, *Looking for the Mountain Monk Zhensheng but Not Finding Him*[116]
*Qibai was a literary monk from Yue (Guangdong) whose companions included the poets Yao He (fl. 831), Cao Song (fl. late ninth century), and Li Dong (fl. late ninth century). During the reign of Emperor Xuanzong (r. 847–860), he lived at Jianfu Temple on Mount Jianfu (in Poyang, Jiangxi). The temple was later associated with the Yunmen branch of Chan. Sixteen of his poems remain extant. Upon his death, his friend Li Dong lamented in part, "When I meet a mountain or face the moon, /I'm stricken with grief./Overwhelmed, I cannot speak,/For they are just like the master." Another friend, the famous monk Guanxiu (832–912), visited the mountain soon afterward and wrote, "Who will bow at this new grave?/Desolation, by Wei River side."[117]

gaze-at-the-mind (kanxin)—the same term as used for Shenxiu's approach, which Shenhui and the Southern school criticized as gradualist. Here, the poet displays the usual distrust of that kind of meditation: the mountain monk is *not* sitting on such a rock, and has been guided by white clouds *out* of meditative trance. *Platform Sūtra* 4 explains:

Good friends, there are also those who teach meditation [in terms of] viewing the mind, contemplating tranquility, motionlessness, and nonactivation. You are supposed to make an effort on the basis of these. These deluded people do not understand, and in their grasping become mixed up like all of you here. You should understand that such superficial teachings are greatly mistaken![118]

56. Zhangzhou Luohan Heshang, *Untitled*[119]
*Zhangzhou Luohan Heshang flourished during the reign of Emperor Yizong (r. 860–874). Little is recorded about him, other than that he resided at Luohan Monastery in the coastal district of Zhangzhou (Yunxiao, Fujian), and that he was a disciple of Guannan Daochang and a third-generation disciple of Mazu Daoyi (709–788). This poem is one of two he composed upon attaining enlightenment. In the first poem, he says he began to cultivate Buddhism in the seventh year of the Xiantong reign period (867). Three years later, he asked his master, "What is the source of the Great Way?" Daochang's reply was to hit him hard on the chest. Suddenly, "The ball of doubt shatters, and wolf beasts fall./For the first time, I raise my head and see the round sun."[120]

57. Changsha Jingcen, *Untitled*[121]
*Changsha Jingcen (d. 868) was a disciple of the great master of illogical rhetoric Nanquan Puyuan (748–835), who also taught Zhaozhou Congshen (778–897). His *zi* was Zhaoxian. Jingcen was the first Chan master at Luyuan (Deer Park)

Temple in Tanzhou (Changsha, Hunan); later he wandered about with no fixed address or design, following circumstances. For a time he taught Chan on Mount Changsha (in Hunan), and so became known as the Changsha Monk. He features in numerous Chan exchanges, for example the following from the *Records of Yangshan Huiji* (814–890):

> Changsha and Yangshan were once admiring the moon. Yangshan said, "Every person has this; but they can't use it." Changsha said, "Exactly so. Why don't you use it yourself?" Yangshan replied, "How would you use it?" Changsha gave him a kick to the chest and knocked him over. Yangshan called out, "Ha! You're getting to be just like a big tiger!"

Thenceforward he was known in many quarters as "Big Tiger Cen."[122]

   ten directions (shifang shijie) — the four cardinal directions, the intermediate directions between them, and the nadir and zenith. There is a buddha for each direction.

   This poem appears in *Transmission* 10, and is a source for *gong'an* 46 in *Gateless Pass*. The "hundred-foot pole" (*baizhang gantou*) is a metaphor for reaching a state of pacified mind (*anxin*). One must jump off the pole — abandon all fixed conceptions and attachments — to reach no-mind and enlightenment.

58.   Guanxiu, *Fisherman*[123]

*Guanxiu (832–912), *zi* Deyin, was a major cultural figure in the waning days of the Tang. He was born in Wuzhou (Lanxi, Zhejiang); his secular surname was Jiang. Orphaned at the age of seven, he became an acolyte in a local temple, and later resided for a time in a temple on Mount Shishuang (near Changsha, Hunan) as a disciple of Shishuang Qingzhu (807–888). In the 890s Guanxiu returned to his home region, where he was favored by Qian Liu, future king of Wu-Yue. However, he managed to offend his patron because he refused to reword an already laudatory poem to make it even more flattering. Guanxiu thereupon moved up to the middle Yangtze region, where he came under the protection of the warlord Cheng Rui. Unfortunately, Guanxiu fell out with this patron as well. Depressed, he wrote of his feelings through the medium of a *yongwu shi* (poem on an object) about an inkstone: "This body will have peace only when it's in a box." Finally, he moved all the way west to Shu (Sichuan), where he was welcomed by Wang Jian, king of the region. There Guanxiu was invested as "Great Master of the Chan Moon" (Chanyue Dashi) and ended his days as an honored court poet and teacher. More than five hundred of his poems remain. Famous as a poet, Guanxiu is still perhaps best known for his grotesque but powerful portraits of the Sixteen

Luohan (arhats), which he painted while still under the patronage of Qian Liu. Later, the poet Ouyang Jiong (896–971) described them: "Forms like thin cranes, with ruddy vigor/Heads like crouching rhinoceros, with misshapen skulls." The Song dynasty art historian Guo Ruoxu claimed that Guanxiu's *luohan* were so spiritually powerful that prayers for rain addressed to one temple set were always answered. Guanxiu was also famous as a calligrapher, especially of the dynamic cursive style. Seven of his calligraphies, as well as thirty of his portraits, were in the imperial collections during the Xuanhe era (1119–1126).[124]

Fisherman—a frequent Daoist figure of freedom and harmony with nature here becomes a generalized Buddhist ideal, who is unmoved by the wind and waves of *saṃsāra*. The interest in the poem is in the contrast between the frost and snow that cover his head and the flowering reeds and green mountains around him. The cold suggests his state of mind. When asked what auspicious signs were there on the day Bodhidharma achieved enlightenment, Xutang Zhiyu (1185–1269) answered, "In deep mountains the snow has not melted."[125]

flowering reeds—reeds have general Chan associations, as according to legend Bodhidharma crossed the Yangtze River on one. More specifically, flowering white reeds/rushes (the same word in Chinese) often represent the buddha nature as revealed in the phenomenal world, particularly in a polarity with the moon—the buddha nature in its absolute aspect. Consider the following exchange:

> A monk asked Furong [Daokai (1043–1118)], "In the middle of the night it is full and bright, but at dawn it does not show. Why does it not show?" The master replied, "Filling the boat, the moon rides the void/Fishermen dwell among the flowering reeds."[126]

59. Guanxiu, *Meeting an Old Monk in Deep Mountains*[127]

60. Guanxiu, *Living in the Mountains*[128]
The mind of the mind of the mind (xinxinxin)—repetition of this magnitude is highly unusual in Tang poetry. Most uses of this reduplicative in Chan texts allude to a previous use in the *Treatise on the Destruction of Characteristics*, attributed to Bodhidharma but now known to have been authored by Shenxiu.[129] A *gāthā* contained in it reads in part, "I seek the mind, and do not seek Buddha;/Completely understanding the Three Realms are empty of objects./If you want to seek Buddha, then seek the mind;/Just this mind of the mind of the mind is Buddha."[130] Guanxiu's use of the term is apparently to show that in Chan the mind is not inert and blank, but active, dynamic, and subject to external stimulation. That is, we may take the three words as forming different parts of speech,

and the meaning accumulates through the phrase. Alternatively, the phrase may describe the transmission of Chan truth, from the mind of Buddha to the minds of the patriarchs to the minds of masters and disciples.

past sound and sight (xiyi) — this compound is formed from words found in *Daodejing* 14: "Because the eye gazes but can catch no glimpse of it, it is called elusive (*yi*);/Because the ear listens but cannot hear it, it is called the rarefied (*xi*)." Arthur Waley notes that the words are a traditional description of ghosts and spirits, adopted in Laozi's classic as a description of the Way.[131] Here, Guanxiu says that the mind does *not* lodge in otherworldly stillness but is actively engaged with the rich particularity of life.

61. Guanxiu, *Hearing the New Cicadas; Sent to Guiyong*[132]

Cicadas — these insects have a variety of associations in Chinese poetry. On the one hand, because cicadas are most prevalent in summer and autumn, the sound they make is considered mournful and a harbinger of coming decay. On the other hand, the cicada is a happy symbol of resurrection and transformation, because the larva passes its first years underground, then leaves its shell and emerges as a perfect insect. It is in this latter sense that cicadas appear in Guanxiu's poem. The image is fairly frequent in Chan poetry, for obvious reasons, but perhaps also because the word "cicada" (pronounced *chan*) is (and was in Tang times) a homonym for Chan.[133]

cuckoo (duyu) — the image connotes the sadness of separation; here, of Guanxiu from his friend Guiyong. The provenance is a legend of the late Zhou (ca. 1027–256 B.C.E.) King Duyu of Shu (present Sichuan), who fell in love with his minister's wife. He abdicated in shame, died, and was transformed into a cuckoo. The cuckoo's call is thus considered to be mournful. Another name for the cuckoo, *zigui*, also relates to the allusion: it is a homonym for "Return to me!"

western mountain — context suggests the western paradise of the Amitābha Buddha, the Pure Land of Sukhāvatī.

62. Guanxiu, *Evening Watch*[134]

lotus roundelay — a common trope in classical Chinese poetry is the "lotus song" or "caltrop song" sung by the peasant girls who harvest these water crops in the marshes of south China; often neither the girls nor their boats can be seen — only the music wafting out of the tall grasses reveals their presence. Here, Guanxiu recasts the "lotus song" as music of the Dharma.

63. Guanxiu, *Old Frontier Song*[135]

64. Guanxiu, *Fishing at Zeng Deep*[136]

Quiet scene—the first line contains an extraordinary string of alliteration, alas untranslatable: *jing jing jiang qing wu shi shi*. "Quiet scene" here refers to an enlightened "mental realm"; see the introduction.

    White Snow—an ancient song title. *Huainanzi* 6 says, "Shi Kuang played White Snow, and heavenly birds came down to earth." Thus the singing of the boatmen will bring the divine cranes mentioned in an earlier line. The words also describe the petals in the air, which resemble snow.

65. Guanxiu, *Night Rain*[137]

dead trees (kumu)—the old or dead tree image was briefly described in the introduction. It carries associations of detachment from the world; old or dead trees have a (relative) permanence and constancy that flowering vegetation does not. To Chan adherents the old or dead tree signifies the extinction of attachments, but itself should not be a source of attachment. Carrying the metaphor through, the ideal conclusion is for the dead tree to blossom again (*kumu zai shenghua*). In *Transmission* 17, Master Caoshan Benji (840–901) says, "Don't you see that the king can manage the affairs of the whole country, and from dead wood blossoms may yet be gathered?"[138] In *Blue Cliff* 27, Yunmen Wenyan (862/4–949) is asked, "When the tree withers and the leaves fall, how is it?" He answers, "The body is revealed by a golden wind."[139] Numerous aphorisms of similar meaning employ the dead tree image, like "Dead trees, cold ashes" (*kumu hanhui*); "Dead trees by a frozen cliff/Three winter months without warmth" (*kumu yi hanyan sandong wu nuanqi*); "Blossoms bloom on dead trees in a spring beyond time" (*kumu huakai jiewai chun*); and "In winter the dead tree blooms/In summer, the snowflakes fly" (*sandong kumu xiu jiuxia xuehua fei*). The "iron tree" (*tieshu*) is equivalent.

66. Shenying, *Staying Overnight at the Yanling Fishing Terrace*[140]

*Shenying was a monk during the Xiantong reign period (860–874). This is one of his two extant poems.[141]

    Yanling—the name of a mountain and a stream (in Tonglu, Zhejiang). During the reign of Han Emperor Guangwu (r. 25–57), the Confucian recluse Yan Guang farmed and fished there, in order to avoid government service and remain true to his principles.

    Seven-mile Shoal—Qilizhou, also known as Qilitan (Seven-mile Shoal/Beach) or Qililong (Seven-mile Rapids) is a stretch of shallow, clear water that runs from the Fishing Terrace to Meicheng Village (in Jiande, Zhejiang).

67. Qiji, *Staying at Daolin Temple; Sent to Chan Master Yuelu*[142]

*Qiji (fl. 881), whose secular family name was Hu, was a native of Yiyang (Yiyang, Hunan). Orphaned at the age of seven, he found refuge on Mount Dagui near his home, at Tongqing Temple (where, presumably, Guishan Lingyou [771–853] was still teaching); he was set to work initially as a cowherd. A gifted child, he was said to have scratched poems on the backs of the cows with a bamboo stick. After training in the *Vinaya*, he visited holy sites all over China and received instruction at virtually all of the major Chan centers. He also resided for a number of years near the capital of Chang'an (Xi'an, Shanxi). Among his Chan teachers were Yaoshan Weiyan (745–828) (a disciple of Shitou Xiqian), Lumen Chuzhen (fl. late ninth century), and Huguo Shoujing (fl. late ninth to early tenth century). As did his contemporary Guanxiu (832–912), Qiji resided for a time in the temple of Shishuang Qingzhu (807–888) (on Mount Shishuang near Changsha, Hunan), where he was asked to take on a supervisory role. Most important to him personally was the long period he spent on Mount Heng (in Hunan), which prompted him to call himself the "Śramaṇa of Mount Heng." In later years he settled down in the Jiangling (Jiangling, Hubei) area of the middle Yangtze. Jiangling at that time was the center of the small Nanping state; its king, Gao Zonghui (r. 927–934), welcomed Qiji and appointed him to a position at Longxiang Temple. While in Jiangling, he avoided the powerful and instead kept company with well-known poets and compiled his collected works, *The White Lotus Collection* (preface dated 938). In a poem attributed to his contemporary and fellow monk Qichan (and also to Shangyan) he was described as "The Literary Star That Lights the Sky of Chu." A considerably less grand *hao* was "Poem Bag," given him in ironic reference to the large wen on his neck. Well over five hundred of his poems are extant. Qiji was also well known as a calligrapher: according to the *Register of Calligraphy of the Xuanhe Era*, in the early twelfth century seven of his running-style and two of his standard-style pieces were in the imperial collections.[143]

Chan Master Yuelu—probably the abbot of Mount Yuelu (near Changsha, Hunan), who was a disciple of Baofu Congzhan (d. 928); he appears in *Transmission 22*.

Daolin Temple—in Changsha, Hunan.

Search: you will not find—these lines describe the pointlessness of purposefully seeking spiritual attainment.

traces of my mind—the mind (*xin*) is internal, while traces (*ji*) are its external manifestations as revealed by actions. In this poem, Qiji suggests his discriminating mental consciousness comes to an end in the light of *prajñā* wisdom.

window—this image held enormous importance to Qiji and recurs in many of his poems. By it he emphasizes a separation between ourselves and the world, because our perception is through the filter of our senses. When the window is "open" or "empty," it allows unmediated perception of things as they are. Many Chan poets who use the image specify "six windows," referring to the six senses: eyes, ear, nose, tongue, body, and mind. To open these windows is to see the buddha nature, as in the following amusing dialogue:

> Yangshan [Huiji (814–890)] asked Chan Master Zhongyi Hong'en of Langzhou, "How can I see the buddha nature?" The master replied, "Imagine a room with six windows. Inside is a monkey, and outside is a monkey. [The monkey outside] calls out from the east, 'Monkey! Monkey!' The monkey [inside] will respond. If there are six [open] windows, then the monkeys will call and respond to each other." Yangshan bowed and said, "I understand your example completely. Here is another situation: if the monkey inside is taking a nap, how can the monkey outside see him?" The master came down from his meditation seat, grabbed Yangshan's hand and started a dance, saying, "Monkey! I see you!"[144]

Similarly, in *Blue Cliff* 9, a monk asks Zhaozhou Congshen (778–897), "What is Zhaozhou?" He replies, "East gate, west gate, south gate, north gate."[145] That is to say, he is open in all directions.

68. Qiji, *Old Pine*[146]

Old pine—analogous to the dead tree. Pines and cypresses are evergreens, so relative to other trees they appear unchanging. The Chinese metaphor of the evergreen signifying the man who maintains his principles even in adversity dates at least to the Confucian *Analects* IX, 27: "It is in the cold of winter that one realizes that the pine and cypress have not withered." A monk once asked Zhaozhou Congshen (778–897), "What is the meaning of Bodhidharma coming from the West?" Zhaozhou answerered, "The cypress in the courtyard."[147]

69. Qiji, *Boat Window*[148]

70. Qiji, *Close the Door*[149]

A single line of the patriarchs' words—the term "one word" or "one line" (*yiju* or *yiyan*) in Chan contexts generally indicates a perfect summary statement of universal truth.

71. Qiji, *Written at a Hermitage in Zhenzhou*[150]

Zhenzhou—in Maoxian, Sichuan.

Travelers from the sea—Zhenzhou is 2,000 miles from the ocean; thus the term here is used euphemistically and to fit the parallelism with "fishermen's homes." The "assembly of the sea" (*haizhong*) is a Buddhist term, referring to a great assembly of monks, the whole body of monks. The metaphor is based on the idea of all streams of Buddhism joined and mixed together, just as rivers run to the sea. Thus the "travelers" here are monks. A related term is "Dharma sea" (*fahai*), which is the sum total of Buddhist teachings.

72. Qiji, *White Lotus at Donglin*[151]
    Donglin—Donglin Temple on Mount Lu (in Dehua, Jiangxi), where Huiyuan (334–416) gathered a group of disciples to worship Amitābha and grew white lotus.

    Tuṣita Heaven—often translated as the Heaven of Complete Knowledge (*zhizutian*), this is the fourth Devaloka, Maitreya's heaven of all knowledge, where all bodhisattvas are reborn before rebirth as buddhas.

    Portrait Hall—the temple hall in which the portrait of the founder is displayed.

    Baihe *incense*—an incense produced in the Han dynasty; in literature the term (literally "Hundred Amities") refers to wonderful fragrance in general and fine incense in particular.

    unsullied nature—there is a pun in this couplet. "Unsullied nature" (*buranxing*) refers here most directly to the purity of the lotus. Yet the term was also used to describe the original nature of the mind, before the tainting influence of life in the world of causation; thus it is identical to the buddha nature.

73. Qiji, *Rain on a Summer Day; Sent to a Friend in Administrative Service*[152]
    Lotus Peak—although several peaks with similar-sounding names are found in China (the most spectacular is Lotus Flower Peak at Mount Huang in Anhui), the use here is a general reference to Buddhism. "White Lotus Peak" is also common.

    Rushing streams (puliu)—as the rain stops, the aggravations and worries caused by sensory desires no longer afflict him. See the note on "waterfalls" above.

74. Qiji, *Amusing Myself*[153]
    Stone Monk—Shitou Xiqian (700–790).

75. Zilan, *Facing Snow*[154]
*Zilan (fl. 889–904) wrote twenty-six poems that are extant. He presented his writings to the court of Tang emperor Zhaozong. Only some have Buddhist content, while the rest are mainstream secular compositions.[155]

76. Zilan, *Evening Scene*[156]
tribunal hall—the town hall, where the magistrate holds court.

77. Shangyan, *Staying Overnight at a Mountain Temple at Qingyuan Gorge*[157]
*Shangyan (fl. late ninth century), *zi* Maosheng, was a member of the same clan as Xue Neng (metropolitan degree 847), a poet and official who became Minister of Works. Shangyan became a monk in Jingmen (Danyang, Hubei). Thirty-four of his poems are extant. His poetry was extremely important to him, as these lines suggest: "When all actions are forgotten, I can't forget poetry/When I enter into a poem, it seems there's something on which to rely." His works include a poem of remembrance for the eccentric poet and Daoist hermit Lu Guimeng (d. ca. 881), which helps to date him. In addition, two poems by his friend Qiji (fl. 881) help to pinpoint the geographic area where he spent at least the latter part of his life. In the first, Qiji commemorates Shangyan's new home: "On the south face of Mount Lu, to the west of Juzhou/You build a new hermitage, as high as the bamboo." Mount Lu is Mount Yuelu (near Changsha, Hunan), near where Changsha Jingcen had taught a generation earlier. Juzhou is an island in the nearby Xiang River. In the second, Qiji laments Shangyan's death, also on the mountain.[158]
Qingyuan Gorge—also known as Feilai (Flying) Gorge (in Qingyuan, Guangdong, not far from the city of Guangzhou).
belt stones—traditional Chinese often wore ornaments of semiprecious stone or other material to fasten their belts; these might jangle as they walked. The custom is similar to the wearing of *netsuke* in old Japan.
wisdom eye (huiyan)—one of the five Buddhist "eyes." Opening it gives one the "wisdom" (*prajñā*) to see the emptiness of things and *dharmas*.
Starry River—the Milky Way.

78. Qichan, *Herdboy*[159]
*Qichan (fl. late ninth century) was a contemporary and acquaintance of Qiji and Shangyan. Two poems by Qiji have his name as Xichan. He was said to have resided at Pingfeng Cliff, which probably refers to Mount Pingfeng, also known as Mount Xiaci or Mount Cuiping (in Zhongxian, Sichuan), as there are other references to Shu (Sichuan) sites in his poetry. This peak is one of the twelve

that make up the Wu Mountains, in the eastern corner of the modern province. Twelve of Qichan's poems are extant.[160]

Herdboy—to "ride the ox" is a metaphor for Buddhist attainment. The herdboy represents the seeker of the Dharma, and the ox is the mind. The water buffalo/ox already had religious significance in pre-Buddhist India. The term "King of Bulls" was associated by the Buddhists with buddhas and bodhisattvas in general, and Śākyamuni in particular. Nanquan Puyuan (748–834) was particularly fond of the image. When asked where he would be in a hundred years, he answered, "I'll be a water buffalo down the hill."[161] Changqing Da'an (793–883) compared both his religious quest and his enlightenment to an ox:

> All I did was to look after an ox. If he got off the road, I dragged him back; if he trampled the flowering grain in others' fields, I trained him by flogging him with a whip. For a long time how pitiful he was, at the mercy of men's words! Now he has changed into the white ox on the bare ground, and always stays in front of my face. All day long he clearly reveals himself. Even though I chase him, he doesn't go away.[162]

In the Song period, several sets of cow herding pictures with verse commentaries were produced to describe the process of Chan enlightenment; the "Ten Pictures of Cow Herding" attributed to Kuo'an Shiyuan (fl. twelfth century) became the most popular.[163]

Not "real" and not "not-real"—the nonduality of reality and emptiness.

79. Xuanbao, *Roads*[164]
    *Xuanbao (Tang dynasty; n.d.) left a single poem.
        Shu—approximately the area of Sichuan, in the southwest.
        Qin—approximately the area of Shanxi, in the northwest.

80. Anonymous monk, *Old Plum Tree*[165]
    *Anonymous monk (Tang dynasty).

81. Shushan Kuangren, *Death Gāthā*[166]
    *Shushan Kuangren (fl. late ninth to early tenth century), also known as Guangren, was from Jizhou (Jishui, Jiangxi). He traveled widely in China, studying with numerous well-known Chan masters, including Guishan Lingyou (771–853) and Xiangyan Zhixian (ninth century). He became a disciple of Dongshan Liangjie (807–869) and "deeply entered the mysterious principles." Patience does not seem to have been one of Kuangren's virtues, as his *Eminent Monks* biography

suggests: "Kuangren once asked Xiangyan a question, but thought Xiangyan's answer somewhat missed the mark. Kuangren then said, 'I suffered calluses in coming here, but have I gained any relief?' He then spat on the ground and left." Kuangren became abbot at Mount Shu in Fuzhou (Linchuan, Jiangxi). To describe his diminutive physical stature and quick intellect, he was nicknamed "The Dwarf Ācārya." A monk asked him, "Where will you go one hundred years from now?" The master replied, "Thick grass will be beneath my back, and my four legs will point to Heaven." It was said that after he died a white deer came and knelt down before his tomb, which onlookers understood as a sign of grief.[167]

rootless tree (wugen shu)—the *Flower Garland Sūtra* includes the following: "There is a tree named 'Rootless.' It does not grow from the roots, but its branches, leaves, blossoms, and fruits all flourish."[168] In *Transmission* 23, the Tang master Shimen Huiche is asked, "What is the monk's teaching?" He answers, "Understand how to join with the rootless tree, and you can carry a lamp beneath the sea."[169] Chinul associated it with the "true mind"; see the introduction.

Yellow leaves (huangye)—the image perhaps alludes to "Yellow leaves to stop the crying of a baby" (*huangye zhiti*), from a parable in the *Nirvāṇa Sūtra*. When their baby was crying, his parents hurriedly waved yellow poplar leaves in front of him, saying, "Don't cry! Don't cry! We'll give you gold!" The baby thought it was real gold, and stopped crying.[170] Thus the yellow leaves represent the expedient means (*fangbian*) used by Buddha to lead people to salvation. In Kuangren's poem, if this allusion is intended, the rootless tree is the buddha nature, and all expedients return to it in the end.

82. Lingquan Guiren, *Peonies*[171]

*Lingquan Guiren (fl. tenth century) was a late Tang to Five Dynasties/Ten Kingdoms monk from the southeastern Yangtze region. He was a disciple of Shushan Kuangren (fl. late ninth to early tenth century) and second-generation disciple of Dongshan Liangjie (807–869). He became abbot of Lingquan Monastery in Luoyang (Luoyang, Henan). One of his poems expresses his grief over the death of the satirical writer Luo Yin (833–909), which helps to ascertain his dates. He appears in a few brief Chan dialogues in the transmission-of-the-lamp anthologies. "A monk asked, 'What is the monk's teaching?' The master answered, 'When riding an ox, put on your straw hat/When crossing a river, put on your riding jacket.'"[172]

Peony—in China, generally considered the king of flowers. It was said that in late spring in the Tang dynasty capital, carriages and horses thronged the roads as wealthy aristocrats searched for the finest blossoms.[173] The roots of the peony were used for medicinal purposes. Perhaps the incongruity of the combination—the flashy, ephemeral blossom with the mundane yet useful root—is what attracted Chan practitioners to the image. Yunmen Wenyan (862/4–949) was once asked by a monk, "What is the pure Dharma body?" He answered, "A bed of peonies."[174] Compare the following exchange featuring Nanquan Puyuan (748–834):

> Governor Lu Xuan spoke to the Master, saying, 'Sengzhao (384–414) is very strange indeed. He said that Heaven and Earth share the same root, and that the ten thousand things are the same substance.' The Master pointed to the peony blossoms in the courtyard and said, 'Governor! When people today see these blossoms, it is as if they see them in a dream.' The Governor could not understand what he was saying.[175]

Wuling—the area around the tombs of five Han dynasty emperors, outside the Tang capital Chang'an (Xi'an, Shanxi). In the Tang dynasty Wuling was a wealthy residential district.

83. Kezhi, *Sent to an Elder Monk on the Fan River* [176]
*Kezhi (859–934) was from Mount Dafang in Fanyang (Pingshan, Hebei); his secular surname was Ma. A child prodigy, he was drawn to a religious vocation by age twelve; his first Buddhist studies were in the *Vinaya,* with masters Fazhen and Renchu. At his elder monks' invitation, he began preaching in Hengyang (Quyang, Hebei) while still a teenager. When he was nineteen, he undertook ordination at Mount Wutai (Wutai, Shanxi), and "felt the spirit brightness of the Jewel shining on his body." Proficient at poetry, he presented his compositions to the Tang court in the third year of the Qianning reign period (897) and was rewarded with a purple cassock. After serving in various temples, he returned home to care for his aged mother. Each day he begged the finest dainties for her and would chant scriptures. At the end of three years, suddenly a huge snake appeared in the house; it held up its head and stared, as if it had something to say to him. A local monk suggested it was a dragon. Kezhi thereupon burned incense and addressed it, saying, "If you are indeed a benevolent dragon spirit, I wish that I may meet a *dānapati* (almsgiver/patron)." A few days later, he was summoned to serve Liu Shouguang, soon to found the brief Later Liang dynasty (907–923). Emperor Ming of the Later Tang (r. 926–934) named Kezhi abbot of Zhangshou Temple in Luoyang in 929. Nine of his poems are extant. According to his *Eminent Monks* biography, this poem was particularly popular.[177]

Fan River—to the south of the Tang capital Chang'an (Xi'an, Shanxi).

fool—Laozi, *Daodejing* 49: "The Sage, in his dealings with the world, seems like one dazed with fright;/For the world's sake he dulls his wits."[178]

Chu—south central China, far from the Fan River in the north.

Sui—the Sui dynasty (589–618), three hundred years earlier than the time of the poem's composition.

Taibai—the planet Venus, called Taibai when referring to the evening star and Qiming when referring to the morning star, is sometimes depicted as an old man (as in the Ming dynasty novel *Journey to the West*).

84. Yunmen Wenyan, *Words of Criticism*[179]

*Yunmen Wenyan (864–949) is credited as the founder of the Yunmen house of Chan. He was from Jiaxing (Jiaxing, Zhejiang)[180] and his secular surname was Zhang. He is one of the most often-quoted of the Tang masters. Wenyan left home to enter a religious life at seventeen; by twenty he was an ordained monk. His first Chan encounter was with Muzhou Daozong (fl. late ninth century), a disciple of Huangbo Xiyun (d. 849). He tried for three days to gain audience with the master but was rebuffed. Finally he sneaked inside, whereupon Muzhou grabbed him and said, "Speak! Speak!" Just as Wenyan was about to answer, Muzhou pushed him roughly outside and slammed the door on his leg, breaking it. That moment of excruciating pain triggered Wenyan's enlightenment. He built upon this experience under Xuefeng Yicun (822–908), whose disciple and Dharma heir he became. After a pilgrimage south to Caoqi (in Guangdong) to the grave of the Sixth Patriarch, he remained in the area for the rest of his life. There he received the protection and patronage of the Liu family, which ruled the small kingdom of Nanhan after the fall of Tang. In 938 he was granted the title Great Master Supporting Truth (Kuangzhen Dashi). He founded a flourishing Chan community on Mount Yunmen and taught there for nearly thirty years. He was a hard taskmaster, and frequently beat and shouted at his many disciples. Yunmen Wenyan adopted a radical antilanguage stance—he once compared all the teaching in the Buddhist canon to medicine administered to a dead horse— and forbade his students from recording his words. Those dialogues that have come down to us were supposedly transmitted by his disciple Xianglin Chengyuan, who wore a paper robe and surreptitiously took notes. Wenyan is particularly noted for his one-word answers to questions, a technique that later came to be known as the One-Word Gate. When a monk asked the master what was the eye of the true Dharma, he replied, "*Pu!* (Everywhere!)."[181]

A pearl in a robe (yizhu)—a metaphor for the buddha nature within a person, which is obscured by deluded thinking. The source is a parable in the *Lotus Sūtra* about a poor beggar who does not realize a pearl is sewn into his robe, until a wise man points it out.[182]

Even the Buddhist Dharma can become an impediment if the practitioner be-comes too attached to it and considers it a precious thing outside his own mind. This entire poem is quoted in *Blue Cliff* 61, and *Blue Cliff* 25 includes the lines, "In truth, though gold dust is precious, when it falls into your eyes it becomes a blinding obstruction."[183]

85. Tong'an Changcha, *The Mind Seal*[184]

*Tong'an Changcha (d. 961) was a disciple of Jiufeng Daoqian (d. 923). He was abbot of Tong'an Monastery on Mount Fengqi in Hongzhou (Nanchang, Jiangxi). A monk once asked him, "What is the meaning of Bodhidharma coming from the West?" He replied, "Because the rhinoceros plays with the moon, colored stripes appear on his horns./Since the elephant is startled by the thunder, colored spots enter his tusks." This unusual answer appears to invoke the interpenetration of all things. Several exchanges featuring Changcha are recorded, but he is best known for his poem series "Ten Abstruse Conversations," recorded in *Transmission* 29 and elsewhere, which discusses the process of awakening from ten different per-spectives. The poems qualify as *gong'an* themselves, and certain lines were fre-quently quoted.[185] The five translated poems include the first, and four of the last five of the set. Although difficult, these poems taken together appear to be a cau-tion against intellectualizing the Chan enlightenment process. Changcha adopts a contrarian approach, denying the validity of common orthodoxy in order to challenge practitioners' preconceptions.

mind seal—the verification of enlightenment given by a master to a student.

red-hot brazier—here, the egocentric mind, which yet contains the lotus (bud-dha nature).

86. Tong'an Changcha, *Reaching the Root*[186]

Void King (*kongwang*)—Buddha.

Snowy Mountains—a general term for the Himalayas. The usage here can be traced to *Nirvāṇa Sūtra* 14, in a story about one of the Buddha's past lives, when he was known as the "Bodhisattva of Snowy Mountains" or the "Boy of Snowy Mountains":

> At that time I lived in the Snowy Mountains. These mountains were fresh and pure; flowing springs bathed the earth, forests and medicinal plants filled the land. . . . At that time, I resided alone there, eating only fruits. When I had eaten, I bridled my mind and thought only of meditation. Countless years passed in this way.[187]

not a single thing—an allusion to Sixth Patriarch Huineng's famous quatrain.

87. Tong'an Changcha, *Returning to the Source*[188]

Return to the root, come back to the source (fanben huanyuan) — the general process of enlightenment. More specifically, however, it is the title of the ninth of the Ten Oxherding Pictures, and so implies enlightenment that is close but not achieved. Consider the oft-cited poem for this ninth stage, by Kuo'an Shiyuan (fl. twelfth century):

Return to the root, come back to the source — already wasted effort;
Instead, strive directly to become like one deaf and dumb.
Within his hut, he's unaware of anything outside;
Streams flow away on their own, flowers are red of themselves.[189]

the origin (benlai) — the "original mind" (benlai xin), "original nature" (benlai xing), or "original face" (benlai mianmu) is the buddha nature, innate enlightenment.

nowhere to dwell (wuzhu) — the concept of "nonabidingness," which signifies the impermanence of things, is key to all Mahāyāna teachings. The *Vimalakīrtinirdeśa sūtra* says, "From nonabidingness all *dharmas* are created."[190] Chan tended to focus on its implications for the thinking process: since thoughts, concepts, and language are nonabiding, the practitioner in contemplation and daily life should cultivate an attitude of nonattachment to them. Seen from this perspective, no-mind is exactly the realization of nonabidingness; thus no-mind is also described as a "nonabiding place" (wuzhuchu). Zhaozhou Congshen (778–897) once advised a monk, "You cannot abide in the place of Buddha; quickly pass by the place with no Buddha."[191]

When both guest and host are silent — this line alludes to the "Fourfold Relation of Guest and Host" (si binzhu), ascribed to Linji Yixuan (?–866) and the Linji School. In this scheme, first, guest sees host; second, host sees guest; third, host sees host; and fourth, guest sees guest. Literally the "guest" is the questioner in a Chan dialogue, while the "host" is the master. At their most basic, the four relationships describe possible outcomes of teaching sessions: the student understands, but the teacher does not; the teacher understands, but the student does not; both teacher and student understand; neither teacher nor student understands.[192] Yet the relations between the two participants also may connote a range of metaphoric polarities. The line in the present poem remains ambiguous: does it indicate that the enlightenment process has been a success or a failure? The silence of guest and host suggests the former, but this is immediately undercut by Changcha's comment that it is "perfect delusion."

When the ways of lord and vassal merge—an allusion to the "Fivefold Relation of Lord and Vassal" (*junchen wuwei*) ascribed to Dongshan Liangjie (807–869) and elaborated by Caoshan Benji (840–901) and the later Cao-Dong School. Chinese Cao-Dong masters frequently focused on the relationship between universality (*zheng*) and particularity (*pian*). Caoshan Benji defined the former as "the world of the Void, in which there is nothing from the beginning," and the latter as "the world of appearance, which consists of ten thousand forms and images."[193] Yet the two are not separate, but nondual and interpenetrating. Caoshan Benji described five ranks (*wuwei*) of universality and particularity to present the enlightenment process. The "Fivefold Relation of Lord and Vassal" mirrored this plan, with the "lord" signifying universality and the "vassal" as particularity: the vassal turns toward the lord; the lord sees the vassal; the lord is alone; the vassal is alone; and the lord and vassal are in union. In the present poem, the fifth and highest of the lord/vassal relations is cited, but then Changcha denies its completeness.

88.   Tong'an Changcha, *Motivating Power*[194]

wooden man/stone girl—wood and stone are inert materials, but the wooden man and stone girl have life and energy, just as in no-mind the practitioner is not attached to thought while engaging in dynamic thought. It says in the *Samādhi as Reflection from the Precious Mirror:* "While the wooden man is singing,/The stone maiden starts to dance./This cannot be reached by our consciousness./ How can you give any thought to this?"[195] Similarly, the "Song Confirming the Way" says, "Call and ask the wooden man at the Function Barrier/When the search for Buddha will succeed."[196] The source of the wooden man image is very early. The Daoist text *Liezi* (compiled fourth century, but including much earlier material) describes a meeting between King Mu and a great artisan. The artisan presented a puppet that could run, dance, and sing, yet was constructed entirely of wood, lacquer, and paint.[197] Similarly, *Nirvāṇa Sūtra* 17 equates heavenly principle with an artisan, and all sentient beings with the mechanical wooden man he constructs.[198]

Over and over scoop it up—to "to scoop up the moon in the water" (*shuizhong laoyue*) generally suggests useless activity. Compare "monkeys search for the moon in the water," described above. Xutang Zhiyu (1185–1269) said, "Studying the mind to reach the origin is like sitting in a well to gaze at the sky; probing principle to comprehend one's nature is like scooping up the moon in the water."[199] Yet Changcha adds the words "and you will understand" to his line. Perhaps he means that repeated experience of the world will reveal its illusory nature, and thus lead the practitioner to a search for the truth. When Yuanwu Keqin (1063–

1135) posed the question "What is the means to ascend to truth?" he answered by quoting Changcha's couplet.[200] Linji master Fenyang Shanzhao (947–1024) intoned it at the moment of his enlightenment.[201]

89. Tong'an Changcha, *One Reality*[202]
White egrets standing in the snow — this metaphor, as well as "the bright moon on [white] rush blossoms," refers to nondual polarities like the universal and the phenomenal, or original and actualized enlightenment. Compare the following lines, from *Samādhi as Reflection from the Precious Mirror*: "As snow is contained in a silver bowl, and as a white heron hides in the bright moonlight, when you classify them they are different from each other, but when you unify them they are the same in the Source."[203] Linji master Dahui Zonggao (1089–1163) once asked, "What is difference within sameness? 'When the white egret stands in the snow it has a different color.'"[204] Other sets of images are also employed, like "the white horse enters rush flowers" (*baima ru luhua*) and "white egrets stand on the sandbar/Facing them, rush flowers bloom" (*bailu shating li/luhua xiangdui kai*).

Song Dynasty (960–1279)

90. Dongshan Xiaocong, *Death* Gāthā[205]
*Dongshan Xiaocong (d. 1030) was from Shaozhou (Qujiang, Guangdong); his secular surname was Lin (one source has Du). He became a disciple of Wenshu Yingzhen (fl. tenth century) at Mount Wenshu in Dingzhou (in Hunan) in the Yunmen branch of Chan. Xiaocong later became abbot at Mount Dong in Yunzhou (in Jiangxi). On the slope of a peak there he planted a forest of pine trees. Whenever one took root and grew, he would sit and chant a chapter of the *Diamond Sūtra*. He thus called himself "The Pine-planting *Bhikṣu*" and the peak "Diamond Peak." Someone once asked him, "The peak is here, but where is the diamond?" Xiaocong pointed to a tree and said, "I planted this pine myself."[206]

hidden in Dipper stars — a reference to a *gong'an* featuring Yunmen Wenyan (864–949): "A monk asked, 'What word penetrates to the Dharma body?' The master [Yunmen] answered, 'Hide your body in the Big Dipper.'"[207] It is recorded in Sima Qian's (ca. 145 B.C.E.–ca. 85 B.C.E.) *Records of History* 27, in a chapter concerning Chinese astronomy:

The Dipper is the chariot of the Emperor [of Heaven] and travels the central sky. Looking down, [the Emperor] orders the four directions, divides *yin* and *yang*, creates the four seasons, balances the five elements, causes the movement of time, fixes the divisions of time—all these derive from the Dipper.

Thus one interpretation of Yunmen Wenyan's enigmatic directive is for the practitioner to become the ruler of the cosmos. Seen in this light, the *gong'an* relates to others that focus on the "master" (*zhurengong*) of the mind/body, which is another name for the buddha nature.

hoe blade—a symbol for Xiaocong's life of manual labor, and by extension, his religious cultivation of the Everyday Way.

91.   Xuedou Zhongxian, *Foolishness Is Prized in the Way* [208]
*Xuedou Zhongxian (980–1052), *zi* Yinzhi, was from Suizhou (Suining, Sichuan); his secular surname was Li. He became a monk after he was orphaned at an early age, and eventually developed into a major figure in the Yunmen branch of Chan. He was a failure in his Chan studies until he met Zhimen Guangzuo (fl. early eleventh century). Guangzuo asked him, "Without a single thought arising, what can be said to be wrong?" When Zhongxian was about to answer, Guangzuo suddenly hit him in the mouth with his whisk, triggering enlightenment. Later, while on a journey to the Hangzhou (Hangzhou, Zhejiang) region, Zhongxian met scholar and official Zeng Hui, who gave him an introduction letter to the abbot at Mount Lingyin. Three years later, Zeng happened to be in the area and came to call on Zhongxian, but none of the monks there knew who he was. Finally he found Zhongxian among the throng and asked about the letter. Zhongxian drew it intact from his sleeve and said, "Thank you for your good intentions, sir, but we footloose monks are not postmen." Zhongxian later attracted a group of disciples of his own as abbot of Zisheng Temple on Mount Xuedou in Mingzhou (near Ningbo, Zhejiang). Zhongxian was granted the imperial title Great Master of Bright Awakening (Mingjue Dashi). Soon before he died, his grief-stricken attendant monk requested a parting *gāthā*. Zhongxian merely replied, "My only regret in this life is that I talked too much." He is best known for compiling a group of 100 *gong'an* featuring major Chan masters and adding a verse commentary to each; about 60 years later Yuanwu Keqin (1063–1135) augmented the text with his own commentaries to form the *The Blue Cliff Record*.[209]

Subhūti—one of the ten major disciples of Buddha; he is said to have been the best exponent of *śūnyatā*, or emptiness. He is the principal interlocutor in the *Prajñāpāramitā Sūtras*.

This poem is quoted in Yuanwu Keqin's (1063–1135) commentary in *Blue Cliff* 6, prefaced by the following story:

Haven't you read how as Subhūti was sitting in silent meditation in a cliffside cave, the gods showered down flowers to praise him? The venerable Subhūti said, "Flowers are showering down from the sky in praise; whose doing is this?" A god said, "I am Indra, king of the gods." Venerable Subhūti asked, "Why are you offering praise?" Indra said, "I esteem the Venerable One's skill in expounding the transcendence of wisdom." Subhūti said, "I have never spoken a single word about wisdom; why are you offering praise?" Indra said, "You have never spoken and I have never heard. No speaking, no hearing—this is true wisdom." And again he caused the earth to tremble, and showered down flowers.[210]

92. Jingtu Weizheng, *Untitled*[211]

*Jingtu Weizheng (986–1049), *zi* Huanran, was from Xiuzhou (Jiaxing, Zhejiang); his secular surname was Huang. He was in the short-lived Fayan branch of Chan. He entered religion after being orphaned at a young age. After studies at Mount Tiantai, he became a disciple of Jingtu Weisu on Mount Jing (in Yuhang, Zhejiang). When Weisu became abbot at the Jingtu Monastery on Mount Gongzhen (in Lin'an, Zhejiang), Weizheng accompanied him as his assistant, and eventually became abbot himself. Weizheng remained unconcerned with worldly affairs; his favorite pastime was riding an ox. Whenever he left the monastery, he would hang his water bottle and begging bowl on the ox's horns. Although the townspeople jostled to see him, he remained completely unperturbed, and gained the nickname Yellow Ox Zheng. His eccentricities did not end there: "He also liked to admire the moon. He would kneel down in a big tub and float on the water. Spinning his tub in circles, he would chant and laugh until dawn. He was always as natural as this."

Weizheng was a master calligrapher and painter, and his pieces were sought after by collectors. Yet he laughed at scholars who copied the inscriptions of past masters, saying, "They all think that brush and ink are precious, and so their art always shows intention. In contrast, children's calligraphy and painting contain many pure strokes, which can be followed." Weizheng was once asked why he never talked about Chan. He answered: "Language is useless. I'm too lazy to be willing to use its twists and turns. Day and night I'm vexed that the ten thousand things are spread out all around—yet language has limit while this Dharma has none. This is the Buddha's so-called Storehouse of Unlimited Creation."

On a high summer day in 1049, Weizheng said to his assembled disciples, "It's said 'activity' is always matched by 'stillness'—that even before it begins it has an end. My activity has continued for sixty-four years and now comes to stillness. But really now, do activity and stillness in fact exist?" He then tranquilly passed away.[212]

93. Shishuang Chuyuan, *Entering the Capital by Boat*[213]

*Shishuang Chuyuan (987–1040), *hao* Ciming, was from scenic Quanzhou (Guilin, Guangxi); his secular surname was Li. A student in his early life, he became a monk at the age of twenty-two. He became a disciple of Linji master Fenyang Shanzhao (947–1024) at Taizi Monastery in Fenyang (Fenzhou, Shanxi). Chuyuan's zeal was such that he meditated day and night, and when drowsiness overcame him, pierced his flesh with an awl in order to focus his mind through pain. Thus he came to be called "The Lion of West River." He became abbot at a series of temples around Tanzhou (Changsha, Hunan), including the Chongsheng Chan Monastery on Mount Shishuang, and gained the respect of the imperial court. He also became close friends with Hanlin academician Yang Yi (974–1020), known generally as Yang Danian, an important poet and prose stylist who also was the major editor of the *Record of the Transmission of the Lamp Compiled in the Jingde Period*. Chuyuan was a key figure in Chan history, especially the Linji branch. It was he who brought Linji Chan to the south, which began its greatest flowering. He also served as editor of his master's writings. He was posthumously given the title Great Teacher of Benevolent Light (Ciming Dashi). Two of Chuyuan's disciples created offshoots of their own. Huanglong Huinan (1002–1069) started a short-lived Huanglong line that was transmitted to Japan by the monk Eisai as Oryo Zen. Yangqi Fanghui (992–1049) had a more lasting influence: his line of Linji Chan absorbed all other branches by the end of the Song dynasty and became the basis for Rinzai Zen in Japan.[214]

Capital—a metaphor for where the mind's "master" (*zhurengong*) dwells, like the emperor in his capital city; that is, the buddha nature within one's own mind.

94. Yuanjian Fayuan, *Untitled*[215]

*Yuanjian Fayuan (991–1067), also known as Fushan Fayuan, was from Zhengzhou (Zhengxian, Henan); his secular surname was Wang. A monk by age nineteen, he became a disciple of Shexian Guixing at Guangjiao Monastery in Ruzhou (Yexian, Henan), in the Linji branch of Chan. Guixing was a hard taskmaster, as the story of Fayuan's arrival illustrates. Though the weather was bitterly cold, Guixing cursed and reviled all the visiting monks to drive them out, and even doused them with water. Only Fayuan and Tianyi Yihuai (993–1064) persevered and dared challenge the master. Impressed, Guixing accepted them. Things went badly for Fayuan. One day, when Guixing was away from the temple, the monks asked Fayuan to cook them some porridge. Just when the porridge was ready, Guixing returned, and he angrily accused Fayuan of stealing temple goods to obtain personal favor. Fayuan was driven out but remained firm of purpose. That he might still hear Guixing's Dharma lectures, he lived for more than half a year under a covered walkway at the foot of the mountain. Eventually Fayuan's resolution won the master over, and he was brought back in honor. Guixing made him his successor, saying, "The dead tree has blossomed, and soon will welcome spring color. Then *you* can instruct *me.*" Later Fayuan was abbot for many years on Mount Fu in Shuzhou (in Qianshan, Anhui). One of his many students was Ouyang Xiu (1007–1072), a statesman, historian, literary critic, poet, and leading personality of his time. Fayuan was posthumously given the title Chan Master of the Round Mirror (Yuanjian Chanshi).[216]

Golden scales—the Tang monk Chuanzi (Boatman) Decheng of Xiuzhou (in Zhejiang) once said, "I have been rowing and stirring the clear waves, but a golden fish is seldom found."[217] The image also appears in *Blue Cliff* 49: "Sansheng [Huiran] asked Xuefeng [Yicun (822–908)], 'When the golden-scaled fish has passed through the net, what will it eat?' The master answered, 'I'll tell you when you have escaped from the net.'"

95. Yuanjian Fayuan, *Death* Gāthā[218]
Frost and snow/entering a red-hot brazier—enlightenment. As used in *Blue Cliff* 69: "Robed monks who have passed through the forest of thorns and brambles are like a pinch of snow on a red-hot brazier." Just as a snowflake in a hot brazier disappears immediately, leaving no trace behind, so too *prajñā* wisdom removes deluded thinking and leaves "not a single thing." Compare the "lotus in the fire" in Tong'an Changcha's poem above.

96. Huanglong Huinan, *Leaving the Temple and Departing from Mount Lu*[219]
*Huanglong Huinan (1002–1069) was from Xinzhou (Shangrao, Jiangxi); his secular surname was Zhang. He became a Buddhist novice at the age of eleven and a monk at nineteen, and received the Dharma seal from Yunmen master Huaicheng (fl. early eleventh century). Yet Linji master Yunfeng Wenyue (998–1062) at Mount Lu believed Huaicheng's teachings were dead words — "good-looking but useless" — and told Huinan to go see Shishuang Chuyuan (987–1040). The young monk was furious and threw a pillow at Wenyue (a more dangerous action than it sounds — Chinese pillows were often made of wood or ceramic!). Eventually Huinan became Chuyuan's disciple, and was enlightened at the age of thirty-five. When Huinan was abbot of Guizong Temple on the southern slope of Mount Lu (near Jiujiang, Jiangxi), there was a fire for which he was blamed and imprisoned for two months. He was later pardoned, and left the mountain; the present poem was likely composed at that time. Huinan is most associated with Mount Huanglong (in Xiushui, Jiangxi), where he taught for many years. He was the founder of

a short-lived Huanglong lineage that was transmitted to Japan, and was given the posthumous title Chan Master of Universal Awakening (Pujue Chanshi). He is well known in the *gong'an* tradition for his "Three Barriers of Huanglong"—three questions he used to challenge students: "Everyone has his own cause for birth. Where is yours?" "Why is my hand like Buddha's hand?" "Why is my leg like a donkey's leg?" When he received tentative answers, Huinan neither affirmed nor denied them. A disciple asked him why. Huinan replied, "Those who have already passed the barriers just swung their arms and went directly through, and never even noticed there is a watchman. Those who ask the watchman to affirm or deny have not passed the barriers."[220]

crane boat—boat with carved or painted crane decorations.

To stay or go makes no difference—one should remain "unattached" (Ch. *wuzhu*; Skt. *asakta*) to circumstances.

97. Huanglong Huinan, *Instructing Chan Disciples at a High Terrace on Nanyue Mountain*[221]

Nanyue Mountain—Mount Heng, one of China's five sacred mountains, in Hengzhou (Hengshan, Hunan).

part the grass and see the wind—a metaphor for eradicating delusion. Lines in a poem by Huanglong Huinan included in *Blue Cliff* 9 describe Zhaozhou Congshen's (778–897) compassion for those still searching for truth: "Zhaozhou entered the weeds to look for the man/And cared not that his whole body was drenched in muddy water."

Tianhuang's cake—a *gong'an* featuring Tianhuang Daowu (748–807) and his student Longtan Chongxin, describing the exchanges that piqued the latter's interest in Chan. Chongxin originally came of a family of cake sellers. The text continues:

> The master's [Chongxin's] home was in the lane by the temple, and often he would make offerings of ten cakes. [Dao-]wu received the offerings, and each time after he had eaten, he would hold back one cake and say, "I give this to you for the protection of your sons and grandsons." One day the master thought to himself, "I brought the cakes, so why does he turn around and give them back to me? Does he mean something else?" He then went and asked. [Dao-]wu replied, "It was you who brought the cakes, so why are you complaining?" The master heard this and seemed to understand a hidden meaning. He thereupon left home to become a monk.[222]

Zhaozhou's tea—a *gong'an* featuring Zhaozhou Congshen (778–897):

Zhaozhou asked a monk who was newly arrived, "Have you ever been here before?" The monk answered, "Yes, I have." The master said, "Go drink tea." He then asked another monk, "Have you ever been here before?" The monk said, "No, I haven't." The master said, "Go drink tea." Later the abbot asked Zhaozhou, "Why did you say to both the one who had been and the one who had not been here before, 'Go drink tea'?" The master called the abbot, who answered. The master then said, "Go drink tea."[223]

Numerous commentators understand the response "Go drink tea" as a reprimand. Linji master Kaifu Daoning (1053–1113) explains, "Zhaozhou's disciples can't tell the difference between high and low, so he nourishes them one and all with a cup of poor tea. Those who can taste its flavor will then know that within cold ashes the fragrant elixir of immortality is perfected."[224]

Nanquan—a *gong'an* featuring Nanquan Puyuan (748–834), in *Transmission* 8:

One evening when Master Nan-ch'üan was enjoying the moonlight, a monk asked him when one could be equal to the moonlight. The master said, "Twenty years ago I attained that state." The monk continued, "What about right now?" The master went immediately to his room.[225]

Lingyun—Lingyun Zhiqin (fl. ninth century), who was enlightened upon seeing peach blossoms.

Dharma forest (conglin)—a euphemism for a temple or assembly of monks.

98. Fachang Yiyu, *Parting from a Monk*[226]
*Fachang Yiyu (1005–1081) was from Zhangzhou (Longxi, Fujian); his secular surname was Lin. He left home to become a monk early in life, and studied under famous masters including Yuanjian Fayuan (991–1067) and Shishuang Chuyuan (987–1040). Eventually Yiyu became a disciple of Beichan Zhixian in the Yunmen branch of Chan. He is most associated with the Fachang Chan Monastery in Hongzhou (Fenning, Jiangxi), where he was abbot for many years. His biographies record brilliant verbal battles with Huanglong Huinan (1002–1069) and Baojue Zuxin (1025–1100), in which he easily held his own. Yet he was disappointed in his followers, as the story of his death illustrates. Yiyu was a close friend and teacher to Xu Xi (*zi* Dezhan) before the latter became an important civil official. The day before he died, he sent Xu a parting *gāthā:*

This year I'm seventy-seven,
And should pick a day to leave.

Last night I asked my Tortoise Brother,
Who said tomorrow is a good day.[227]

Dezhan was shocked. He called for Old Lingyuan [Weiqing (d. 1117)], and together they rushed over. Yiyu was sitting on his bed, transferring temple affairs and miscellaneous objects to the monk administrator. He said, "I've been abbot of this mountain for thirty years. To protect and maintain its continuity, I've managed everything alone. Now I'm going. You two manifest spirit brilliance." He then raised his staff, and continued, "Now tell me, to whom shall I give this?" Dezhan and Lingyuan held their breaths, and said nothing in reply. Yiyu then threw the staff on the ground, pillowed his head in his arm, and passed away.

Indeed, charts reveal only two disciples of Yiyu, neither of whom had disciples of their own.[228]

99. Fachang Yiyu, *The Fisherman Gives up Fishing*[229]
chase the waves/and on the ripples ride (suibo zhulang)—This phrase appears to impart two distinct meanings in Chan texts. First, it criticizes those who are thrown about by the waves of karma and thus are deluded. Second, it describes a process by which nature is allowed to take its own course. In the latter sense, it became one of the "Three Propositions of the Yunmen School," used to initiate students. It was loosely interpreted as "from causes succeed to things" (*suiyuan jiewu*) and "take medicine to fit the disease" (*yingbing yuyao*). In practice this was justification for guiding students using flexible and varying methods that fit their capacities.

100. Baojue Zuxin, *Reading the* Record of the Transmission of the Lamp[230]
*Baojue Zuxin (1025–1100), *hao* Huitang, was from Shixing (Nanxiong, Guangdong); his secular surname was Wu. He began Buddhist studies as a novice at age ten and formed the intent to become a monk at age nineteen, when a temporary blindness he suffered was cured following his prayers to the bodhisattva of compassion, Avalokiteśvara (Guanyin). He subsequently spent a long period traveling to study with various masters. It appears he also had a sense of humor. When he visited Mount Lu (near Jiujiang, Jiangxi), local magistrate Peng Ruli asked him, "When people are about to die, do they gain some secret meaning?" Zuxin answered, "They do." The magistrate continued, "Can you tell me what it is?" Zuxin said, "I'll tell you when you're dead." Zuxin's formal studies included three years with Linji master Yunfeng Wenyue (998–1062) and four years with Huanglong Huinan (1002–1069)—all with no result. Then, while studying with

Shishuang Chuyuan (987–1040), he was enlightened while reading dialogues in *Transmission*. He returned to the circle of Huanglong Huinan and eventually became Huinan's successor. His students included the key Neo-Confucian philosopher Cheng Yi (1033–1108) and the famed poet Huang Tingjian (1045–1105).

> Huang Shan'gu [Tingjian] once asked Chan Master Huitang Zuxin of Longxing Commandery for guidance. The Master said, "It is just as Confucius said, 'My friends, I know you think that there is something I am keeping from you. There is nothing at all that I keep from you.'[231] How do you understand this?" Shan'gu was about to answer, when the Master said, "Wrong! Wrong!" One day they were walking in the mountains, and the clifftop osmanthus was in bloom. The Master said, "Do you smell the fragrance of the osmanthus flowers?" Shan'gu said, "Yes." The Master said, "There is nothing at all that I keep from you!" Shan'gu understood, and was enlightened.

Zuxin was posthumously given the title Chan Master of Treasured Awakening (Baojue Chanshi).[232] About a century later, through his line, Linji Chan was first transmitted to Japan.

Record of the Transmission of the Lamp—compiled in 1004 by the monk Daoyuan, this book records the dialogues of six hundred masters and the names of more than a thousand others.

101. Baojue Zuxin, *A Newly Transplanted Sunflower*[233]
Sunflower—just as sunflowers always face the sun, the practitioner should remain focused on the buddha nature. Cao-Dong master Hongzhi Zhengjue (1091–1157) writes, "Sunflowers face the sun/Willow catkins follow the wind."[234]
Shanglin Park—a famous garden built in Qin times to the west of the capital Chang'an (Xi'an, Shanxi) and enlarged by emperor Wu (r. 140–86 B.C.E.) of the Han dynasty.

102. Baiyun Shouduan, *White Cloud Mountain on a Summer Day*[235]
*Baiyun Shouduan (1025–1072) was from Hengyang (Hengyang, Hunan); his secular surname was Zhou (one source has Ge). He became a monk at the age of twenty and was enlightened while studying with Linji master Yangqi Fanghui (992–1049). After accompanying his teacher for a number of years, Shouduan served as abbot in several temples associated with the Yangqi line of Linji Chan. He was fond of striking metaphors. Describing the universality of Buddha, he said, "There are no cold places in a wok of soup." Another day he ascended the dais in the hall and said:

Birds have two wings to fly, and there is no "near" or "far" for them. Once they leave a place, there is no "future" or "past." You robed monks always just pick up your spoons or put down your chopsticks, and say you know there'll be a time when you ascend the peak. Yet why then are you so anxious and unsettled? You don't understand that the practitioner of the Way has no distant concerns. To have such brings grief near to hand.

Shouduan is most associated with Haihui Temple on Mount Baiyun (White Cloud) (near Tongcheng, Anhui), which he founded.[236]

103. Miaozong Daoqian, *Summer Night*[237]
*Miaozong Daoqian (1043–1106?), *hao* Canliaozi (Man of Emptiness), was in the Yunmen branch of Chan, having been a disciple of Dajue Huailian (1009–1090). He was from Yuqian (Lin'an, Zhejiang) and had the lay surname Hua (one source has He). Daoqian for many years maintained close ties with the poet, critic, and statesman Su Shi (1037–1101). When Su Shi was prefect of Hangzhou (Hangzhou, Zhejiang) and Daoqian dwelt at the Zhiguo Monastery on nearby West Lake, the two spent many happy hours appreciating the landscape and discussing religion. Daoqian even appeared in his dreams, as Su explains:

> When I was in Huangzhou, Canliao came from Wuling to visit, and stayed with me at Eastern Slope. One day, I dreamed that Canliao was chanting a new poem. When I awoke, I recorded the two lines, "Cold Food Days and Pure Brightness Festival are both past;/By a stone spring and an acacia fire, time is made new." Seven years later, I had gone out to govern Qiantang (Hangzhou), and Canliao had just begun to dwell at the Zhiguo Monastery on the lake. The monastery had a spring that poured out from a fissure in the rocks. The water was sweet and cold—perfect for tea. The day after Cold Food Days, some guests and I floated in a boat from the Lonely Mountain and went to see Canliao. We drew water and started a fire, and brewed "Huangbo tea." Suddenly I remembered the poetic omen I had dreamed seven years before. All of the guests were shocked, and sighed in admiration. They understood that since there was a record, the story must be true.

In 1094, when Su was exiled in a political struggle between reformers and traditionalists, Daoqian was accused by the authorities of writing treasonous poetry and was punished as well—forced to return to lay life for seven years. Near the end of the Chongning reign period (1102–1107), Daoqian retired to Mount Qian in his home region, where he died. He was given the imperial title Chan Master of Wondrous Universality (Miaozong Chanshi) early in the reign of Song emperor Zhe (r. 1086–1101). He was a prolific poet whose collected poems are still extant.[238]

104. Kaifu Daoning, *Bamboo Shoots*[239]

*Kaifu Daoning (1053–1113) was from Huizhou (Wuyuan, Anhui); his secular surname was Wang. As a young man he was a Daoist, but took his baths at a local temple. One day, when he was about to wash his feet, he happened to hear a monk intoning lines from the *Diamond Sūtra*. He forgot where he was and what he was doing, and without thinking trailed his feet in the hot water. The shock triggered an illumination experience. He became a monk at Mount Jiang (near Nanjing, Jiangsu), and in subsequent years studied at all the major Chan centers. Eventually he became a disciple of the famous Wuzu Fayan (1024–1104) in the Yangqi line of Linji Chan. He was "suddenly and completely enlightened to the Dharma source" when he heard Fayan discourse on *gong'an* of the Tang masters. Daoning became abbot of Kaifu Chan Temple in Tanzhou (in Hunan). He is reported to have been a brilliant teacher, his lectures concise and direct. Just before he died, he assembled his disciples and said in part, "My golden body is here today, gone tomorrow. If any of you says I'm entering *nirvāṇa*, you are not my disciple! And if any of you says I am *not* entering *nirvāṇa*, you're not my disciple either! Look around here, and you'll know where I've ended up." It was Daoning's line that later produced Wumen Huikai (1183–1260), compiler of the *Gateless Pass*.[240]

without frustration (shoujie) — there is a pun here. The term in general usage means to maintain (moral) principle. Another meaning of *jie* is a segment, as of bamboo; thus *shoujie* is literally "to maintain its segments" — to grow naturally and without interference.

dragon transformation — a *gong'an* in *Blue Cliff* 60 featuring Yunmen Wenyan (862/4–949): "Yunmen used his staff to instruct the assembled monks, saying, 'The staff transforms into a dragon, which swallows the entire universe; where are all the rivers and mountains of the great world to be found?'"[241] In enlightenment, the universe can be held in the hand like a staff.

A comment in Daoning's discourse records relates directly to the present poem. When explaining why so many people meet the Buddha but still do not recognize him, he said, "If you cut down the bamboo before the frost, it will never transform into a dragon by the riverside."[242]

105. Yun'gai Zhiben, *Untitled*[243]

*Yun'gai Zhiben (1035–1107) was from Yunzhou (Gao'an, Jiangxi); his secular surname was Guo. He became a monk at nineteen at Ciyun Monastery near his home, and traveled widely. He became a disciple of Baiyun Shouduan (1025–1072) and remained with him more than ten years. Zhiben's fame began to spread. When he was invited by the prefect of Shuzhou (in Anhui) to lecture, Shouduan led the entire community to see him off. As Zhiben rode away, he turned and said, "I will not refuse what I deserve." Shouduan laughed, and said to the other monks, "A noble talent of the Buddhist world—when the family's rich, the little sons are proud!" As an abbot, Zhiben taught at a series of temples, including that at Mount Yun'gai in Tanzhou (near Changsha, Hunan). He employed a pithy style of rhetoric reminiscent of the Tang masters. A monk asked, "Can one use the mind to investigate the mind?" Zhiben commented, "That's like a foreigner studying Chinese." Zhiben is described as frank and direct, inattentive to worldly concerns, and possessed of courage greater than that of his contemporaries. In later years he retired to Mount Jia (in Hubei).[244]

   walkers in the night (*yexing ren*)—walking abroad at night was restricted by law. Thus the metaphorical use of the term in *Transmission* 15: "Zhaozhou [Cong-shen (778–897)] asked, 'When is the time when those who have died the Great Death return to life?' The master [Touzi Datong (845–914)] replied, 'You are not permitted to walk at night, but must reach there by dawn.'"[245] The Great Death (*dasi*) is no-mind; "to walk at night" is to practice the Chan Way.

106. Yun'gai Zhiben, *Sending off the Honorable Palace Library Editor Tang Songming on His Return to Guan Stream*[246]

107. Furong Daokai, *Death Gāthā*[247]
   *Furong Daokai (1043–1118), a major teacher of Cao-Dong Chan, was from Yizhou (Feixian, Shandong); his secular surname was Cui. As a young man he studied Daoism, and even abstained from grain—a frequent Daoist practice in the quest for immortality. For a time he became a recluse on Mount Yiyang (in Henan). Eventually he traveled to the Song capital of Bianliang (Kaifeng, Henan) and began Buddhist studies at Shutai Temple. In 1074 he was formally ordained; he wandered widely in ensuing years. On Mount Touzi in Shuzhou (in Anhui) he met the Cao-Dong master Touzi Yiqing (1032–1083), and after speaking with him was suddenly enlightened; he then became Yiqing's disciple. Afterward Daokai went to the mountains, where it was said he lived with tigers as his companions. Once he even took a tiger cub from its lair, but let it go when great roars from the trees told him the mother tiger objected. His teaching career began in earnest in 1082, and he successively served as abbot in half a dozen temples in Henan and Hubei. In 1107, the governor of the capital successfully petitioned the throne to award Daokai a purple cassock and the title Chan Master of Contemplative Illumination (Dingzhao Chanshi). However, Daokai refused these honors, as he had

vowed not to pursue profit or fame, and was consequently banished to Zizhou (in Shandong). He was pardoned in 1111, and soon thereafter built a cottage on the banks of Lake Furong (in Shandong) and founded a religious community. Daokai was a hard man, and conditions were harsh; monks were limited to one cup of rice gruel per day. Many slipped quietly away, but more than a hundred remained to study under the master. Tablets in the imperial hand, one naming the site Huayan Chan Temple, were conferred in ensuing years. Daokai had many disciples, the most notable of whom was perhaps Danxia Zichun (1064–1117), who in turn taught Hongzhi Zhengjue (1091–1157), the most important Cao-Dong figure in the Song period. He once described the method of silent illumination: "The path to entering the Way is to be empty inside and tranquil outside, like water still and frozen. Then all things will brilliantly reflect [each other], and neither submerged nor floating on top, all phenomena will be just thus."[248]

108. Danxia Zichun, *Living in the Mountains*[249]

*Danxia Zichun (1064–1117), also known as Dechun, was from Jianzhou (Zitong, Sichuan); his secular surname was Jia. He undertook the religious life as a novice at Da'an Temple near his home, and at age twenty-seven formally took orders as a monk. He became a disciple of Cao-Dong Chan master Furong Daokai (1043–1118). Furong saw that Zichun had great potential, and said to him:

> "The ancients said, 'Begin the task even before there was an Empty Realm;/Find understanding when Buddha has not yet appeared in the world.' You are dismissed now to complete this, leaving nothing out. There's no use for me to say anything further." At these words Zichun was greatly enlightened, and he subsequently served Furong for many years.

Zichun was described as of a lofty disposition but a stern appearance; while his thoughts were benevolent, his words were sharp. He had little to do with worldly affairs. In 1104 he became abbot at Qixia Temple on Mount Danxia in Dengzhou (Nanzhao, Henan), and later at temples on Mount Dacheng (in Henan) and Mount Dahong (in Hubei). He guided a large number of disciples, including the major Cao-Dong figure Hongzhi Zhengjue (1091–1157). Once he overheard Zhengjue laugh at a monk who misunderstood a *gong'an*. Zichun scolded him, "A single laugh can destroy good cultivation." He admonished the younger man, "If you let go for even a moment, you're like a dead man." Zichun also compiled 100 cases for teaching purposes; commentary was added later by Linquan Conglun to form the *Empty Hall Collection*.[250]

Walking or sitting still—two types of meditation: the contemplative stroll and seated meditation.

109. Changling Shouzhuo, *Living in the Mountains*[251]

*Changling Shouzhuo (1065–1123) was from Quanzhou (Jinjiang, Fujian); his secular surname was Zhuang. He was a disciple of Lingyuan Weiqing (d. 1117), who himself was a disciple of Baojue Zuxin (1025–1100) in the Huanglong line of Linji Chan. He served Weiqing for more than ten years and learned all the old master could teach. He was abbot of several temples (in Anhui and Henan). Stern and severe, he gained the nickname Iron Face (Tiemian). After his death, the emperor sent an envoy to the cremation to bestow a gift of incense and collect any holy *śarīra* (Ch. *sheli*) crystals that might be found. Several five-colored relics as large as beans were indeed recovered, and the envoy carried them back to court in a golden pan. Upon seeing them, the emperor was delighted.[252]

Sound enters beyond sound—the poet understands that what he hears is an object of perception/cognition (*viṣaya*) and hence unreliable, and that "beyond sound" is true sound.

void seems within void—the void is not separate from anything else; it is not a "place" or "idea" beyond reality; thus the void is also void.

110. Changling Shouzhuo, *After Hanshan*[253]

What kind of a thing is existence?—the rest of this poem can be interpreted as an answer to this question; the poet attempts to break down the distinction between "existence" (*youwu*) and "nonexistence" (*wuwu*), "being" (*you*) and "nonbeing" (*wu*), "form" (*se*) and "void" (*kong*)—thus we might paraphrase the line, "Is reality really real?"

clouds return—a traditional belief was that clouds arose from mountain caves. The metaphor here suggests a return to origins.

The finger exists/and so does the horse—a summation of a section of *Zhuangzi* 2:

To use a finger to show that a finger is not a finger is not as good as using a non-finger to show a finger is not a finger. To use a horse to show that a horse is not a horse is not as good as using a nonhorse to show that a horse is not a horse. Heaven and earth are a single finger; the ten thousand things are a single horse.[254]

Zhuangzi here presents his take on the work of the logician Gongsun Long (third century B.C.E.). Gongsun famously said that "a white horse is not a horse," as he distinguished between the concrete particularity of objects and the universal designations we use to categorize them and structure language. Gongsun used the term "pointing fingers" (*zhi*) to refer to the universals.[255] Zhuangzi denies the difference between universals and particulars and allows logical opposites to coexist. Changling Shouzhuo follows suit, thus "The [pointing] finger [that connotes the universal designation of "horse"] exists, and so does the [concrete, particular] horse."

the mind is not,/and the Buddha also is not—the line recalls the following two exchanges from the records of Mazu Daoyi (709–788) in *Transmission 6*:

> One day the Master spoke to his assembly as follows: "All of you should realize that your own mind is Buddha, that is, this mind is Buddha's Mind. . . . Those who seek for the Truth should realize that there is nothing to seek. There is no Buddha but Mind; there is no Mind but Buddha."[256]

> A monk asked why the Master maintained, "The Mind is the Buddha." The Master answered, "Because I want to stop the crying of a baby." The monk persisted, "When the crying has stopped, what is it then?" "Not Mind, not Buddha," was the answer.[257]

The two dicta are complementary: "Not Mind, not Buddha" is "The Mind is the Buddha" seen from the perspective of emptiness.

"this" and "that"—another allusion to *Zhuangzi 2*:

> [The Sage] . . . recognizes a "this," but a "this" which is also "that," a "that" which is also "this." His "that" has both a right and a wrong in it; his "this" too has both a right and a wrong in it. So, in fact, does he still have a "this" and "that"? Or does he in fact no longer have a "this" and "that"? A state in which "this" and "that" no longer find their opposites is called the hinge of the Way.[258]

111. Xingkong Miaopu, *Instructions for My Disciples*[259]

*Xingkong Miaopu (1071–1142) was from Hanzhou (Guanghan, Sichuan). He became a monk under the guidance of Sixin Wuxin (1043–1114) on Mount Huanglong. Miaopu was struck by the example of the Tang monk Chuanzi (Boatman) Decheng, who had passed his days floating in a small boat on the Xiu River in Xiuzhou (near Jiaxing, Zhejiang). Miaopu moved to the same area and built a hermitage in the wild land of Mount Qinglong. He remained there for the rest of his life, playing the metal flute for amusement and writing religious verses for his friends. During the chaos of the middle Song period, when the north was invaded and the Chinese imperial government fled to the south, rebels overran Wuzhen (in Wuxing, Zhejiang). Many people were slaughtered and others ran away. Miaopu, however, carried on as before, and traveled through the war-torn district. His unusual demeanor made the rebels believe he was a spy, and they wanted to kill him. Miaopu told them they could have his head, but first he would like a last ritual meal. When finished, he said matter-of-factly, "Calamity has befallen me. Well, I've been a contented and honest man, and now it's time for me to go." He asked them to bring a sword, then called out in a loud voice, "Strike! Strike!" The rebels were amazed and frightened, and touching their heads to the ground, begged for his forgiveness. They let him go, and refrained from burning the nearby villages as well.[260]

imperial walls — the Forbidden City, where the emperor dwells.

six thieves — the six senses (*liugen*): eyes, ear, nose, tongue, body, and mind. Chan Buddhists held that sensory perceptions and the passions they engender are as illusory as all other things in the world of causation, so to focus on them instead of reaching directly for enlightenment is wasted effort. This is reflected in the surprisingly peaceful dénouement in the poem's second half. Compare the words of Muzhou Daozong (tenth century) in *Transmission* 12, "The soldiers arrayed before Dharma Flower Peak will be recalled when the word *nirvāṇa* is spoken."[261] The *Platform Sūtra* says, "The Dharma of no-thought means: even though you see all things, you do not attach to them, but, always keeping your own nature pure, cause the six thieves to exit through the six gates."[262]

general of the central army — the "master" (*zhurengong* or *zhurenweng*) of the mind/body as a name for the buddha nature was mentioned above. This is identical with the "original man" (*benlai ren*) or the "true man of no rank" (*wuwei zhenren*) of Linji Yixuan. Because this "master" has control, sensory perceptions and passions are not a threat. Here, the "master" is the general, who can give orders such that no conflict will be necessary for "peace" to be achieved. It says in the commentary to *Blue Cliff* 13, "It's easy to obtain a thousand soldiers, but hard to find a single general"; and in *Blue Cliff* 61, "Everyone knows the song of peace."[263] Compare the following *gong'an* in *Gateless Pass* 12:

Master Ruiyan Shiyan (ca. tenth century) called to himself every day, "Master!" and answered, "Yes, sir!" Then he would say, "Be wide awake!" and answer, "Yes, sir!" "Henceforward, never be deceived by others!" "No, I won't!"[264]

112. Xingkong Miaopu, *Death* Gāthā[265]

In dying, Miaopu showed the same independent streak that characterized his life. He called a crowd together and intoned this poem. Then, sitting cross-legged in a tiny boat, he floated down the river to the sea. The crowd followed on the bank. Miaopu pulled the plug in the bottom of the boat, and singing and playing his metal flute, drifted away into the distance. At last, the crowd saw him throw his flute up into the air and go under. Three days later, his body was found on the sand, sitting cross-legged in perfect repose. During his funeral rites, two cranes soared in the sky above.

113. Cishou Huaishen, *The Terrace of Spreading Clouds on Mount Lingyan* [266]
*Cishou Huaishen (1077–1132) was from Shouchun (Shouxian, Anhui); his secular surname was Xia. When he was born, auspicious light filled the house, and he was recognized for his religious potential. His mother allowed him to become a monk at the age of fourteen. Huaishen was in the Yunmen branch of Chan, having become a disciple of Changlu Chongxin (ca. eleventh century) at Zisheng Temple in Jiayao (Jiaxing, Zhejiang). When his teacher moved to Mount Changlu (in Liuhe, Jiangsu), Huaishen accompanied him. Beginning in 1113, he became abbot of numerous temples, moving frequently, and enjoyed imperial patronage. He was known for his strict adherence to monastic rules, his humility, and his attention to teaching the younger monks. He is most associated with Yaofeng Monastery on Mount Lingyan. At his last post, Yuanjue Temple (in Jiangxi), a monk asked him, "What is the word after death?" Huaishen replied, "Wait five days and see." In fact, five days later Huaishen grew ill and died. [267]

root of clouds (yun'gen)—a euphemism for rocks, with extensive connotations. It is written in *The Mustard Seed Garden Manual of Painting*, the most comprehensive and influential painting manual of the Qing dynasty:

> In estimating people, their quality of spirit (*qi*) is as basic as the way they are formed; and so it is with rocks, which are the framework of the heavens and of earth and also have qi. That is the reason rocks are sometimes spoken of as *yun'gen* (roots of the clouds). Rocks without *qi* are dead rocks, just as bones without the same vivifying spirit are dry, bare bones. How could a cultivated person paint a lifeless rock? [268]

hang them on the wall—there are two referents here. First, when a monk arrived at a temple, he hung his priest's staff, robe, and/or begging bowl on a hook on the wall; the hooks had a prescribed order that indicated the monk's place in temple activities and meditation. Second, the line recalls the Chan aphorism, "All of the Buddhas of the Three Ages hang their mouths on the wall" (*sanshi zhufo kou gua bishang*), which suggests the uselessness of words in achieving truth. The message: be quiet and practice.

114. Cishou Huaishen, *Walking Song to Instruct Monks at Zifu Temple*[269]

115. Cishou Huaishen, *Written at Ke Pavilion on West Lake at Hangzhou*[270]

    Xiangyan—the Chan master Xiangyan Zhixian (fl. ninth century) failed to answer when Guishan Lingyou (771–853) asked him what was his original being before birth. In great doubt and distress, he thereupon burned all his books and notes and withdrew into solitude. He suddenly attained enlightenment when he heard the sound of a tile shard knocking against a bamboo stalk.[271]

116. Baofeng Weizhao, *Untitled*[272]

    *Baofeng Weizhao (1084–1128) was from Jianzhou (Jianyang, Sichuan); his secular surname was Li. In his teens he left home to study Buddhism in the regional capital of Chengdu (Chengdu, Sichuan); he became a monk at the age of nineteen. One night, he heard passersby calling to each other in a storm and gained a measure of understanding. He traveled to Mount Dahong and became a disciple of Cao-Dong master Furong Daokai (1043–1118). When his teacher moved to Shandong in the northeast, Weizhao followed. En route, the driver lost his way. Weizhao raised his staff to strike him and was suddenly enlightened. Perhaps it was the unexpected switching of roles—now *he* was the master trying to make the student understand—that was the catalyst. He later taught in several Chan centers, including Letan (in Qing'an, Jiangxi). After his death, his cremation "revealed holy *śarīra* crystals like strings of pearls, and his tongue and teeth were not destroyed."[273]

    Weizhao inscribed this poem on a portrait of his teacher, Furong Daokai.[274]

117. Dahui Zonggao, *Leavetaking*[275]

    *Dahui Zonggao (1089–1163) was from Xuanzhou (Xuancheng, Anhui); his secular surname was Xi. He was the key figure in Song dynasty Linji Chan and was largely responsible for the systematization and popularization of the *gong'an* (public case) technique; see the introduction. When in his teens he enrolled in the local school for Confucian classics, but was sent home and forced to pay a fine after he and a classmate beaned the teacher's hat (with the teacher under it) in a game of "inkstone toss." He became a monk at the age of seventeen. He studied Chan with several masters before joining Linji master Yuanwu Keqin (1063–1135). Zonggao was enlightened in 1124 while at Tianning Temple in the Song capital of Bianliang (Kaifeng, Henan), the moment he heard his teacher say, "Whence come all the buddhas? A fragrant breeze comes of itself from the south/In the palace pavilion a light coolness is born." His master could see that the young monk sat in "a place of purity, where all dust of affliction is stripped away." Yet

Keqin was not satisfied, and remarked, "It's not easy to reach this mind ground where you are, but too bad that once dead you do not live again. Not to doubt words and language is a big mistake." It took another period of training, a second experience of liberation, and close questioning from the master before Zonggao was granted the Dharma seal. Zonggao quickly became an important figure in Chan in the north. In 1127 the north of China was taken over by Jin invaders, and the Song was reconstituted as the Southern Song in the area that remained under Chinese control. Zonggao moved first to Yunmen Monastery (in Jiangxi) and then in 1134 to Yangyu Monastery (in Fujian). Three years later Zonggao was summoned by the prime minister to oversee Nengren Chan Monastery on Mount Jing (near Yuhang, Zhejiang), not far from the new Song capital of Lin'an (Hangzhou, Zhejiang); thus he is also known as Jingshan Zonggao. However, he was caught up in the factional fighting at the court and incurred the wrath of the quisling prime minister Qin Kuai (1090–1155). He was banished for more than ten years to Hengzhou (in Hunan), where he devoted himself to writing his own collection of annotated *gong'an*, *Treasury of the True Dharma Eye* (a title later borrowed by Dōgen). He was returned to favor in 1158 and allowed back to the capital area. At this time he wrote his well-known criticisms of the Cao-Dong "silent illumination" method. In 1163, he was given the imperial title Chan Master of Great Wisdom (Dahui Chanshi). One night that year, the streak of a meteor was seen west of the Bright Moon Hall, where Zonggao had retired, and he noticed a slight illness. He died in the summer.[276]

the bucket's bottom falls out—the "lacquer bucket" (*qitong*) refers to those mired in ignorance, as lacquer is pitch black; when "the bucket's bottom falls out" (*tongdi tuo*) one breaks through to the light—sudden enlightenment. Dahui Zonggao often used the broken bucket metaphor as the successful end of the *gong'an* process.[277]

life's root breaks—death. However, the poet uses the words metaphorically, as equivalent to the bucket's bottom falling out. Compare Zhaozhou Congshen's (778–897) concept of the "great death" in *Blue Cliff* 41.

118. Hongzhi Zhengjue, *For Layman Li*[278]

*Hongzhi Zhengjue (1091–1157) was from Xizhou (Xixian, Shanxi); his secular surname was Li. His mother, it was said, became pregnant after dreaming that a monk from Mount Wutai placed a bracelet on her right arm. When her baby was born, the skin of his right arm showed a mark in the shape of a bracelet, and bright light emanating from the house startled passersby. He became a novice at ten and a monk at fourteen. He traveled widely in his late teens, including a period spent on Mount Xiang near Luoyang (Luoyang, Henan) studying with

Furong Daokai's (1043–1118) disciple Kumu Facheng (1071–1128). While there he had his initial enlightenment experience. He later became a disciple of Danxia Zichun (1064–1117), under whom his enlightenment was completed and affirmed. Zichun tested the young monk with a question similar to that which had led to his own enlightenment: "What is the self *before* the Empty Realm?" Zhengjue answered, "The toad at the bottom of the well has swallowed the moon;/In the third watch, he does not rely on (*jie*) curtains against the night light." Zichun said, "Not quite. Speak again." When Zhengjue was about to reply, Zichun hit him with his whisk and said, "Speak again. Don't 'rely' [on anything]." At this, Zhengjue was suddenly enlightened. Beginning about 1121, he served as abbot at half a dozen temples. When he was at Mount Changlu (in Liuhe, Jiangsu), he purportedly was able to convince marauding bandits to withdraw merely by the force of his personality and benevolent words. Zhengjue is particularly associated with Mount Tiantong (near Ningbo, Zhejiang), where he served for thirty years, refusing all invitations to come down. Thus he is also called Tiantong Zhengjue. He became one of the most influential Chan teachers of his generation, known in particular for his espousal of the Cao-Dong "silent illumination" (*mozhao*) method; see the introduction. When he died, despite their ideological differences, Dahui Zonggao rushed to Mount Tiantong to participate in the funeral rites. The Song emperor conferred upon Zhengjue the posthumous title Chan Master of Vast Wisdom (Hongzhi Chanshi). Zhengjue was famed as a writer and poet. He was the compiler of two collections of *gong'an* that later provided much of the source material for the *Records of Serenity,* edited by Wansong Xingxiu (1166–1246) and first published in 1224.[279]

dead meditation (kuchan) — "dead meditation" is an abbreviation for "dead wood meditation" (*kumu chan*), which means to become as immobile and non-thinking as a dead tree. The phrase is associated with the "silent illumination" method of Cao-Dong Chan, although it also was used as a criticism by Linji *gong'an* proponents.

Dhāraṇī Gate — *dhāraṇī* (Ch. *zongchi*, transliterated as *tuoluoni*) refers to mystical forms of prayer and is a synonym for *mantra*.

119. Hongzhi Zhengjue, *Sending off Monk Hui Upriver to Buy Hemp and Rice*[280]
the price of rice — an allusion to a *gong'an* in *Transmission* 5: "A monk asked Qing-yuan [Xingsi (?–740)], 'What is the great meaning of Buddhism?' Qingyuan said, 'What is the price of rice in Luling?'"[281] The poem may be understood as an interpretation of the *gong'an.* Although here and now it is not possible to know the price of rice in Luling, once you arrive there it will be obvious.

120. Hongzhi Zhengjue, *Written at Cloud Retreat at Letan*[282]

    Letan—a famous Chan center (in present Qing'an, Jiangxi). Mazu Daoyi (709–788) died there, and Dongshan Liangjie (807–869) taught there. Several temples were nearby, including Dongshan Temple, Letan Temple, and Baofeng Temple.

121. Hongzhi Zhengjue, *Begging Song for the Bell Ringer*[283]

122. Hongzhi Zhengjue, *Returning to My Old Home in the Southern Hills*[284]

    bird/fish—the final line is a reference to the first of Tao Qian's (365–427) Daoist-inspired "Returning to My Home in the Country" poems: "The tame bird longs for his old forest;/The fish in the house pond thinks of his ancient pool." For Tao, returning home brought a spontaneous freedom that living in the world of human striving could not.

123. Hongzhi Zhengjue, *Death* Gāthā[285]

    Dreams, illusions, flowers in the air—a line from the "Trust in the Mind Inscription" attributed to Third Patriarch Sengcan: "Dreams, illusions, flowers in the air:/Why bother to grasp them?"[286] The *Śūraṃgama sūtra* is the source for the "flowers in the air" term: "It's like a man with an eye disease seeing flowers in [empty] space. If the disease is removed, then the flowers will disappear."[287]

    The white bird—compare the second couplet here with Zhengjue's "Lancet of Seated Meditation," quoted in the introduction.

124. Baiyang Fashun, *Attainment*[288]

    *Baiyang Fashun (1076–1139) was from Mianzhou (Mianyang, Sichuan); his secular surname was Wen. He was a disciple of Longmen Qingyuan (a.k.a. Foyan Qingyuan) (1067–1120) in the Yangqi line of Linji Chan. Fashun wrote this poem immediately after his enlightenment, as proof of his experience. He once said to the community:

> It's easy to be close to the mire of causation, but it's hard to accomplish the Way. If you don't understand what is before your eyes, then the ten thousand worldly ties will remain distinct. You'll see only vast, vast *viṣaya* winds withering the forest of goodness; and hot, hot fires of mind burning the *bodhi* tree.

    Although he did serve as an abbot at least twice, Fashun mostly lived an ascetic, wandering life, taking with him only his staff and a straw hat.[289]

    Attainment (touji)—to merge with (touhe) Chan essence or potentiality (Chanji).

125. Huayan Zujue, *Untitled*[290]

*Huayan Zujue (1087–1150), also known as Zhidu Zujue, was from Longyou (Leshan, Sichuan); his secular surname was Yang; his *hao* included Jue Huayan and Chi'an. A Confucian student and admirer of the Tang literatus Han Yu in his youth, he once wrote an essay denouncing Buddhism, but then was suddenly afflicted with boils and sores and could not walk. He recovered only after he had repented and decided to become a monk. He immersed himself in Huayan Buddhism and soon was lecturing to assemblies in Chengdu (Chengdu, Sichuan). Yet he found his religious understanding lacking, so left to undertake Chan studies under ex-prime minister Zhang Shangying (a.k.a. Layman Wujin) (1043–1121) in Jingnan (Jiangling, Hubei). Wujin thought Zujue showed promise, and sent him to continue his studies under the guidance of Yuanwu Keqin (1063–1135) on Mount Jiang (near Nanjing, Jiangsu). This poem was written just after Zujue *thought* he had attained enlightenment while listening to Yuanwu Keqin lecture:

> When Yuanwu saw it he just let out a big laugh. The next day he asked Zujue, "Where did yesterday's *gong'an* come from?" As Zujue was about to reply, Yuanwu yelled, "The Buddhist Dharma is not this way!" After this event, Zujue continued his studies for another five years.[291]

126. Huayan Zujue, *Untitled*[292]

After his further period of study, Zujue had another enlightenment experience. He wrote this poem as proof, and sent it to his teacher, Yuanwu Keqin. Yuanwu laughed, showed it to the community, and said, "Jue Huayan is complete!" By imperial order Zujue became abbot at Zhongyan Temple in Meizhou (Meishan, Sichuan). He was a prolific author.

127. Botang Nanya, *Living in the Mountains*[293]

*Botang Nanya (fl. twelfth century), also known as Longxiang Nanya, was a disciple of Lai'an Dingru (1092–1153) in Fuzhou (in Fujian); he taught the Linji *gong'an* method as abbot at a series of temples in Wenzhou (Yongjia, Zhejiang) but is most associated with Longxiang Temple, which is on an island in the river there. It was sixth of the Ten Temples of the Southern Song period, which were second in importance only to the Five Mountains.

> Nanya ascended the dais in the hall and said, "The Great Mechanism must be worked directly;/The Great Function must be started suddenly./Even secrets as wordless as striking arrows,/Must be killed with one blow of the hammer. Why doesn't my royal arsenal have such a hammer?"

"Striking arrow secrets," or more literally, "biting arrow secrets" (*niezu zhi ji*), are Chan ideas or principles that are beyond words.

Nanya said of this poem, "True clarity is reflected herein. If you can attain it, then it will be like meeting universal certainties spread out below your bright window. You who are within the Longxiang Temple gate should then kill them with one blow of the hammer."[294]

128. Ci'an Shoujing, *Untitled*[295]

*Ci'an Shoujing (fl. mid-twelfth century) was a disciple of Linji master Dahui Zonggao (1089–1153) and taught the *gong'an* method. A native of Fuzhou (in Fujian), he was abbot of temples both there and in Quanzhou (also in Fujian). Shoujing's style was earthy and direct, and even a little contrary, as when he proclaimed, "To discuss mysteries and speak of wondrousness—just piss! Just piss! To use blows and shouts—just salt to assuage a thirst!" Another example:

> Shoujing ascended the dais in the hall and said, "The Way is the Unchanging Way; the Mind is the Unchanging Mind. When all of you hear me talk like this, you say, 'I understand.' At most it takes you thirty days, at least twenty-nine. Yet above your heads is heaven, and below your feet is earth; your ears hear sound, and your noses breathe air. If suddenly the waters of the four seas were above your heads, and poisonous snakes pierced through your eyes, and toads entered through your nostrils, what would you do then?"[296]

Iron trees will blossom—a *gong'an* in *Blue Cliff* 40. Iron trees are equivalent to dead trees; see above.

129. Chichan Yuanmiao, *Untitled*[297]

*Chichan Yuanmiao (1111–1164) was from Wuzhou (Jinhua, Zhejiang); his secular surname was Wang. While still a schoolboy he realized a religious vocation and left to search out famous Buddhist masters. He studied Chan in Hangzhou (Hangzhou, Zhejiang) and resided in nearby temples. For a long period he was in Shishi Zuxiu's community and was Zuxiu's disciple in Linji Chan. Zuxiu once praised him, "I'm not impressed by your Chan,/And I'm not impressed by your Dao./But I *am* impressed by a pair of hands and a pair of eyes—/Just right for building a home of your own." However, Yuanmiao was by nature careless and unrestrained, so he needed a long period of immersion in the tradition of the past Chan masters. Eventually his Chan matured and he engaged in debates with Dahui Zonggao (1089–1163). After Zonggao's death, he oversaw the funeral rites.[298]

130. Chichan Yuanmiao, *A Priest's Staff*[299]

Staff—the monk's walking staff was such a common piece of equipment that it took on multiple meanings. It was support (of the Dharma); the journey (to enlightenment); and synecdochically, the individual monk himself. The master's staff was his symbol of authority, and, related to its use to beat sense into dull disciples, a trigger to enlightenment. It might even serve as an all-encompassing symbol for the "Chan of the patriarchs," much like Buddha's flower or the axiom of "Bodhidharma coming from the West." Wumen Huikai (1183–1260) wrote in *Gateless Pass* 44,

> Comment: It helps me wade across a river when the bridge is down. It accompanies me to the village on a moonless night. If you call it a staff, you will enter hell like an arrow. Verse: The depths and shallows of the world,/Are all in its grasp./It supports the heavens and sustains the earth;/Everywhere, it enhances the doctrine.[300]

As Fenyang Shanzhao (947–1024) said, "Understand the staff, and the monk's traveling days are over."[301]

sinners, saints (fansheng)—"saints" are beings at advanced levels of religious cultivation, like buddhas, bodhisattvas, and arhats; "sinners" are the rest of us ordinary human beings. As one approaches the highest truth, the distinction disappears; in other words, even buddhas and bodhisattvas are, in the end, expedient means. Thus the phrase "sinners and saints are the same" (*fansheng yiru*).

kill them all—concepts such as "buddhas" and "demons" in the end can be hindrances to enlightenment, if they become attachments. Compare the famous *gong'an* by Linji Yixuan:

> If you meet a buddha, kill the buddha; if you meet a patriarch, kill the patriarch. If you meet an arhat, kill the arhat. If you meet your parents, kill your parents. If you meet your kinfolk, kill your kinfolk. Then for the first time you will gain emancipation, will not be entangled with things, will pass freely anywhere you wish to go.[302]

The story of Danxia Tianran (739–824) burning statues of Buddha for warmth holds a similar message.[303]

diamond eye of wisdom—the wisdom eye.

131. Gong'an Zuzhu, *Untitled*[304]

*Gong'an Zuzhu (fl. 1163–1190), *hao* Dun'an, was from Nanping in China's southwest (Baxian, Sichuan). This poem is found in *Wonderful Events in Temple Forests,* which describes him as a prickly personality who kept people at a distance, and notes that his teachings were popular in the Xiang region (Hunan). He was a disciple of Wan'an Daoyan (1094–1164) in Linji Chan, and a second-generation disciple of Dahui Zonggao (1089–1163). The source also says that he used this poem to describe himself.[305] For an explication, see the introduction.

132. Meng'an Ge, *Reaching the Shore*[306]
*Meng'an Ge (fl. twelfth century) was from Wuhu (Wuhu, Anhui); his secular surname was Ding. He was in the lineage of Linji master Tianli Zhen. He can be approximately dated by reference to Huihong (1071–1128), a master in the Huanglong line of Linji Chan and a renowned poet and critic, mentioned in the title of the series from which this poem is taken. The set uses fishing to describe various perspectives on Chan attainment.[307]

133. Zhiweng, *Instructions for My Disciples*[308]
*Zhiweng (ca. 1150–1230) is likely identical with a Chan painter of that name who was probably a monk and disciple of Yanqi Guangwen (1189–1263) in the Dahui line of Yangqi Linji Chan; paintings attributed to him include one of the Sixth Patriarch cutting wood and another of a layman's moment of enlightenment at the feet of a master.[309] Lineage charts show a Zhihong Jian as a disciple of Guangwen; Zhiweng (Old Man Zhi) may be a shortened version of this name. Zhihong Jian was a temple abbot at least twice, once at Zhenru Temple in Qingyuan (Ningbo, Zhejiang) and once at Mount Tiantong (near Ningbo). His entry in *Supplemental Record of Pointing at the Moon* 4 supports this identification: in the contents he is called Zhiweng Jian, while in the text he is Zhihong Jian.[310] Another poem attributed to Zhiweng is found in *Recorded Occasions in Sung Poetry*.[311]

134. Jidian Daoji, *Untitled*[312]
*Jidian Daoji (1150–1209) was from Linhai (Linhai, Zhejiang); his secular surname was Li. He was a popular figure known by various names, including Huyin (Hermit of the Lake), Fangyuansou (Old Man of the Square Earth and Round Heaven), Jidian (Lunatic Ji), and Jigong Huofo (Old Ji the Living Buddha). It was said that his mother dreamed she had swallowed a sunbeam, and so became pregnant with him. He became a monk at age eighteen at Lingyin Temple, near the shores of West Lake at the Southern Song capital of Lin'an (Hangzhou, Zhejiang). However, he was not one for keeping the precepts, preferring wine, meat, and wild behavior, so the monks there cursed him, spit at him, and drove him out. He spent his days wandering around the town, and recited sūtras in exchange for food and wine. "He enjoyed turning somersaults while not wearing

any underwear, revealing his body for all to see. People laughed at him, but he remained quite pleased with himself." He eventually became a disciple of Xiatang Huiyuan (1103–1176) at Huqiu (Tiger Hill) in Suzhou (Suzhou, Jiangsu), in the Yangqi line of Linji Chan. Much of his life was spent at Jingci Temple on West Lake. Local people in the capital believed him to be an arhat or a bodhisattva. His life became intertwined with legend—fantastic stories abound. Once, it was said, Jingci Temple burned down and wood was needed for its rebuilding. Daoji magically transported himself to the Yanling mountains (in Tonglu, Zhejiang). He covered the mountains with his cassock, uprooted all the trees, and floated with them all the way back to Hangzhou. Daoji also became a familiar figure in popular literature. A play called *The Drunken* Bodhi (*Zuiputi*) by Zhang Dafu (fl. seventeenth century) presents Daoji as a wild eccentric who yet aids the poor and downtrodden. A full-length novel called *The Biography of Old Ji* (*Jigong zhuan*) appeared at the end of the Qing dynasty. In recent times tales about him have been made into popular television series. He died, sitting in meditation, at age sixty.[313]

Maitreya—the bodhisattva who is destined to be Buddha of the Future. In China he is most familiarly depicted as a bare-bellied, laughing fat man; the iconography derives from that of Budai Heshang (The Monk with the Linen Bag), a ninth-century Chinese figure who was considered one of Maitreya's incarnations.[314]

Vairocana (Pilu)—the Buddha of Universal Light, the cosmic manifestation of Buddha. "To stand atop Vairocana's head" represents the highest level of attainment—to become a buddha.

Ten Sages (shisheng)—advanced levels for the perfection of bodhisattvas, equivalent to the Ten Stages (*shidi*). Sources differ as to the total number of levels; some count as many as fifty-two to fifty-five. The use here posits forty levels, with the "Ten Sages" corresponding to levels thirty-one to forty. After the fortieth is reached, there are an additional one or two levels of buddha enlightenment, making forty-one or forty-two levels in all.

Three Worthies (sanxian)—basic levels for the perfection of bodhisattvas. Each of the three is in fact a group of ten, thus the "Three Worthies" include the first thirty levels.

135. Jidian Daoji, *Untitled*[315]

136. Jidian Daoji, *Untitled*[316]

137. Jidian Daoji, *Death* Gāthā[317]

138. Zheweng Ruyan, *Sending off a Friend*[318]

*Zheweng Ruyan (1151–1225) was from Taizhou (Ninghai, Zhejiang); his secular surname was either Zhou or Guo. He became a monk at age eighteen in a Pure Land monastery near his home. He later became a disciple of Fozhao Deguang (1121–1203) in the Yangqi line of Linji Chan. Deguang often said that Ruyan was the only student who truly grasped his teaching. Ruyan taught the *gong'an* method as abbot at half a dozen temples in south China. In 1218 he was invited to be abbot at Mount Jing (in Yuhang, Zhejiang) and given the imperial title Chan Master of the Buddha Mind (Foxin Chanshi). His popular *hao* Zheweng (Old Man of Zhe-[jiang]) derived from a belief among many monastics that he was the holiest man in the region. During his pilgrimage to China, the great Japanese Zen master Dōgen (1200–1253) studied for a time with Ruyan at Mount Jing.[319]

139. Laike, *Untitled*[320]

*Laike (Scabby Potential) (fl. twelfth century), or sometimes Bingke (Sick Potential), was a substitution for this monk's actual religious name, Zuke (Patriarch Potential), in reference to a skin disease from which he suffered. His secular name was Su Xu and his *zi* was Zhengping. He was from the scholarly Su family of Danyang; his father was Su Jian and his brother Su Yang. Laike's primary residence was Mount Lu (near Jiujiang, Jiangxi). His literary reputation earned him a place in Lü Benzhong's (fl. 1119) list of representative poets of the Jiangxi School. The poetry compendium *Jade Splinters of the Poets* (dated 1244) describes him as follows: "Contemporary monk-poets include Zuke, who contracted a serious illness; people call him Laike." The same source notes that the great Neo-Confucian philosopher Zhu Xi (1130–1200) wrote out this poem in his own hand and had it carved on stone at his home. Laike is mentioned in "Passing Wusha and Gazing on Datang Stone Peak" by Yang Wanli (1127–1206), which helps to roughly date him: "The mountain is like Master Ke, with scabs on top." Laike also appears to have been friends with Qin Zhan, a son of the poet Qin Guan (1049–1100).[321]

when lutes have no strings—it was written that the poet Tao Qian (365–427) didn't understand music, so he made a stringless lute. Whenever he was drunk, he would play the lute to express his feelings. The image often appears in Chan contexts to suggest profound teachings. Chinul compared the image to the "true mind"; see the introduction.

Zhong Ziqi—the *Spring and Autumn Annals* (third century B.C.E.) and other sources relate the story of the lute player Bo Ya's friendship with Zhong Ziqi. When Bo Ya played of Mount Tai, Zhong Ziqi could hear the mountains in the music; when Bo played of flowing rivers, Zhong could hear the water. Zhong Ziqi died, and Bo Ya broke his lute and never played again, for no one else would ever understand his music as well. "One who understands the music" (*zhiyin*) remains a term for an intimate friend. Dahui Zonggao wrote, "Leisurely strum a stringless tune/Clear wind and bright moon will understand the music."[322]

140. Chijue Daochong, *River Lantern*[323]

*Chijue Daochong (1169–1250) was from Wujin (Wujin, Jiangsu); his secular surname was Xun, and he chose the *hao* Chijue (Complete Fool). After he had failed the civil service examinations, Daochong became a monk, first at Miaoyin Monastery in Zizhou (Santai, Sichuan) and later in Chengdu (Chengdu, Sichuan), where he studied the sūtra literature at Dashengci Temple. He then moved back to southeast China and tried to gain admittance to Chan master Songyuan Chongyue's (1132–1202) community, but due to a famine in the region, new monks were not being accepted. Daochong was at last accepted as caretaker of the incense by Linji master Caoyuan Daosheng (fl. twelfth century), whose disciple he eventually became. Yet in the time he spent there, Daosheng only pummeled and clubbed him without mercy. Frustrated, Daochong felt he was making no progress and regretted that he had not been able to meet Songyuan Chongyue. Declaring that whenever he itched, he would scratch, he left Daosheng for Lingyin Temple in Lin'an (Hangzhou, Zhejiang), where Chongyue dwelled. He arrived during the hot and sultry days of the eighth month, when monks were normally confined to their temples. Daochong's stammered entreaties at the gate were answered only with abuse, and he was not allowed entry. One day Daochong's presence was reported to Chongyue, who said, "I have already opened the door—it's just that he has missed it." When the master's words were related to him, Daochong was as if struck deaf and dumb. He later became abbot of several major temples in south China, including Lingyin Temple itself. In his last years he wanted only to retire to the mountains, but his fame was such that imperial commands for him to lecture and teach were unceasing. His final post was at Fahua Temple on Mount Jing (in Yuhang, Zhejiang). When it became clear that he was dying, a monk begged for a parting *gāthā*. Daochong laughed, and said, "The word after death cannot be discussed. Every one of you should just set about your task." He is described as a simple, placid, and compassionate man, so reticent that it seemed he could not speak at all. Yet when he took his seat to examine the monks, his words "hit them like spears, or like rolling thunder and flashing lightning."[324]

white autumn—white was the color cosmologically associated with autumn in Five Elements theory.

141. Wumen Huikai, *The Lazy Water Buffalo*[325]

*Wumen Huikai (1183–1260) was from Qiantang, near the Song capital at Lin'an (Hangzhou, Zhejiang); his secular surname was Liang. After meetings with various masters, he moved to Wanshou Temple in Pingjiang (in Jiangsu) and became Yuelin Shiguan's (1143–1217) disciple in Linji Chan. When Huikai first met Shiguan, the old master set him to ponder this famous *gong'an*: "A monk asked Zhaozhou, 'Has a dog the buddha nature?' Zhaozhou answered, 'No.'" After six years Huikai still had not found understanding, and he cursed and reviled himself for his failure. He swore, "If I sleep again [before I succeed], then may my body rot away!" Every time he felt sleepy he would walk the corridors or knock his head against a temple pillar. One day, while standing next to the altar in the hall, he heard the drum calling the monks to their meal and was suddenly enlightened. He later was abbot at half a dozen major temples. Chan anthologies feature his wonder-working abilities. During the Chunyou period (1241–1253), he retired to a hill near West Lake in his home region. One day, a stone at the bottom of the hill suddenly rolled upward and a spring of sweet water burst forth. People said that since Huikai had previously been at Mount Huanglong (Yellow Dragon Mountain), a dragon must have followed him from there. A great drought afflicted south China at the time, and the court invited him to preach the Dharma and pray for rain. After Huikai took his seat, but even before he had said a word, a heavy rain indeed fell. Emperor Li of Song (r. 1225–1265) then bestowed upon Huikai a golden robe and the title Chan Master of the Buddha Eye (Foyan Chanshi). Huikai is best known as the compiler of the the *Gateless Pass* collection of 48 *gong'an*, which he prepared for the emperor's birthday in 1229. The title alludes to Xuansha Shibei's (835–908) line, "No-gate is the gate of emancipation; no-mind is the mind of the man of Dao."[326] One of his students was the pilgrim monk Shinchi Kakushin (1207–1298), who introduced *Gateless Pass* to Japan. Huikai was very short of stature, and *Supplemental Biographies of Eminent Monks* states he made a secret prayer that if he were reborn in the future, he wished to be taller. On the night he died, a pregnant woman in Qiantang, surnamed Sun, dreamed that Huikai approached her, carrying a lantern. The next day she gave birth to a boy, who grew up to be the Linji master Zhongfeng Mingben (1263–1323).[327] Huikai seemed to get his wish, for in his biographies Mingben is described as much taller than average, and with bigger feet.

142 Wumen Huikai, *Wontons*[328]

turned to mush—a similar image in Buddhist texts is salt water: the salt no longer has form or characteristics, but its essence is pervasive. See, for example, the "Inscription on the Mind King" attributed to Fu Dashi (497–569).[329]

143. Xutang Zhiyu, *Casting the Seal*[330]

    *Xutang Zhiyu (1185–1269) was from Siming (Ningbo, Zhejiang); his secular surname was Chen and his *hao* included Xutang (Empty Hall) and Xigengsou (Old Man Who's Ceased Plowing). He became a monk at age sixteen, and eventually traveled to Mount Jing (near Hangzhou) and became a disciple of Yun'an Puyan (1156–1226) in Linji Chan. Possessed of an imposing personality, beginning in 1229 he taught as abbot in more than ten temples, most of them important government-sponsored establishments, and gained the favor of two emperors. His teaching career was interrupted only once: in 1258, when he was abbot at Mount Ayuwang in Mingzhou (near Ningbo, Zhejiang), he came into conflict with the government and was forced to retire. This interregnum was short, and he ended his days again as an influential abbot, at Mount Jing where he had spent so many years. One of his students was the pilgrim monk Nampo Jōmyō (1235–1309), better known by his title Daiō Kokushi, who founded a Rinzai (Linji) teaching line upon his return to Japan. Through this relationship, Zhiyu has been revered there, and his collected works have been widely read. Zhiyu was an able painter, and a number of his self-portraits can be found today in the two monasteries of Myōshin-ji and Daitoku-ji in Kyoto.[331]

    Casting the Seal—this poem and the next are to be read as a pair. Zhiyu compares the seal of office presented to a general setting out on a campaign with the mind seal of Chan practice.

144. Xutang Zhiyu, *Melting the Seal*[332]

    cloud shadows (yunying)—shadows of objects are already insubstantial; how much more so the shadows of objects that are themselves insubstantial? Thus the image was useful for discussing emptiness. *Transmission* records the meditation experience of the important early Tiantai monk Nanyue Huisi (514–577). When his way forward was blocked, anxiety set in. He thought, "Affliction comes from karma. Karma is born from the arousal of the mind. When the mind source does not arise, then what does the outside world look like? The karma of affliction and the body are both like cloud shadows." With this realization his former anxiety disappeared.[333]

145. Xutang Zhiyu, *Hearing the Snow*[334]

    hearing with the mind (xinwen)—the Bodhisattva Samantabhadra says to the Buddha in the ten-fascicle *Śūraṃgama sūtra*, "World-honored One, I employ hearing with the mind, and thereby discern all wisdom-based views of living beings."[335]

146. Xutang Zhiyu, *Asking for a Cat*[336]

Cat—whenever this animal is mentioned in the Chan context, the following *gong'an* featuring Nanquan Puyuan (748–835) comes to mind:

> Once the monks in the east and west wings of the monastery were quarreling over the possession of a cat. The master appeared on the scene, picked up the cat, and said, "If any one of you can say something to the point, he will save this cat's life; if nobody can, I'll chop it in two." No one said anything, so the master chopped it in two. Later, Zhaozhou [Congshen (778–897)] returned. The master told him about the incident, and what had been said. At once Zhaozhou took off a grass sandal, put it on top of his head, and went out. The master said, "Had you been here, you would have saved the cat's life!"[337]

Nanquan's action runs counter to the basic Buddhist rule against taking life, yet he has an even more urgent problem: the poor cat has become the cause of disputation among the monks, a sign that their thinking remains egocentric. This is the line taken by Linji master Hengchuan Xinggong (1222–1289) in his poetic commentary on the story: "One chop of the sword makes two pieces,/ And releases two monks from disputation./If not for the grass sandal worn on the head,/The cat would have had no rebirth!"[338] In the present poem, Zhiyu is apparently giving what would have been his answer to Nanquan: "I want the cat so that I can watch it be a cat."

a golden promise—an allusion to "one promise worth a thousand golds" (*yinuo qianjin*), a saying derived from the biography of Ji Bu in Sima Qian's (c. 145–c. 85 B.C.E.) *Records of History*. Ji Bu's word was considered more valuable than a thousand pieces of gold.

147. Wuwen Daocan, *Home of the Great Teacher*[339]

*Wuwen Daocan (1213–1271) was from Yuzhang (some sources say Qinhe) in present-day Jiangxi Province; his secular surname was Tao and his *hao* was Liutang. He became a monk after failing the imperial civil service examinations. A disciple of Linji master Xiaoweng Miaokan (1177–1248), he was invited to teach at Jianfu Chan Temple in Raozhou (in Jiangxi) in 1254 and was abbot at Huazang Chan Temple on Mount Lu (near Jiujiang, Jiangxi). He was an accomplished poet.[340]

Great Teacher (chaoshi)—a master who surpasses (*chao*) his own teacher. *Blue Cliff* 11 quotes Baizhang Huaihai's (720–814) words to Huangbo Xiyun (d. 849): "If your view equals your teacher, you have less than half your teacher's virtue;

only when your wisdom goes beyond your teacher are you worthy to pass on the transmission."[341]

148. Wuwen Daocan, *Untitled*[342]

149. Hengchuan Xinggong, *Untitled*[343]
*Hengchuan Xinggong (1222–1289), also known as Rugong, *zi* Zipu, was from Yongjia (Wenzhou, Zhejiang); his secular surname was Lin. His father died when he was still a child. By nature pure and innocent, and unsuited to the vulgar world, he soon stopped eating meat. He became a monk at age fifteen. At Lingyin Temple in the capital of Lin'an (Hangzhou, Zhejiang), he was guided by Linji master Shitian Faxun (1171–1245) and later by Chijue Daochong (1169–1250). But his doubt remained, and he made no progress. He then moved to Mount Tiantong (near Ningbo, Zhejiang), where he was enlightened with the guidance of Mieweng Wenli (1167–1250), whose disciple he became. Later he held the highest place in the order of monks at Jingci Temple in Lin'an, under abbot Duanqiao Miaolun (1201–1261). Miaolun thought he would make a worthy abbot and recommended him to the prime minister. Xinggong was consequently invited to lead Lingyan Temple on Mount Yandang in Rui'an (Rui'an, Zhejiang). He quickly came to be considered a reflection of the ancient masters, due to his use of a brilliant yet down-to-earth rhetoric. Mild-mannered and sincere, he guided his community with benevolence and never employed forceful methods. Even when students openly defied him in debate, Xinggong would not punish them; instead, he encouraged them to reflect until their obstinacy disappeared. Thus while many disregarded him at first meeting, they later came to appreciate his greatness. He retired to a shepherd's hut on the mountain, where he remained for several years. After the Song dynasty fell and the Yuan was founded, he unwillingly accepted an imperial command to teach at Mount Ayuwang in Mingzhou (near Ningbo, Zhejiang), where he attracted a large following.[344]

Stone rams — probably sculptures before a tomb.

This poem is the last from a set of twenty untitled poems. Xinggong described the inspiration behind them in his Chan records: "The poems that Hanshan wrote had no titles, and described the original truth of heaven. I live alone in a mountain hut. The foundation of what my eyes see and ears hear all flows out from the pure [buddha] nature; [I am] unconscious of form and language. Twenty poems."

150. Hengchuan Xinggong, *Death* Gāthā[345]
Zhaozhou's wall — in the "Records of Zhaozhou," a monk asks, "What is the meaning of Bodhidharma coming from the west?" Zhaozhou Congshen (778–897)

answered, "A bottle gourd has been hanging on the eastern wall for a long time." Originally associated with Daoist immortality elixirs, the bottle gourd image in Chan/Zen often represents the freedom of enlightenment, expecially when depicted in water. Xuetang Daoxing (1089–1151) describes the Function Realm (Ch. *jijing*) as "naturally empty but alive," "like a bottle gourd on the water, bobbing about without restraint or hindrance: push it and it moves off, press it and it spins away—it is truly free."³⁴⁶

Buddhas of the Three Ages (sanshi fo)—entering a Chinese Buddhist temple, one typically sees a set of three images in the main hall: Dīpaṃkara, the Buddha of the Past; Śākyamuni, the Buddha of the Present; and Maitreya, the Buddha of the Future.

151. Yuejian Wenming, *To My Barber*³⁴⁷
*Yuejian Wenming (1231–?) was a disciple of Linji master Xiyan Liaohui (1198–1262). He was abbot of several temples in Jiangxi, including Jianfu Chan Temple in Raozhou, and left a short Chan record. Although in a minor and short-lived line, he did have one recorded disciple, Dongshan Chong. He remained active until ca. 1300.³⁴⁸

152. Yuejian Wenming, *Meditation Deportment at Mount Tiantong*³⁴⁹

153. Yuejian Wenming, *Picking Tea*³⁵⁰
thick wood (conglin)—besides its literal meaning, the term is also a euphemism for a group of monks, or a Buddhist temple.

This poem is perhaps inspired by the following famous *gong'an:*

Guishan [Lingyou (771–853)] and Yangshan [Huiji (814–890)] were picking tea. The Master [Guishan] said, "All day we've been picking tea, but I've only heard your voice, and not seen your form." Yangshan shook the tea bush. The Master remarked, "You've only achieved the function, but have not achieved the substance." Yangshan asked, "Can you explain?" The Master was silent for a long time. Yangshan then said, "You've only achieved the substance, but have not achieved the function." The Master replied, "I absolve you from thirty blows!" Yangshan countered, "If you beat me I will submit to it, but who then can I beat?'" Guishan said, "I absolve you from thirty-three blows!"³⁵¹

154. Yuetang Zuyin, *Skull Beneath a Pine*³⁵²
*Yuetang Zuyin (1234–1308) was from Nankang (Xingzi, Jiangxi); his secular surname was Zhou. He was orphaned at thirteen, so became a monk. After an initial

awakening while reading the *Flower Garland Sūtra,* he continued his studies with Bieshan Zuzhi (1200–1260) at Mount Tiantong and Duanqiao Miaolun (1201–1261) at Jingci Temple in Hangzhou, before attaining enlightenment under Miaolun's successor there, Jieshi Zhipeng. Eventually he gained the notice of the Yuan court and was presented with a seal and a golden cassock, as well as an honorific title, Chan Master of Penetrating Wisdom (Tonghui Chanshi). In 1306 he became abbot of Lingyin Temple in Hangzhou. He once said to a monk, "The innumerable buddhas are all on your tongue; the sacred teachings of the Tripiṭaka are all beneath your feet. Why don't you take a look at the ground?" Just as the monk was about to do so, the master shouted at him.[353]

Skull in the grass,/body in a dream—an allusion to a story in the *Zhuangzi.* While on a journey, Zhuangzi found an old skull and sympathetically asked how it lost its life. He then lay down to sleep, using the skull as a pillow. In the night the skull came to him in a dream and chastised him for assuming that life is preferable to death: "Among the dead there are no rulers above, no subjects below, and no chores of the four seasons. With nothing to do, our springs and autumns are as endless as heaven and earth. A king facing south on his throne could have no more happiness than this!"[354]

The skull appears frequently in Chan discourse, and is similar to the dead tree image. The most well-known use is in the commentary to the second case of the *Blue Cliff Record,* which reads in part:

Haven't you read how a monk asked Xiangyan [Zhixian (d. 898)], "What is the Path?" Xiangyan said, "In a dead tree, dragon murmurings." The monk asked, "What is a man of the Path?" Xiangyan said, "Eyeballs in a skull." Later the monk asked Shishuang [Qingzhu (807–888)], "What are 'dragon murmurings in a dead tree'?" Shishuang said, "Still having joy." The monk asked, "What are 'eyeballs in a skull'?" Shishuang said, "Still having consciousness."[355]

Cold Food Days—in traditional practice, no fires were lit for three consecutive days coinciding with the observance of the Qingming (Pure Brightness) Festival, so food was eaten cold. Qingming, set at 105 days after the winter solstice, is the time when people visit the tombs of their ancestors.

Beimang—a mountain north of the ancient city of Luoyang, and a favored site for tombs.

155. Yunwai Yunxiu, *Reading a Record of My Teacher's Words*[356]
  *Yunwai Yunxiu (1242–1324) was from Changguo (Dinghai, Zhejiang); his secular surname was Li. He was a disciple of Cao-Dong master Zhiweng Deju (late

thirteenth century). Yunxiu was abbot at several temples and wrote a commentary to the Cao-Dong text *Samādhi as Reflection from the Precious Mirror*. He was described as small of stature, but strong of personality and an energetic and ingenious teacher. "The master was never haughty or rude, was not greedy for things or selfish about food, and whenever he received donations, he would immediately pass them on to other people. Thus his students' respect for him grew even more. At the two daily meals of rice gruel, he always joined the community in the refectory." Numerous Korean and Japanese pilgrims were guided by Yunxiu. Several of his Chinese disciples gained a measure of renown; one of them, Dongling Yongyu (d. 1365), became a temple abbot in Japan.[357]

thousand-day wine—wine so strong it makes one drunk for a thousand days.

156. Songyan Yongxiu, *Writing out the* Diamond Sūtra *in Blood*[358]

*Songyan Yongxiu (fl. late thirteenth century) was a disciple of Bieshan Zuzhi (1200–1260) at Mount Tiantong. He contributed 11 poems to the influential *Wind and Moon on Rivers and Lakes Collection* (*Jianghu fengyue ji*), which presents 270 poems by 79 monks of the late thirteenth century to the early fourteenth century.[359]

Jetavana Garden—a park near Śrāvastī that was frequently visited by Śākyamuni. His sermon in the *Diamond Sūtra* is set there. The site became the most influential of the early Buddhist monasteries in India.

Yuan Dynasty (1279–1368) and Ming Dynasty (1368–1644)

157. Gulin Qingmao, *Sending off Attendant Jin to Visit His Teacher*[360]

*Gulin Qingmao (1262–1329) was from Leqing (in Zhejiang); his secular surname was Lin. Besides reaching eminence as a Chan master, he was well known as a calligrapher. It was recorded that the night before his birth, his mother dreamed a bodhisattva gave her a lotus flower and said, "Celebrate the birth of your son, who will be the eyes of the world." Qingmao became a monk at age thirteen, at Guoqing Temple on Mount Tiantai. He became a disciple of Linji master Hengchuan Xinggong (1222–1289). In 1298 he accepted a post as abbot of Baiyun Chan Temple on Mount Tianping (near Suzhou, Jiangsu) and resided there for nine years before moving to the nearby Kaiyuan Temple. In 1312 he was given the imperial title Chan Master of Universal Awakening to Buddha Nature and Support of the Faith (Fuzong Pujue Foxing Chanshi). He subsequently was abbot at several other temples in the southeast. In his later years he was influential and respected at court and among the literati, and had several thousand followers. He died at Baoning Temple in Jinling (Nanjing, Jiangsu).[361]

A smack beneath the ribs — a *gong'an* about the enlightenment of Linji Yixuan (d. 866?). Linji had been a member of the Huangbo Xiyun (d. 849) community. When Linji asked, "What is the real meaning of Bodhidharma coming from the west?" Huangbo struck him. Linji initially did not understand, but was later enlightened when Master Gao'an Dayu on Mount Lu commented that the blow was an act of motherly kindness.[362]

Three answers to the call — a *gong'an* featuring National Teacher Nanyang Huizhong (d. 775) and his attendant Danyuan Yingzhen (fl. eighth century):

The National Teacher called his attendant three times, and three times the attendant responded. The National Teacher said, "I long feared that I was betraying you, but really it was you who were betraying me."[363]

Interpretations vary, but it appears that the transgression was against the teacher-student relationship. Huanglong Huinan (1002–1069) held it was a test that Yingzhen successfully passed, as evidenced by his commentary poem:

The National Teacher thrice called his attendant;
He beat the grass just to startle the snake.
Who knew that below the green pine in the valley
Lay the herb of immortality?[364]

The essentials and the mysteries — 1) The essentials are *yaomiao* or *yaoji*: the essential principles of *dharmas*. It says in the *[Larger] Boundless Life Sūtra*, "Deeply enter all *dharmas*, clearly examine the essentials."[365] The mysteries are *xuanzhi*: fundamental meanings beyond the power of language. It says in the *Records of Linji*, "Followers of the Way, grasp it and put it in action; no names or words are appended to it. This is called 'mysterious principle.'"[366] 2) The terms may refer to a baffling passage concerning the "three mystic entrances and three essentials" (*sanxuan sanyao*) in the *Records of Linji*: "Each word we say should possess the three mystic entrances, and each mystic entrance must possess the three essentials, manifested in temporary appearance and action. What do you understand by this?"[367]

smile — an allusion to a well-known (but apocryphal) story about Buddha. The version in *Gateless Pass* 6 reads:

When Shakyamuni Buddha was at Mount Grdhrakuta, he held out a flower to his listeners. Everyone was silent. Only Mahakashyapa broke into a broad smile. The Buddha said, "I have the True Dharma Eye, the Marvelous Mind of Nirvana, the True Form of the Formless, and the Subtle Dharma Gate, independent of words and transmitted beyond doctrine. This I have entrusted to Mahakashyapa."[368]

The story appears in no sūtra. The apparent first use was in the eleventh century.[369]

158. Zhongfeng Mingben, *Sweeping the Floor*[370]

*Zhongfeng Mingben (1263–1323), *hao* Zhongfeng (Middle Peak) and Huanzhu Daoren (Man of Dao of the Illusory Domicile), was from Qiantang (in Zhejiang); his secular surname was Sun. His mother died when Mingben was nine, and he became a monk at age fifteen. He went to Linji master Gaofeng Yuanmiao (1238–1295) for instruction. Yuanmiao was aloof, stern, and coldly severe, not to mention neglectful of his appearance: when his hair grew long he did not cut it, and when his robe was in tatters he did not change it. Yet he could see Mingben's vast potential, and after he closed his door to other students, he continued to instruct the young monk. Mingben became Yuanmiao's disciple. Avoiding invitations to become a temple Chan master, Mingben traveled widely, keeping no fixed address. Every place he laid his head he would call his Illusory Domicile. He gained a reputation for holiness and became known as the Old Buddha of Jiangnan. In later years he settled at Mount Tianmu (near Hangzhou, Zhejiang) and attracted a large number of followers. An able poet, he exchanged verses with the famous painter Zhao Mengfu (1254–1322) and other literati. Zhao honored Mingben as his teacher, and painted his portrait. Mingben gained the patronage of two emperors and was given a golden cassock and the title Chan Master of Buddha Compassion, Complete Illumination, and Pervading Wisdom (Foci Yuanzhao Guanghui Chanshi). Soon before he died, he told his disciples, "The Illusory Domicile leaks at the top and has holes in the sides; the fence is collapsing and the walls are falling. I can't live there much longer." His memorial stūpa was built at Shengyong Temple on Mount Tianmu; for hundreds of years, monks there also carefully saved a pair of his large sandals. A portrait of Mingben, showing him as an eccentric, long-haired, and corpulent figure, was carried to Japan by his disciple Enkei Soyū (1285–1344), where it remains in Kōgenji temple in the province of Hyōgo.[371]

Dharma flowers,/five-petaled—the following verse is attributed to Bodhidharma:

Originally I came to this land
To transmit Dharma and save beings from delusion.
A flower blooms with five petals
Of itself the fruit will ripen.[372]

There have been two different interpretations. First, Bodhidharma is the flower and the rest of the patriarchs are the petals; together they represent the Chan teachings. Second, the flower is Chan as a whole and the petals are the Chan branches: Linji, Gui-Yang, Yunmen, Fayan, and Cao-Dong.

broom — The image here likely derives from the following exchange between Zhaozhou Congshen (778–897) and Daci Huanzhong (780–862) on the meaning of *prajñā*:

> Zhaozhou asked Daci, "What is the substance of *prajñā*?" Daci repeated, "What is the substance of *prajñā*?" Zhaozhou laughed heartily and left. Next morning, when Daci saw Zhaozhou sweeping the yard, he asked, "What is the substance of *prajñā*?" As soon as Zhaozhou heard this, he threw down his broom and went away, clapping his hands and laughing.[373]

159. Zhongfeng Mingben, *Embracing the Pure Land*[374]
mind pearl — the buddha nature innate in human nature and the world is the jewel (Skt. *maṇi*), normally a bright pearl. Xuansha Shibei (835–908) said, "The entire universe is one bright pearl. What is there to interpret or to understand?"[375]

160. Wujian Xiandu, *Instructions for Chan Meditation*[376]
*Wujian Xiandu (1265–1334) was from a literati family in Xianju (in Zhejiang); his secular surname was Ye. By nature intelligent and refined, already as a child he gave up eating meat, and obtained his parents' permission to become a monk. He eventually became a discile to Linji master Fangshan Wenbao (d. 1135) at Ruiyan Temple in Taizhou near his home. Yet during the time he remained with Wenbao he could not attain a breakthrough. So he abandoned temple life altogether and built a solitary hut high on Hua Peak on Mount Tiantai, in the same place that Gao'an Shanwu (1074–1132) had lived many years earlier. In this harsh and remote environment, he followed an arduous regimen of self-cultivation. One day, after performing his daily labor, he achieved illumination, and "all of the obstructions of his life disappeared like the melting of ice." He remained there alone for the next forty years. He gained a reputation for holiness, and was given the title Chan Master of True Awakening (Zhenjue Chanshi) by imperial order. He was even popularly thought to be a reincarnation of Gao'an Shanwu. He willingly in-

structed those students dedicated enough to climb the mountain and search him out. "In manner the master was as lofty as the distant stars, looking down on the dust of the mundane world."[377]

161. Wujian Xiandu, *Following the Rhymes of Chan Master Yongming*[378]
Chan Master Yongming—Fayan master Yongming Yanshou (904–975) was compiler of the *Records of the Source Mirror*. He sought a syncretism of Chan with other forms of Buddhism, like Pure Land and Tiantai. He also wrote sixty-nine "Poems on Living in the Mountains." Several Chan figures, including Wujian Xiandu, modeled their own poems on Yanshou's; a combined anthology was published in 1700.[379]

162. Wujian Xiandu, *Following the Rhymes of Chan Master Yongming*[380]
forget the road back—expedient means can be forgotten once the goal is reached.
    Knowledge Sea (xuehai)—the great body of acquired knowledge, where the hundred streams of knowledge collect.

163. Wujian Xiandu, *Following the Rhymes of Chan Master Yongming*[381]

164. Chushi Fanqi, *Sending off Temple Librarian Sui Back to Lingyin*[382]
*Chushi Fanqi (1296–1370) was from Mingzhou (Xiangshan, Zhejiang); his secular surname was Zhu and his *zi* was Tanyao. He lost his parents when he was four, and the family fortunes declined. He became a novice at age nine and a monk by sixteen, and traveled widely before becoming a disciple of Linji master Yuansou Xingduan (1255–1341) at Mount Jing (near Yuhang, Zhejiang). His calligraphy was superior (the artist Zhao Mengfu [1254–1322] was an early patron), so as a young monk he was invited to the capital to assist in writing out the Buddhist canon. While there, one night he woke to the sound of drums from the western gate tower. His perspiration falling like rain, he was suddenly enlightened. Fanqi served as abbot in several temples, including Baoguo Temple in Hangzhou (in Zhejiang) and Tianning Yongqi Temple (in Jiaxing, Zhejiang), where he directed the construction of a seven-story pagoda. Legend has it that when the pagoda was almost complete, it suddenly began to lean and seemed in danger of collapse. By the power of Fanqi's prayer, ghosts and spirits set it straight again. In 1359 Fanqi withdrew to a hermitage near the temple and called himself the Old Man of the West Studio. The Mongol Yuan court granted him the title Chan Master of the Buddha Sun, Universal Illumination, and Wise Disputation (Fori Puzhao Huibian Chanshi). After the founding of the Ming dynasty (1368–1644), he also received

imperial favor, perhaps due in part to his friendship with Song Lian (1310–1381), a poet, critic, and political advisor to the founding emperor of the Ming.[383]

Before moving their tongues — the true scriptures are wordless scriptures. For example, the *Laṅkāvatāra sūtra* says that during his fifty years of teaching, the Buddha "never spoke a single word": his sermons were mere "skillful means," "golden leaves to stop the crying of an infant," empty talk from a "golden mouth."[384]

sweet dew (ganlu) — the nectar (Skt. *soma*) of the gods, which wards off old age and death and thus is also called no-death (Skt. *amṛta;* Ch. *busi*). It is a metaphor for the Buddhist teachings.

165. Yu'an Zhiji, *Autumn Night in a Mountain Tower*[385]

*Yu'an Zhiji (1311–1378) was from Wuxian (in Jiangsu); his secular surname was Gu and his *zi* Yizhong. As a boy he became an acolyte at the nearby Haiyun Temple, studying both Buddhist and secular texts. One day he heard a monk lecturing about Dharma realms. Before the talk had reached its end, Zhiji burst out, "A true Dharma realm is as perfect as the Great Void, but as soon as you describe it in words, it becomes filthy!" He began Chan training with Xiaoyin Dasu (1284–1344) in Jianye (Nanjing, Jiangsu). While there, he gained a reputation for literary brilliance and the patronage of the powerful. He was enlightened as he watched falling leaves in the courtyard. With light heart, he traveled to Mount Jing (near Yuhang, Zhejiang) and was examined closely by Linji master Yuansou Xingduan (1255–1341), who bestowed the Dharma seal. In 1342 he took his first of several positions in the region as temple abbot, in a career that eventually saw him in charge at Mount Jing itself. The last Yuan dynasty emperor granted him the title Chan Master of Bright Disputation, Orthodox Religion, and Vast Wisdom (Mingbian Zhengzong Guanghui Chanshi). During the chaos surrounding the collapse of the Yuan, when the people were in great distress, he organized the transport of provisions for their relief. In 1373, when the new Ming dynasty court summoned ten Buddhist figures to lecture at Tianjie Temple in the capital of Jianye, Zhiji was granted the premier place.[386]

the night divides in two — midnight is reached.

166. Tianru Weize, *Miscellaneous Words on Living in the Mountains*[387]

*Tianru Weize (d. 1354) was from Ji'an (Yongxin, Jiangxi); his secular surname was Tan. He was a disciple of Linji master Zhongfeng Mingben (1263–1323) on Mount Tianmu (near Hangzhou, Zhejiang). Although asked many times to serve as abbot at major temples, he always adamantly refused. In 1342 patrons and friends bought a piece of land in the city of Suzhou (in Jiangsu) and built a hermitage for him. It was called Shizilin (Lion Forest) in honor of a lion-shaped rock standing in the garden, and is still a major tourist site today. Weize remained there the rest of his life, and wrote prolifically on religious topics. By imperial order he was granted a gold cassock and the title Chan Master of Buddha Mind, Universal Succor, and Great Disputation (Foxin Puji Dabian Chanshi).[388]

Su Embankment—a dike built by the statesman and poet Su Shi (1037–1101) on West Lake in Hangzhou (in Zhejiang).

Six Bridges—a series of small arched bridges on the dike in the outer lake.

167. Tianru Weize, *Sending off Yu Xiaolin, a Monk from My Hometown*[389]

168. Tianru Weize, *Winter*[390]

169. Tianru Weize, *Instructions for My Friends*[391]

170. Jitan Zongle, *Funeral Poem*[392]
*Jitan Zongle (1318–1391), *hao* Quanshi, was from Taizhou (in Zhejiang); his secular surname was Zhou. Orphaned early, for a time he was forced to beg for food. At the age of eight he joined Tianning Temple (in Qiantang, Zhejiang), where Linji Chan master Xiaoyin Dasu (1284–1344) tested him on the *Heart Sūtra* and pronounced the boy "a brilliant flame on a dark road." Zongle was ordained a monk at age twenty and became Dasu's disciple. During his years with Dasu, he voraciously read and mastered Buddhist texts and developed his own literary talent. A mountain recluse during the last years of the Yuan dynasty, in the founding year of the Ming (1368) he became abbot at his old temple. Zongle impressed the first Ming emperor with his ritual poetry and Dharma lectures, and so was ordered to prepare annotated editions of several sūtras. In 1377 the emperor commanded Zongle to lead a group of thirty monks on an expedition to India to collect additional Buddhist texts. Zongle's facility with Sanskrit was instrumental in the group's success. Upon his return, he was named abbot of Tianjie Temple in the early Ming capital (Nanjing, Jiangsu) and gained major influence in national Buddhist affairs. However, he became embroiled in political factionalism and was for a time banished. He retreated to Fengyang (in Anhui) and built a quiet hermitage beneath the pines. He was recalled in 1387, and again invited by the court to become abbot of Tianjie Temple. He remained in imperial favor to the end of his life. In 1390, he pleaded old age and retired to Shifo Temple (in Jiangpu, Jiangsu), where he died the next year.[393]

This poem was written after the death of the empress dowager in 1390. Just before the funeral was to begin, there was a violent thunderstorm. The emperor was unhappy at this ill omen and ordered Zongle to produce a *gāthā* to ease her journey.

171. Dai'an Puzhuang, *Rhyming with Old Patriarch Guiyuan's Mountain Song*[394]

*Dai'an Puzhuang ("Universal Reverence") (1347–1403), *zi* Jingzhong, *hao* Dai'an (Idiot's Hut), was from Xianju in Taizhou (Xianju, Zhejiang); his secular surname was Yuan. He became a monk at Mount Tiantong (near Ningbo, Zhejiang) and then a disciple to Linji master Liaotang Weiyi (fl. late fourteenth century) at Tianning Temple (in Qiantang, Zhejiang). In 1379 he took the first of several posts as abbot. Not only did his Buddhist lectures unlock the meaning of the Way "as fast as thunder and lightning," but he was equally at home discussing Neo-Confucianism. In the spring of 1393, he was called to the capital to expound the Dharma in the inner court. He was rewarded with an imperial gift of a cassock and an abbot's post at Xingsheng Wanshou Temple on Mount Jing (near Yuhang, Zhejiang). While chatting with guests there late one night, he heard the temple bell and drum, and contentedly passed away. *Supplemental Biographies of Eminent Monks* records his final words: "It's hard! It's hard! A lovely maiden of sixteen is climbing the high mountain, and this old monk can't help her!"[395]

Pine Gate (songmen)—a euphemism for Buddhism.

172. Dai'an Puzhuang, *Sending off Attendant Yao*[396]

Xianglin—Xianglin Chengyuan was a follower of Yunmen Wenyan (864–949) who purportedly wore a paper cassock on which he secretly recorded the master's teachings. "Black as lacquer" describes the cassock covered in writing, but also suggests ignorance, as in the "lacquer bucket" image.

Three times three isn't nine—the line seems to say that in enlightenment normal logic will not apply. The line probably alludes to *Blue Cliff* 35, wherein the monk Wuzhu asks the bodhisattva Mañjuśrī how numerous are the congregations of the faithful in the north. Mañjuśrī answers, "In front three by three; in back, three by three."[397] Wuzhu does not understand.

nine times nine is eighty-one—another Yunmen allusion. When he was asked, "What is the road upward?" he pithily replied, "Nine times nine is eighty-one."[398]

173. Zibo Zhenke, *Crossing Cao Stream*[399]

*Zibo Zhenke (1543–1603) was from Juqu (Jurong, Jiangsu); his secular surname was Shen, his *zi* Daguan, and his *hao* Zibo Laoren (Old Man of the Purple Cypress). He and his close friend Hanshan Deqing (1546–1623), along with Pure Land master Yunqi Zhuhong (1535–1615), were known as the "dragon-elephants" of late Ming Buddhism. Zhenke grew up wild, and his parents could not control him. He later admitted he had been a crude youngster with a fiery temper, who "knew only drinking wine and eating meat," who "relied on drunkenness to vent his anger," and whose companions were "pig and dog butchers." He left home at age 16 and wandered as far north as the Great Wall, so beginning a lifetime habit of restless travel. At age 17, while he was taking shelter from a rainstorm beneath one of the Suzhou city gates, his life was transformed when he met a monk named Mingjue from nearby Huqiu (Tiger Hill). He was formally ordained two years later. Zhenke is generally considered to have been in the Linji lineage, but like other major Ming Buddhist figures, he was in fact a syncretist, merging Chan with Pure Land Buddhism, and even Neo-Confucianism and study of the *Book of Changes*. He was by all accounts an unusual and charismatic man. He is described as stern of appearance and ascetic and uncompromising in demeanor; he forced himself to walk until he could travel 200 *li* (60 miles) in a day, slept at night in a seated posture for many years, and once wrote a temple inscription in his own blood. In 1586 he first met Deqing, at the latter's retreat on Mount Lao (in Shandong). It appears that Deqing introduced Zhenke to his connections at the imperial court, including the empress dowager. With support from his patrons, beginning in 1589 Zhenke led a group to edit and recut the blocks for a ten-thousand-fascicle version of the Buddhist canon, known now as the *Mount Jing Canon*. He also organized the rebuilding of temples and monasteries. Zhenke remained engaged with the ruling class, and this was his eventual undoing. He was implicated in the so-called "Yaoshu" (Weird Book) incident of 1603: an anonymous pamphlet was circulated that claimed that Prince Changxun intended to usurp the throne. Zhenke was arrested, and died in prison. His funeral at Mount Jing was overseen by his dear friend Deqing.[400]

Cao Stream—the course ran below Mount Shuangfeng (in Qujiang, Guangdong). This was an important Chan site, as it was near the residence of Sixth Patriarch Huineng.

south of the peaks—Lingnan, in southeast China (roughly comprising Guangdong and Guangxi). It is remembered in Chan discourse for the mocking comment made by Fifth Patriarch Hongren when he first met Huineng: "If you're from Lingnan then you're a barbarian. How can you become a Buddha?"[401]

174. Hanshan Deqing, *Sending off Chan Monk Gao Back to Cihua*[402]
*Hanshan Deqing (1546–1623), *zi* Chengyin, was from Quanjiao (in Anhui); his secular surname was Cai. He was the most important figure in late Ming Buddhism and was famous as a preacher, writer, and political insider. The young Deqing gained an interest in Buddhism from his mother, and entered Bao'en

Temple in Jinling (Nanjing, Jiangsu) at age eleven, over the objections of his father. After training in a mixture of Chan and Pure Land teachings, in the early 1570s he began a period of travel. He settled for a time in a hut at Longmen, near the northern summit of the sacred Mount Wutai (at Wutai, Shanxi). As he relates in his autobiography, as spring arrived he was distracted by the sound of the thundering torrents, "like ten thousand galloping horses." He chose a footbridge near a stream and meditated there every day, until one day he suddenly forgot his body and the sound disappeared. In 1577 he received the patronage of the empress dowager, a devout Buddhist. By 1582 his lectures on the *Flower Garland Sūtra* drew ten thousand people daily; he had earlier laboriously written out the sūtra in his own blood, in honor of his parents. In 1583 he moved to a new retreat on Mount Lao (in Jimo, Shandong). The empress dowager soon donated money to build Haiyin Temple nearby, and arranged the gift of a complete Buddhist canon. He was drawn into court politics and became embroiled in the controversy over choosing the heir-apparent. In 1595 he was denounced and imprisoned, then defrocked and dispatched to serve as a soldier at Leizhou (in Guangdong). This was only a temporary setback, as his admirers included many of the leading literati and officials of the day. Although not formally reinstated as a monk until 1605, Deqing was able to continue his religious work almost uninterrupted. In 1601 he began to rebuild the temple complex at Caoqi (in Qujiang, Guangdong), once home to the Sixth Patriarch; this work would consume him for ten years. He returned to Caoqi in 1622 and died there a year later. "The water in Cao Stream suddenly dried up, all the birds cried mournfully, and by night there was a light that illuminated heaven." His "flesh-body" (mummy) was kept at the temple as an object of reverence, and is still there today.[403]

Cihua — Cihua Temple (in Dangyang, Hubei).

175. Hanshan Deqing, *Living in the Mountains*[404]

176. Hanshan Deqing, *Night Departure on Ling River*[405]
   Ling River — in Jiangxi Province.

177. Hanshan Deqing, *Living in the Mountains*[406]

178. Hanshan Deqing, *Sitting at Night, Enjoying the Cool*[407]

179. Miyun Yuanwu, *Death Gāthā (#1)*[408]
   *Miyun Yuanwu (1566–1642), *zi* Juechu, *hao* Miyun (Dense Clouds), also known as Tiantong Miyun, was from Changzhou (Yixing, Jiangsu); his secular surname

was Jiang. By nature an unaffected and straightforward man, Yuanwu spent his early years plowing the fields. At age twenty-six he first read the *Platform Sūtra* and was drawn to a religious life. One day he was carrying a load of firewood to town, when on the mountain path ahead he saw *another* man bent over carrying *his* load of wood. For the whole day he was in a daze. Three years later he settled his wife and family, and became a Buddhist novice under Linji master Huanyou Zhengchuan (1549–1614) at Longchi Monastery in Changzhou. There he was ordained as a monk at age thirty-one. Yet each time he asked for instruction he was cursed and reviled, to the point that he became despondent and ill. Zhengchuan merely said, "If you reach the field, then lay your body down." Then when he was thirty-eight, Yuanwu was suddenly enlightened while crossing over Mount Tongguan on a bracing autumn day. His mind "was opened, and obstructions disappeared like melting ice." After Zhengchuan's death, Yuanwu took his place as abbot of Longchi Monastery; subsequently he taught at several other major temples in south China. His lectures ranged from lucid explanations of *gong'an* and Buddhist terms to gestures like spitting on the floor. When he was abbot of Jingde Temple on Mount Tiantong (near Ningbo, Zhejiang), the community comprised more than three thousand monks. At the end of his career there, he was favored with an imperial gift of a purple robe and the abbacy of Bao'en Temple in the southern capital (Nanjing, Jiangsu). He soon pleaded old age and ill health, and retired. The day before he died, after meting out a blow in response to a monk's question, he gave his last instruction: "A thousand words or ten thousand words, all come from self-understanding. If you don't understand yourself, you won't understand being hit by a stick."[409]

Sumeru Peak—in Indian cosmology, Mount Sumeru (or Mount Meru) is the universal central peak. "Yan'guan [Qi'an (?–842)] said to the assembled monks, 'The Void is the drum, and Mount Sumeru is the drumstick; which of you can beat it for me?' The assemblage had no response."[410]

winds—the "Eight Winds" (*bafeng*) that stimulate affliction: gain, loss, defamation, eulogy, praise, ridicule, sorrow, and joy.

180. Miyun Yuanwu, *Death Gāthā (#2)*[411]
I am the sole master (weiwo duzun)—the first words of Śākyamuni after his birth were, "In heaven above and on earth below, I am the sole master." This announcement is made by every buddha.

181. Wuyi Yuanlai, *Seeing Plum Blossoms at Drum Mountain for the First Time*[412]
*Wuyi Yuanlai (1575–1630) was from Luzhou (Shucheng, Anhui); his secular surname was Sha. He became a monk at Mount Wutai (in Jiangxi) at the age of

sixteen. Five years later he joined Wuming Huijing (1548–1618), who taught at Shouchang Temple in Jianfu (Xincheng, Jiangxi). Yet at first Yuanlai was unimpressed, as the old abbot shouldered a hoe and wore a straw hat like a farmer. He left and spent three years meeting with other masters; he also wrote a discourse on the *Heart Sūtra*. Yuanlai later returned to Huijing, who told him the discourse missed the true meaning of Chan. Yuanlai burned the manuscript and became Huijing's disciple in Cao-Dong Chan. One night, when he had risen to go to the privy, he saw someone climbing a tree, heard a great noise, and was suddenly enlightened. His body was light and his mind danced; it was as if he had put down a heavy burden. In 1602 Wuyi Yuanlai moved to Mount Bo (in Guangfeng, Jiangxi), so he is sometimes called Boshan Yuanlai. There he restored Nengren Temple and revived the moribund monastic community. He later was abbot at several other temples, including Yongquan Temple on Mount Gu (Drum Mountain) in Fuzhou (Minxian, Fujian), where he taught up to a thousand disciples. He died at Tianjie Temple in Jinling (Nanjing, Jiangsu).[413]

ask about the ford (wenjin)—to find a guide to enlightenment, who will help you "cross over."

182. Wuyi Yuanlai, *Thoughts on Climbing Drinkwater Ridge*[414]

183. Yongjue Yuanxian, *Living in the Mountains*[415]
*Yongjue Yuanxian (1578–1657) was from Jianyang (in Fujian); his secular surname was Cai. As a young man he studied the Confucian classics and became a "flowering talent" (*xiucai*—the first of the civil service examination degrees), but when he heard a monk chanting the *Lotus Sūtra*, he was inspired to become a Buddhist. He burned all his Confucian books and devoted himself to Chan study. However, he remained in the secular world, studying as a layman with Wuming Huijing (1548–1618) at Shouchang Temple in Jianfu (Xincheng, Jiangxi). At age forty he left his wife and children to become a monk, and was accepted as Huijing's disciple in Cao-Dong Chan. Soon thereafter Huijing died, and Yuanxian continued his training under Wuyi Yuanlai (1575–1630) and others. He first became an abbot at Yongquan Temple on Mount Gu in Fuzhou (Minxian, Fujian) when he was fifty, teaching a syncretism of Chan and Pure Land Buddhism and even espousing the compatibility of Buddhism and Confucianism—yet he drew the line at Daoism: "Cultivating the arts of chaos merely destroys life." Thereafter he was abbot of numerous temples, authored more than twenty works, and taught hundreds of disciples. During the Manchu invasion he directed large-scale charity work, providing food for the living and funerals for the dead.[416]

Lush cassia can beckon the recluse—an allusion to lines in the "Summons for a Gentleman Who Became a Recluse," a poem in the famous *Songs of Chu* (ca. third century B.C.E.–second century C.E.).

184. Yongjue Yuanxian, *Celebrating the Completion of Discordless Hermitage on an Early Spring Day*[417]
willow eyes—the appearance of newly budding willow leaves.

   time has no winter and summer—a gong'an in *Blue Cliff* 43, featuring Dongshan Liangjie (807–869): "A monk asked Dongshan, 'When cold and heat arrive, why do they avoid meeting?' Dongshan said, 'Why not go to the place without cold or heat?' The monk said, 'What is the place without cold or heat?' Dongshan said, 'In times of cold, the *ācārya* freezes; in times of heat, the *ācārya* burns.'"[418] An *ācārya* (Ch. *asheli*) is an important monk teacher, a model monk.

185. Yongjue Yuanxian, *Small Pond*[419]

186. Yongjue Yuanxian, *Lying Meditation*[420]
lotus clock—see the note to "clepsydra" above.

187. Yongjue Yuanxian, *In Praise of the Wooden Fish*[421]
Wooden fish—percussion instruments used by monks in chanting and rituals. Often these were in the stylized shape of fish. The origin of the use of a fish is unknown; one explanation is that a fish has its eyes open day and night, and so is an example to monks to be watchful.

   Rhythm flows from where a heart would be—a pun. The center of the wooden fish was hollowed out, so that it is literally "heartless" (*wuxin*)—the same term as used for "no-mind."

   Sanskrit song (fanbai)—a sixth-century source defines types of chanting: "In Indian custom, any singing of the Dharma is called *pai*; as for this country, chanting sūtras is called *zhuandu* [circuit-reading], and singing praises is called *fanbai* [Sanskrit song]."[422]

188. Yongjue Yuanxian, *Traveling to White-water Mountain Monastery*[423]
"sparrow-tongue" tea—a type of tea with very small rolled leaves.

189. Yongjue Yuanxian, *My Seventieth Birthday*[424]
Mulberry groves might rise from the sea—from a story in the fourth-century *Record of Spirits and Immortals* about the passage of long periods of time. Two immortals

meet, and the first says, "Since I last waited on you, I've seen the Eastern Sea three times turn into a mulberry grove." The other replies, "The sages all say in the ocean you can repeatedly kick up the dust."[425]

190. Sanyi Mingyu, *Lodging on North Mountain; Presented to Abbot Wei*[426]
*Sanyi Mingyu (1599–1665) was from Qiantang (in Zhejiang); his secular surname was Ding. At twenty-three he became a monk, and then a disciple of Zhanran Yuancheng (1561–1625) in Cao-Dong Chan. He was enlightened in the following intriguing way:

> Chan Master Sanyi Mingyu, of Yu'an Temple in Hangzhou, formerly studied with Yunmen [Zhanran Yuancheng]. One day, while diligently keeping a vow of silence, he entered the temple hall. Suddenly Yunmen came in and yelled at the top of his voice, "Put it down!" Unconsciously Mingyu raised his eyebrows and laughed.

Mingyu became abbot at numerous temples, including Xiansheng Temple in Yuezhou (Shaoxing, Zhejiang). During the war between Ming and Qing forces, he visited the battlefields to give aid to the living. He later retired to West Lake to care for his elderly mother; when she died, he was blind with grief.[427]

SOURCE NOTES

Abbreviations and their referents are as follows:

4-shi — quadrisyllabic poem. Variable number of couplets, four syllables per line.

5-j. — pentasyllabic *jueju* quatrain. Four lines, five characters per line.

6-j. — hexasyllabic *jueju* quatrain. Four lines, six characters per line.

7-j. — heptasyllabic *jueju* quatrain. Four lines, seven characters per line.

5-lü. — pentasyllabic *lüshi* regulated verse. Eight lines, five characters per line, syntactic parallelism required in inner couplets.

7-lü. — heptasyllabic *lüshi* regulated verse. Eight lines, seven characters per line, syntactic parallelism required in inner couplets.

5-gu. — pentasyllabic *gushi* ancient verse. Variable number of couplets, five characters per line.

7-gu. — heptasyllabic *gushi* ancient verse. Variable number of couplets, seven characters per line.

Irr. — irregular line-length form. Often, but not always, these are songs.

1. Source: T51n2076 *Jingde Chuandeng lu* 14:311. Form: 7-j.

2. Bio.: T51n2076 *Jingde Chuandeng lu* 14:309.

3. Faure, *Rhetoric of Immediacy*, 167–168.

4. Source: T51n2076 *Jingde Chuandeng lu* 30:461. Form: Irr.

5. McRae, *Platform Sutra*, 66.

6. Source: QTS 23:806.9069. Form: 5-j.

7. Pulleyblank, "Linguistic Evidence." For additional citations, see Henricks, *Poetry of Han-shan*, 3–26.

8. Bio.: T50n2061 *Song Gaoseng zhuan* 19:831; T51n2076 *Jingde Chuandeng lu* 27:433; Li Fang, *Taiping guangji* 55:338.

9. Source: QTS 23:806.9073. Form: 5-j.

10. Source: QTS 23:806.9065. Form: 5-lü.

11. T12n374 *Da Niepan jing* 29:536.

12. T22n1425 *Mohe Sengqi lü* 7:284.

13. T51n2076 *Jingde Chuandeng lu* 16:328.

14. T51n2076 *Jingde Chuandeng lu* 15:324.

15. Source: QTS 23:806.9068. Form: 5-gu.

16. T12n360 *Foshuo Wuliangshou jing* 2:274.

17. T12n374 *Da Niepan jing* 9:420.

18. T8n235 *Jin'gang banruo boluomi jing* 1:749.

19. Source: QTS 23:806.9091. Form: 5-gu.

20. X69n1321 *Mazu Daoyi chanshi guanglu* 1:3; T51n2076 *Jingde Chuandeng lu* 10:276.

21. Source: QTS 23:806.9083. Form: 5-lü.

22. Source: QTS 23:806.9096–9097. Form: 5-lü. The reduplicative *lulu* in line 3 is obscure.

23. Source: QTS 23:807.9105. Form: 5-gu.

24. Bio.: T50n2061 *Song Gaoseng zhuan* 19:832; T51n2076 *Jingde Chuandeng lu* 27:433.

25. T9n262 *Miaofa lianhua jing* 2:12.

26. T51n2076 *Jingde Chuandeng lu* 2:214.

27. T48n2003 *Foguo Yuanwu chanshi Biyan lu* 4:175.

28. T48n2003 *Foguo Yuanwu chanshi Biyan lu* 8:206.

29. Source: QTS 23:807.9106. Form: 7-j.

30. For a translation, see Mueller, "The Larger Sukhavativyuha Sutra"; T12n360 *Foshuo wuliang shou jing* 1:270.

31. T13n417 *Banzhou sanmei jing* 1:899.

32. *Shōbōgenzō* 29; translated in Bielefeldt, "Mountains and Waters Sūtra."

33. T47n1991 *Jinling Qingliangyuan Wenyi chanshi yulu* 1:591.

34. Source: QTS 23:807.9107. Form: 5-gu.

35. T19n945 *Da foding rulai miyin xiuzheng liaoyi zhupusa wanxing shoulengyan jing* 3:117.

36. An alternate text has *wushi* (my master).

37. Source: *QTS* 23:807.9108. Form: 5-gu.

38. On the cult of arhats, see Faure, *Rhetoric of Immediacy*, 266–272.

39. *QTS* 6:198.2030.

40. Source: *QTS* 23:807.9110; # 2 of 2. Form: 5-j.

41. Bio.: T50n2061 *Song Gaoseng zhuan* 19:831; T51n2076 *Jingde Chuandeng lu* 27:433.

42. Source: Zhu, *Wang Fanzhi shi yanjiu* 2:174. Form: 5-j.

43. Bio.: Li Fang, *Taiping guangji* 82:525; Nienhauser, ed., *Indiana Companion*, 862–863 (entry by Charles Hartman).

44. Source: Zhu, *Wang Fanzhi shi yanjiu* 2:16–19. Form: 5-gu.

45. T13n412 *Dizang pusa benyuan jing* 5:781–782.

46. Source: Zhu, *Wang Fanzhi shi yanjiu* 2:347–348. Form: 5-j.

47. Source: Zhu, *Wang Fanzhi shi yanjiu* 2:361. Form: 4-shi.

48. Source: Zhu, *Wang Fanzhi shi yanjiu* 2:361–363. Form: 4-shi.

49. Source: *QTS* 23:808.9121. Form: 5-lü.

50. Bio.: *QTS* 23:808.9120; Cen Shen's poems are in *QTS* 6:198.2038, 199.2055. A passing reference to a *Vinaya* Master Jingyun of Ximing Temple is found in T50n2061 *Song Gaoseng zhuan* 15:802. Ximing Temple was located in the Tang capital of Chang'an (Xi'an, Shaanxi).

51. Source: *QTS* 23:809.9124. Form: 5-lü.

52. Bio.: T50n2061 *Song Gaoseng zhuan* 15:799; *QTS* 23:809.9123. Guanxiu's poem is in *QTS* 23:827.9319.

53. Source: *QTS* 23:809.9125. Form: 7-j.

54. T51n2095 *Lushan ji* 1:1027.

55. Source: *QTS* 23:809.9130. Form: 7-j.

56. Source: *QTS* 23:809.9127. Form: 7-lü.

57. T51n2076 *Jingde Chuandeng lu* 26:421.

58. Source: *QTS* 23:820.9245. Form: 5-gu.

59. Bio.: T50n2061 *Song Gaoseng zhuan* 29:891; Nielson, "Chiao-jan," particularly 18, 22.

60. Source: *QTS* 23:815.9178. Form: 7-j.

61. Watson, *Chuang Tzu*, 58.

62. Source: *QTS* 23:819.9234. Form: 7-j.

63. Yampolsky, *Platform Sutra*, 178.

64. Source: *QTS* 23:821.9267. Form: 5-lü.

65. Source: *QTS* 23:816.9190. Form: 5-lü.

66. Source: *QTS* 23:817.9203. Form: 5-lü.

67. Watson, *Chuang Tzu*, 104.

68. Yampolsky, *Platform Sutra*, 181.

69. Waley, *Way and Its Power*, 141.

70. T47n1985 *Zhenzhou Linji Huizhao chanshi yulu* 1:497.

71. Source: *QTS* 23:817.9206. Form: 5-lü.

72. T48n2003 *Foguo Yuanwu chanshi Biyan lu* 2:153; translated in Cleary and Cleary, *Blue Cliff*, 84.

73. Source: *QTS* 23:820.9249. Form: 5-gu.

74. Source: *QTS* 23:815.9182. Form: 5-j.

75. Source: *QTS* 23:820.9147–9148; this poem is also attributed to Kezhi. Form: 7-j.

76. Bio.: T50n2061 *Song Gaoseng zhuan* 15: 801.

77. See Chaves, *Mei Yao-ch'en*, 114–125.

78. Source: Tan, *Pang Jushi yanjiu*, 443.

79. Bio.: Tan, *Pang Jushi yanjiu*, 30–74, 337; X69n1336 *Pang Jushi yulu*.

80. Source: Tan, *Pang Jushi yanjiu*, 486.

81. Source: Tan, *Pang Jushi yanjiu*, 461.

82. Source: Tan, *Pang Jushi yanjiu*, 454.

83. T4n217 *Piyu jing* 1:801.

84. McRae, *Platform Sutra*, 54.

85. Source: X83n1578 *Zhiyue lu* 18:501; also X65n1278 *Chanzong za duhai* 7:94. Form: 7-j.

86. Bio.: T50n2061 *Song Gaoseng zhuan* 11:776; T51n2076 *Jingde Chuandeng lu* 7:254.

87. X83n1578 *Zhiyuelu* 9:501.

88. Source: X80n1565 *Wudeng huiyuan* 4:90; X65n1278 *Chanzong za duhai* 6:87.

89. Bio: X80n1565 *Wudeng huiyuan* 4:90; also T51n2076 *Jingde Chuandeng lu* 9:268, which does not include the poem.

90. Source: *QTS* 17:574.6693; this poem is also attributed to Sun Ge. Form: 5-j.

91. Bio.: Nienhauser, ed., *Indiana Companion*, 257–259 (entry by C. Witzling); He and Xie, *Lidai mingseng*, 479–483; *QTS* 23:814.9165.

92. Source: *QTS* 17:571.6620. Form: 5-j.

93. Source: *QTS* 17:572.6632. Form: 5-lü.

94. Source: *QTS* 17:574.6682. Form: 7-j.

95. Source: *QTS* 23:813.9150. Form: 5-lü. For "icy rocks," the translation follows the alternate character *ping*, "ice" instead of *yin*, "shade."

96. Bio.: *QTS* 17:572.6634; 23:813.9149.

97. Source: *QTS* 23:813.9152. Form: 5-lü.

98. X76n1517 *Lichao shishi zijian* 2:154.

99. Source: *QTS* 23:813.9155. Form: 5-lü.

100. Source: *QTS* 23:814.9163; this poem is also attributed to Kezhi. Form: 5-lü.

101. Source: T51n2076 *Jingde Chuandeng lu* 11:285. Form: 7-j.

102. Bio.: T51n2076 *Jingde Chuandeng lu* 11:285; X80n1565 *Wudeng huiyuan* 4:104.

103. T51n2076 *Jingde Chuandeng lu* 7:255.

104. X70n1401 *Gaofeng Yuanmiao chanshi chanyao* 1:708; the text is translated in part in Miura and Sasaki, *Zen Dust*, 246–247.

105. Source: T47n1986B *Ruizhou Dongshan Liangjie chanshi yulu* 520; also T51n2076 *Jingde Chuandeng lu* 15:321.

106. Bio.: T47n1986B *Ruizhou Dongshan Liangjie chanshi yulu*; T50n2061 *Song Gaoseng zhuan* 12:780; T51n2076 *Jingde Chuandeng lu* 15:321.

107. Source: T47n1986B *Ruizhou Dongshan Liangjie chanshi yulu* 1:525 Form: 5-j.

108. T47n1986B *Ruizhou Dongshan Liangjie chanshi yulu* 1:525.

109. T51n2076 *Jingde Chuandeng lu* 11:285.

110. Source: QTS 23:823.9280; #2 of 8. Form: 5-lü.

111. Bio.: T50n2061 *Song Gaoseng zhuan* 16:807; X77n1522 *Xinxiu kefen liuxueseng zhuan* 16:212.

112. T47n1986B *Ruizhou Dongshan Liangjie chanshi yulu* 1:520.

113. Source: QTS 23:823.9281; #6 of 8. Form: 5-lü.

114. Waley, *Way and Its Power*, 141.

115. Source: QTS 23:823.9281; #8 of 8. Form: 5-lü.

116. Source: QTS 23:823.9276. Form: 5-lü.

117. Bio.: QTS 21:723.8293; 23:830.9357.

118. McRae, *Platform Sutra*, 57.

119. Source: T51n2076 *Jingde Chuandeng lu* 11:288. Form: 5-j.

120. Bio.: T51n2076 *Jingde Chuandeng lu* 11:288; X80n1565 *Wudeng huiyuan* 4:106.

121. Source: T51n2076 *Jingde Chuandeng lu* 10:274. Form: 7-j.

122. Bio.: T51n2076 *Jingde Chuandeng lu* 10:274; T47n1990 *Yuanzhou Yanshan Huiji chanshi yulu* 1:585; X80n1565 *Wudeng huiyuan* 4:94.

123. Source: QTS 23:835.9412. Form: 7-j.

124. Bio.: T50n2061 *Song Gaoseng zhuan* 30:897; X80n1565 *Wudeng huiyuan* 6:137; X76n1517 *Lichao shishi zijian* 8:213; QTS 22:761.8638, 23:829.9347; Nienhauser, ed., *Indiana Companion*, 509–510 (entry by Edward Schafer); He and Xie, *Lidai mingseng*, 504–508.

125. T47n2000 *Xutang heshang yulu* 2:1000.

126. X78n1556 *Jianzhong jingguo Xudeng lu* 26:798.

127. Source: QTS 23:828.9334; #1 of 2. Form: 7-j.

128. Source: QTS 23:837.9426; #8 of 24; all 24 poems were also included in X66n1298 *Chanmen zhuzushi qiesong* 2:740–741. Form: 7-lü.

129. See McRae, *Northern School*, 325, n. 159.

130. T48n2009 *Shaoshi liumen* 1:369.

131. Waley, *Way and Its Power*, 159.

132. Source: QTS 23:831.9378. Form: 5-lü.

133. For Ancient Chinese (ca. 600 C.E.) pronunciations, see Zhou Fagao, *Hanzi gujin yinhui*.

134. Source: QTS 23:837.9438. Form: 5-j.

135. Source: QTS 23:827.9321; #2 of 4. Form: 5-gu.

136. Source: QTS 23:837.9429. Form: 7-lü.

137. Source: *QTS* 23:837.9437. Form: 5-j.

138. T51n2076 *Jingde Chuandeng lu* 17:336.

139. T47n1988 *Yunmen Kuangzhen chanshi guanglu* 1:550.

140. Source: *QTS* 23:823.9283. Form: 7-j.

141. Bio.: *QTS* 23:823.9283.

142. Source: *QTS* 24:845.9564; #1 of 2. Form: 7-lü.

143. Bio.: T50n2061 *Song Gaoseng zhuan* 30:897; *QTS* 24:848.9602, 848.9609–9610; Nien-hauser, ed., *Indiana Companion*, 249–251 (entry by Edward Schafer) ; He and Xie, *Lidai mingseng*, 492–495.

144. T47n1990 *Yuanzhou Yangshan Huiji chanshi yulu* 1:585.

145. T48n2003 *Foguo Yuanwu chanshi Biyan lu* 1:149.

146. Source: *QTS* 24:839.9458. Form: 5-lü.

147. T51n2077 *Xu Chuandeng lu* 6:500.

148. Source: *QTS* 24:841.9496. Form: 5-lü.

149. Source: *QTS* 24:843.9529. Form: 5-lü.

150. Source: *QTS* 24:840.9482. Form: 5-lü.

151. Source: *QTS* 24:839.9459. Form: 5-lü.

152. Source: *QTS* 24:841.9493. Form: 5-lü.

153. Source: *QTS* 24:841.9497. Form: 5-lü.

154. Source: *QTS* 23:824.9289. Form: 7-j.

155. Bio.: *QTS* 23:824.9286.

156. Source: *QTS* 23:824.9289. Form: 7-j.

157. Source: *QTS* 24:848.9604. Form: 5-lü.

158. Bio.: *QTS* 24:843.9527, 846.9571, 848.9598, 848.9601.

159. Source: *QTS* 24:848.9610. Form: 5-lü.

160. Bio.: *QTS* 24:843.9520, 848.9608. Another poem addressed to him is by Xuzhong; see *QTS* 24:848.9606.

161. T51n2076 *Jingde Chuandeng lu* 8:259.

162. Miura and Sasaki, *Zen Dust*, 319; T51n2076 *Jingde Chuandeng lu* 9:267.

163. X80n1565 *Wudeng huiyuan* 20:420; X64n1270 *Shiniu tusong*. Two other sets are attributed to Qingju Haosheng and Zide. For a discussion of the cow-herding metaphor, see Suzuki, *Manual of Zen Buddhism*.

164. Source: *QTS* 24:850.9622. Form: 5-lü.

165. Source: *QTS* 24:851.9629. Form: 7-j.

166. Source: T51n2076 *Jingde Chuandeng lu* 17:340. Form: 5-j.

167. Bio.: T50n2061 *Song Gaoseng zhuan* 13:785; T51n2076 *Jingde Chuandeng lu* 17:339; X80n1565 *Wudeng huiyuan* 13:268.

168. T10n279 *Dafang guangfo Huayan jing* 78:434.

169. T51n2076 *Jingde Chuandeng lu* 23:396.

170. T12n374 *Daban niepan jing* 20:485.

171. Source: *QTS* 23:825.9294. Form: 7-lü.

172. Bio.: T51n2076 *Jingde Chuandeng lu* 20:368; X80n1565 *Wudeng huiyuan* 13:278.

173. Li Zhao, *Tangguo shibu* 2.

174. T47n1988 *Yunmen Kuangzhen chanshi guanglu* 1:552.

175. T51n2076 *Jingde Chuandeng lu* 8:258; T48n2003 *Foguo Yuanwu chanshi Biyan lu* 4:178; translated in Chang, *Original Teachings*, 160.

176. Source: *QTS* 23:825.9291. Form: 5-lü.

177. Bio.: T50n2061 *Song Gaoseng zhuan* 7:748.

178. Waley, *Way and Its Power*, 202.

179. Source: T47n1988 *Yunmen Kuangzhen chanshi guanglu* 3:576. Form: 5-j.

180. His biography in *Jingde Chuandeng lu* 19, probably erroneously, says Jiaxing in Suzhou (Wuxian, Jiangsu).

181. Bio.: X79n1560 *Chanlin seng baozhuan* 2:494; T41n2076 *Jingde Chuandeng lu* 19:356; X80n1565 *Wudeng huiyuan* 15:303; Chang, *Original Teachings*, 268.

182. T9n262 *Miaofa lianhua jing* 4:29.

183. Cleary and Cleary, *Blue Cliff*, 166, 348; T48n2003 *Foguo Yuanwu chanshi Biyan lu* 3:166, 7:193.

184. Source: T51n2076 *Jingde Chuandeng lu* 29:455; #1 of 10. Form: 7-lü.

185. Bio.: T51n2076 *Jingde Chuandeng lu* 17:342; X80n1565 *Wudeng huiyuan* 6:132.

186. Source: T51n2076 *Jingde Chuandeng lu* 29:455; #6 of 10. Form: 7-lü.

187. T12n374 *Da niepan jing* 14:449.

188. Source: T51n2076 *Jingde Chuandeng lu* 29:455; #7 of 10. Form: 7-lü.

189. X64n1269 *Shi niutu song* 1:774

190. T14n475 *Weimojie suoshuo jing* 2:547.

191. T51n2076 *Jingde Chuandeng lu* 27:437.

192. T47n1985 *Zhenzhou Linji Huizhao chanshi yulu* 1:500; translated in Watson, *Master Lin-chi*, 55–56.

193. T47n1987b *Fuzhou Caoshan Benji chanshi yulu* 1:536; Chang, *Original Teachings*, 46.

194. Source: T51n2076 *Jingde Chuandeng lu* 29:455; #8 of 10. Form: 7-lü.

195. T47n1986B *Ruizhou Dongshan Liangjie chanshi yulu* 1:526; translated in Chang, *Original Teachings*, 48. For a translation of the entire text, see Lu, *Chan and Zen Teaching*, 2:149–157.

196. T51n2076 *Jingde Chuandeng lu* 30:460; the entire text is translated in Lu, *Ch'an and Zen Teaching*, 3:116–145.

197. Guangwen Editorial, *Zhuzi huiyao, Liezi* vol.:64–65. From *Liezi* 5.

198. T12n375 *Da niepan jing* 17:719.

199. T47n2000 *Xutang heshang yulu* 8:1044.

200. T47n1997 *Yuanwu Foguo chanshi yulu* 10:757.

201. X68n1315 *Guzunsu yulu* 10:58.

202. Source: T51n2076 *Jingde Chuandeng lu* 29:455; #10 of 10. Form: 7-lü.

203. T47n1986B *Ruizhou Dongshan Liangjie chanshi yulu* 1:526; translated in Chang, *Original Teachings*, 47.

204. T47n1998 *Dahui Pujue chanshi yulu* 15:876.

205. Source: T51n2077 *Xu Chuandeng lu* 2:477; also X81n1571 *Wudeng quanshu* 33:710. Form: 7-j.

206. Bio.:X79n1560 *Chanlin seng baozhuan* 11:514; X80n1565 *Wudeng huiyuan* 15:520.

207. T51n2076 *Jingde Chuandeng lu* 19:358.

208. Source: T47n1996 *Mingjue chanshi zuying ji* 5:703. Form: 7-j.

209. Bio.: X79n1560 *Chanlin seng baozhuan* 11:514; X80n1565 *Wudeng huiyuan* 15:322; X77n1524 *Buxu Gaoseng zhuan* 7:416.

210. T48n2003 *Foguo Yuanwu chanshi Biyan lu* 1:146; translated in Cleary and Cleary, *Blue Cliff*, 43–44.

211. Source: X65n1278 *Chanzong za duhai* 1:60. Form: 7-j.

212. Bio.: X79n1560 *Chanlin seng baozhuan* 19:529; X77n1524 *Buxu Gaoseng zhuan* 7:413.

213. Source: X69n1338 *Shishuang Chuyuan chanshi yulu* 1:195 Form: 5-j.

214. Bio.: X79n1560 *Chanlin seng baozhuan* 21:532; X80n1565 *Wudeng huiyuan* 12:238; X77n1524 *Buxu Gaoseng zhuan* 7:412; Miura and Sasaki, *Zen Dust*, 212–213.

215. Source: X86n1610 *Yunwo jitan* 1:671. Form: 7-j.

216. Bio.: X79n1560 *Chanlin seng baozhuan* 17:526; X80n1565 *Wudeng huiyuan* 12:243; X77n1524 *Buxu Gaoseng zhuan* 7:415.

217. X84n1580 *Jiaowai Biezhuan* 14:325.

218. Source: X86n1610 *Yunwo jitan* 1:671. Form: 7-j.

219. Source: T47n1993 *Huanglong Huinan chanshi yulu* 635. Form: 5-lü.

220. Bio.: X79n1560 *Chanlin seng baozhuan* 22:534; X80n1565 *Wudeng huiyuan* 17:351; He and Xie, *Lidai mingseng*, 549–552.

221. Source: T47n1993 *Huanglong Huinan chanshi yulu* 1:635. Form: 7-lü.

222. T51n2076 *Jingde Chuandeng lu* 14:313.

223. X80n1565 *Wudeng huiyuan* 4:93.

224. X69n1353 *Kaifu Daoning chanshi yulu* 2:337.

225. T51n2076 *Jingde chuandeng lu* 8:258; translated in Chang, *Original Teachings*, 158.

226. Source: X73n1448 *Fachang Yiyu chanshi yulu* 1:70. Form: 7-j.

227. The third line refers to divination.

228. Bio.: X79n1560 *Chanlin seng baozhuan* 28:546; X80n1565 *Wudeng huiyuan* 16:330.

229. Source: X73n1448 *Fachang Yiyu chanshi yulu* 1:68. Form: 7-j.

230. Source: X69n1343 *Baojue Zuxin chanshi yulu* 1:223. Form: 5-j.

231. Waley, *Analects*, 128.

232. Bio.: X80n1565 *Wudeng huiyuan* 17:353; X79n1560 *Chanlin seng baozhuan* 23:536; X77n1524 *Buxu Gaoseng zhuan* 8:422; X83n1578 *Zhiyue lu* 26:686–688.

233. Source: X69n1343 *Baojue Zuxin chanshi yulu* 1:224. Form: 7-j.

234. T48n2001 *Hongzhi Chanshi guanglu* 3:27.

235. Source: X69n1352 *Baiyun Shouduan chanshi guanglu* 3:320. Form: 5-lü.

236. Bio.: X79n1560 *Chanlin seng baozhuan* 28:548; X80n1565 *Wudeng huiyuan* 19:388.

237. Source: Du, *Chanshi sanbai shou*, 414. From *Canliaozi shiji* 7. Form: 5-j.

238. Bio.: Li E, *Songshi jishi* 91:2196; X77n1524 *Buxu Gaoseng zhuan* 23:520.

239. Source: X69n1353 *Kaifu Daoning chanshi yulu* 2:343. Form: 5-lü.

240. Bio.: X80n1565 *Wudeng huiyuan* 19:399; X77n1524 *Buxu Gaoseng zhuan* 10:439.

241. T48n2003 *Foguo Yuanwu chanshi Biyan lu* 6:192.

242. X69n1353 *Kaifu Daoning chanshi yulu* 2:341.

243. Source: X68n1318 *Xu Guzun suyu yao* 4:438. Form: 7-j.

244. Bio.: X80n1565 *Wudeng huiyuan* 19:393; X77n1524 *Buxu Gaoseng zhuan* 10:440.

245. T51n2076 *Jingde Chuandeng lu* 15:319.

246. Source: X68n1318 *Xu Guzun suyu yao* 4:439; #2 of 2. Form: 7-j.

247. Source: T51n2077 *Xu Chuandeng lu* 10:523. Form: Irr.

248. Bio.: X79n1560 *Chanlin seng baozhuan* 17:527; X80n1565 *Wudeng huiyuan* 14:291; quote translated in Schlütter, "Silent Illumination."

249. Source: X71n1425 *Danxia Zichun chanshi yulu* 1:761; #5 of 5. Form: 5-lü.

250. Bio.: X80n1565 *Wudeng huiyuan* 14:294; X77n1524 *Buxu Gaoseng zhuan* 9:430.

251. Source: X69n1347 *Changling Shouzhuo chanshi yulu* 1:270; #3 of 3. Form: 7-lü.

252. Bio.: X80n1565 *Wudeng huiyuan* 18:375; X83n1578 *Zhiyue lu* 29:711.

253. Source: X69n1347 *Changling Shouzhuo chanshi yulu* 1:270; #1 of 4. Form: 5-lü.

254. Watson, *Chuang Tzu*, 40, with modifications.

255. See Fung, *Chinese Philosophy*, 1:203–214.

256. T51n2076 *Jingde Chuandeng lu* 6:246; translated in Chang, *Original Teachings*, 149.

257. T51n2076 *Jingde Chuandeng lu* 6:246; translated in Chang, *Original Teachings*, 150.

258. Watson, *Chuang Tzu*, 40.

259. Source: T51n2077 *Xu Chuandeng lu* 23:624. Form: 7-j.

260. Bio.: X80n1565 *Wudeng huiyuan* 18:373; X83n1578 *Zhiyue lu* 29:710; Faure, *Rhetoric of Immediacy*, 190.

261. T51n2076 *Jingde Chuandeng lu* 12:291.

262. Yampolsky, *Platform Sutra*, 153.

263. T48n2003 *Foguo Yuanwu chanshi Biyan lu* 2:154, 7:193.

264. Translation from Sekida, *Two Zen Classics*, 53 (with modifications).

265. Source: T51n2077 *Xu Chuandeng lu* 23:624. Form: Irr.

266. Source: X73n1451 *Cishou Huaishen chanshi guanglu* 2:110; #6 of 10. Form: 7-j.

267. Bio.: X80n1565 *Wudeng huiyuan* 16:347; X83n1578 *Zhiyue lu* 28:709.

268. Sze, *Tao of Painting,* 129.

269. Source: X73n1451 *Cishou Huaishen chanshi guanglu* 2:115; #7 of 20. Form: 7-j.

270. Source: X73n1451 *Cishou Huaishen chanshi guanglu* 2:111; #2 of 2. Form: 7-j.

271. The story is recounted in T51n2076 *Jingde Chuandeng lu* 11:284.

272. Source: X65n1278 *Chanzong za duhai* 1:60. Form: 7-j.

273. Bio.: X80n1565 *Wudeng huiyuan* 14:294; X83n1578 *Zhiyue lu* 27:696.

274. T51n2077 *Xu Chuandeng lu* 12:542.

275. Source: T47n1998 *Dahui Pujue chanshi yulu* 11:858. Form: 7-j.

276. Bio.: X80n1565 *Wudeng huiyuan* 19:402; X83n1578 *Zhiyue lu* 31:730; Miura and Sasaki, *Zen Dust,* 163–165.

277. For example, T47n1998A *Dahui Pujue chanshi yulu* 29:938.

278. Source: T48n2001 *Hongzhi chanshi guanglu* 8:97. Form: 7-lü.

279. Bio.: X80n1565 *Wudeng huiyuan* 14:297; X83n1578 *Zhiyue lu* 28:708; Miura and Sasaki, *Zen Dust,* 170–171.

280. Source: T48n2001 *Hongzhi chanshi guanglu* 8:93. Form: 7-j.

281. T51n2076 *Jingde Chuandeng lu* 5:240.

282. Source: T48n2001 *Hongzhi chanshi guanglu* 8:87. Form: 7-j.

283. Source: T48n2001 *Hongzhi chanshi guanglu* 8:96. Form: 5-lü. *Ganzhong* as the temple position of bell ringer also appears in X70n1386 *Shitian Faxun chanshi yulu* 4:352.

284. Source: T48n2001 *Hongzhi chanshi guanglu* 8:89. Form: 7-lü.

285. Source: T48n2001 *Hongzhi chanshi guanglu* 9:120. Form: 4-shi.

286. T48n2010 *Xinxin ming* 1:376.

287. T19n945 *Da foding rulai miyin xiuzheng liaoyi zhupusa wanxing shoulengyan jing* 4:120.

288. Source: X65n1278 *Chanzong za duhai* 3:67. Form: 7-j.

289. Bio.: X80n1565 *Wudeng huiyuan* 20:416; X84n1579 *Xu Zhiyue lu* 1:16.

290. Source: X79n1559 *Jiatai Pudeng lu* 14:378. Form: 5-j.

291. Bio.: X79n1559 *Jiatai Pudeng lu* 14:378, X85n1593 *Chanzong zhengmai* 10:542; X83n1577 *Luohu yelu* 2:388.

292. Source: X79n1559 *Jiatai Pudeng lu* 14:378. Form: 7-j.

293. Source: T51n2077 *Xu Chuandeng lu* 34:702; and X65n1278 *Chanzong za duhai* 8:96. Form: 7-j.

294. Bio.: X80n1565 *Wudeng huiyuan* 20:440.

295. Source: X68n1318 *Xu Guzun suyu yao* 5:466. Form: 7-j.

296. Bio.: X80n1565 *Wudeng huiyuan* 20:423; X84n1579 *Xu Zhiyue lu* 1:21.

297. Source: T51n2077 *Xu Chuandeng lu* 30:673.

298. Bio.: T51n2077 *Xu Chuandeng lu* 30:673; X86n1611 *Conglin shengshi* 2:703; X80n1565 *Wudeng huiyuan* 16:351.

299. Source: X86n1611 *Conglin shengshi* 2:703. Form: 7-j.

300. Sekida, *Two Zen Classics*, 125.

301. X66n1296 *Zongmen nian'gu huiji* 40:230.

302. T47n1985 *Zhenzhou Linji Huizhao chanshi yulu* 1:500; translated by Watson in *Master Lin-chi*, 52.

303. T51n2076 *Jingde Chuandeng lu* 14:301.

304. Source: X86n1611 *Conglin shengshi* 2:701. Form: 5-j.

305. Bio.: X86n1611 *Conglin shengshi* 2:701; X80n1565 *Wudeng huiyuan* 20:439; X84n1579 *Xu Zhiyue lu* 2:33.

306. Source: X65n1278 *Chanzong za duhai* 6:89; #8 of 10 poems in the series "Following the Fish-catching Verses of Chan Master Juefan [Hui]hong." Form: 7-j.

307. Bio.: X82n1571 *Wudeng quanshu* 101:594.

308. Source: X65n1278 *Chanzong za duhai* 2:63. Form: 7-j.

309. Illustrated in Awakawa, *Zen Painting*, plates 14 and 15; on the painter Zhiweng, see 174.

310. Bio.: X84n1579 *Xu Zhiyue lu* 4:51; Komozawa daigaku, *Zengaku daijiten*, 14.

311. Li E, *Songshi jishi* 93:2266.

312. Source: X69n1361 *Jidian Daoji chanshi yulu* 1:615. Form: 7-lü.

313. Bio.: X77n1524 *Buxu Gaoseng zhuan* 19:501; Zhang, ed., *Zhongwen da cidian* (quoting the *Ji Gong Huofo shengzhuan*); Nienhauser, ed., *Indiana Companion*, 220 (entry by Colin Mackerras).

314. See T51n2076 *Jingde Chuandeng lu* 27:434.

315. Source: X77n1524 *Buxu Gaoseng zhuan* 19:501. Form: 7-j.

316. Source: X69n1361 *Jidian Daoji chanshi yulu* 1:617. Form: 7-j.

317. Source: X69n1361 *Jidian Daoji chanshi yulu* 1:618. Form: 6-j.

318. Source: X65n1278 *Chanzong za duhai* 2:65. Form: 7-j.

319. Bio.: T51n2077 *Xu Chuandeng lu* 35:707; X85n1594 *Fozu gangmu* 39:782.

320. Source: X65n1278 *Chanzong za duhai* 6:85. Form: 7-j.

321. Bio.: Li E, *Songshi jishi* 92:2212–2214; Wei, *Shiren yuxie* 20, quoting *Xiqing shihua*; Lü Ben-zhong, *Jiangxi shishe zongpai tu* is contained in Huzi, *Tiaoxi yuyin conghua*.

322. T47n1998 *Dahui Pujue chanshi yulu* 14:868.

323. Source: X70n1376 *Chijue Daochong chanshi yulu* 2:77. Form: 7-j.

324. Bio.: X77n1524 *Buxu Gaoseng zhuan* 11:449; X84n1579 *Xu Zhiyue lu* 4:48.

325. Source: X69n1355 *Wumen Huikai chanshi yulu* 2:366. Form: 7-j.

326. X73n1446 *Xuansha Shibei chanshi yulu* 1:29.

327. Bio.: X77n1524 *Buxu Gaoseng zhuan* 19:500; Miura and Sasaki, *Zen Dust*, 203–205.

328. Source: X69n1355 *Wumen Huikai chanshi yulu* 2:367. Form: 7-j.

329. T51n2076 *Jingde Chuandeng lu*, ch. 30:456–457.

330. Source: Yoshizawa, ed., *Gōko Fūgetsushū* (*Jianghu fengyue ji*), 61–63; also in T47n2000 *Xutang heshang yulu* 7:1034. Form: 7-j.

331. Bio.: X84n1579 *Xu Zhiyue lu* 5:57; Miura and Sasaki, *Zen Dust*, 206–207; Brinker, *Zen in the Art of Painting*, 97.

332. Source: Yoshizawa, ed., *Gōko Fūgetsushū* (*Jianghu fengyue ji*), 63–64; also in T47n2000 *Xutang heshang yulu* 7:1034. Form: 7-j.

333. T51n2076 *Jingde Chuandeng lu* 27:431.

334. Source: Yoshizawa, ed., *Gōko Fūgetsushū* (*Jianghu fengyue ji*), 76–77. Form: 7-j.

335. T19n945 *Da foding rulai miyin xiuzheng liaoyi zhupusa wanxing shoulengyan jing* 5:126.

336. Source: T47n2000 *Xutang heshang yulu* 7:1035. Form: 7-j.

337. T51n2076 *Jingde Chuandeng lu* 8:258.

338. X71n1411 *Hengchuan Xinggong chanshi yulu* 2:200.

339. Source: Du, *Chanshi sanbai shou*, 542; from Wuwen Daocan, *Liutang waiji*. Form: 7-j.

340. Bio.: X69n1372 *Wuwen Daocan chanshi yulu*.

341. Cleary and Cleary, *Blue Cliff*, 74; T48n2003 *Foguo Yuanwu chanshi Biyan lu* 2:151.

342. Source: X69n1372 *Wuwen Daocan chanshi yulu* 1:811. Form: 7-j.

343. Source: X71n1411 *Hengchuan Xinggong chanshi yulu* 2:203; #20 of 20. Form: 5-gu.

344. Bio.: X77n1524 *Buxu Gaoseng zhuan* 12:457; X84n1579 *Xu Zhiyue lu* 5:56.

345. Source: X71n1411 *Hengchuan Xinggong chanshi yulu* 2:205. Form: 4-shi.

346. X83n1576 *Xuetang Xing shiyi lu* 1:764.

347. Source: X70n1392 *Yuejian chanshi yulu* 2:529. Form: 7-j.

348. Bio.: X70n1392 *Yuejian chanshi yulu*.

349. Source: X70n1392 *Yuejian chanshi yulu* 2:529. Form: Irr.

350. Source: X70n1392 *Yuejian chanshi yulu* 2:529. Form: 7-j.

351. T51n2076 *Jingde Chuandeng lu* 9:265; translated in Chang, *Original Teachings*, 204.

352. Source: Yoshizawa, ed., *Gōko Fūgetsushū* (*Jianghu fengyue ji*), 233–244. Form: 7-j.

353. Bio.: T51n2077 *Xu Chuandeng lu* 36:713.

354. Watson, *Chuang Tzu*, 193.

355. Cleary and Cleary, *Blue Cliff*, 15; T48n2003 *Foguo Yuanwu chanshi Biyan lu* 1:142.

356. Source: X72n1431 *Yunwai Yunxiu chanshi yulu* 1:174. Form: 7-j.

357. Bio.: X72n1431 *Yunwai Yunxiu chanshi yulu*; X84n1579 *Xu Zhiyue lu* 3:45.

358. Source: Yoshizawa, ed., *Gōko Fūgetsushū* (*Jianghu fengyue ji*), 493–494. Form: 7-j.

359. Bio.: X83n1574 *Zengji Xu Chuandeng lu* 5:321.

360. Source: X71n1413 *Gulin Qingmao chanshi shiyi qiesong* 2:284; #2 of 2. Form: 7-lü.

361. Bio.: X84n1579 *Xu Zhiyue lu* 6:68.

362. T51n2076 *Jingde Chuandeng lu* 12:290.

363. T48n2005 *Wumenguan* 1:295; translated in Sekida, *Two Zen Classics*, 68.

364. T47n1993 *Huanglong Huinan chanshi yulu* 1:635.

365. T12n360 *Foshuo Wuliang shou jing* 2:273.

366. T47n1985 *Zhenzhou Linji Huizhao chanshi yulu* 1:498.

367. T47n1985 *Zhenzhou Linji Huizhao chanshi yulu* 1:498; translated in Chang, *Original Teachings*, 122.

368. T48n2005 *Wumenguan* 1:293; translated in Sekida, *Two Zen Classics*, 41.

369. In *Tiansheng guangdeng lu*, completed in 1036; see Foulk, "Myth, Ritual, and Monastic Practice," 253.

370. Source: X65n1278 *Chanzong za duhai* 5:80. Form: 7-j.

371. Bio.: X77n1524 *Buxu Gaoseng zhuan* 13:461; X84n1579 *Xu Zhiyue lu* 7:73; Brinker, *Zen in the Art of Painting*, 97–99.

372. T51n2076 *Jingde Chuandeng lu* 3:219; see also McRae, *Platform Sutra*, 108.

373. T51n2076 *Jingde Chuandeng lu* 9:266; X81n1571 *Wudeng quanshu* 7:467.

374. Source: X70n1402 *Tianmu Mingben chanshi zalu* 3:744. Form: 7-j.

375. X74n1445 *Xuansha Shibei chanshi guanglu* 3:21; cited in Faure, *Chan Insights and Oversights*, 166.

376. Source: X70n1396 *Wujian Xiandu chanshi yulu* 2:587. Form: 5-j.

377. Bio.: X77n1524 *Buxu Gaoseng zhuan* 13:460; X84n1579 *Xu Zhiyue lu* 7:76.

378. Source: X70n1396 *Wujian Xiandu chanshi yulu* 2:589; #17 of 69. Form: 7-lü.

379. See Chan'an Jushi, *Gaoseng shanju shi*.

380. Source: X70n1396 *Wujian Xiandu chanshi yulu* 2:588; #3 of 69. Form: 7-lü.

381. Source: X70n1396 *Wujian Xiandu chanshi yulu* 2:590; #38 of 69. Form: 7-lü.

382. Source: X71n1420 *Chushi Fanqi chanshi yulu* 19:651. Form: 7-j.

383. Bio.: X77n1524 *Buxu Gaoseng zhuan* 14:469; X84n1579 *Xu Zhiyue lu* 5:58; He and Xie, *Lidai mingseng*, 581–586

384. Faure, *Chan Insights and Oversights*, 200.

385. Source: X71n1421 *Yu'an Zhiji chanshi yulu* 9:696; #1 of 3. Form: 5-lü.

386. Bio.: X77n1524 *Buxu Gaoseng zhuan* 14:468; X84n1579 *Xu Zhiyue lu* 5:59.

387. Source: X70n1403 *Tianru Weize chanshi yulu* 4:791; #3 of 10. Form: 7-j.

388. Bio.: X84n1579 *Xu Zhiyue lu* 8:84.

389. Source: X70n1403 *Tianru Weize chanshi yulu* 5:801; #4 of 4. Form: 7-j.

390. Source: X70n1403 *Tianru Weize chanshi yulu* 5:801. Form: 7-j.

391. Source: X70n1403 *Tianru Weize chanshi yulu* 5:800; #3 of 3. Form: 5-gu.

392. Source: X82n1571 *Wudeng quanshu* 56:212. Form: 5-j.

393. Bio.: X77n1524 *Buxu Gaoseng zhuan* 14:471; X82n1571 *Wudeng quanshu* 56:211; X84n1571 *Xu Zhiyue lu* 6:70.

394. Source: X71n1418 *Dai'an Puzhuang chanshi yulu* 8:509; #2 of 4. Form: 5-gu.

395. Bio.: X77n1524 *Buxu Gaoseng zhuan* 18:496; X84n1579 *Xu Zhiyue lu* 8:85.

396. Source: X71n1418 *Dai'an Puzhuang chanshi yulu* 6:502. Form: 5-gu.

397. Cleary and Cleary, *Blue Cliff*, 216; T48 n2003 *Foguo Yuanwu chanshi Biyan lu* 4:173.

398. T47n1988 *Yunmen Kuangzhen chanshi guanglu* 1:545.

399. Source: X73n1452 *Zibo zunzhe quanji* 20:320. Form: 7-j.

400. Bio.: X80n1566 *Wudeng huiyuan xulue* 2:496; X84n1579 *Xu Zhiyue lu* 20; Goodrich and Fang, *Ming Biography*.

401. Yampolsky, *Platform Sutra*, 127; T48n2008 *Liuzu dashi fabao tanjing* 1:348.

402. Source: X73n1456 *Hanshan laoren mengyou ji* 37:733. Form: 7-j.

403. Bio.: X84n1585 *Xudeng cungao* 12:795; Goodrich and Fang, *Ming Biography;* Hsu, *Buddhist Leader in Ming China;* Ho and Xie, *Lidai mingseng*, 619–624.

404. Source: X73n1456 *Hanshan laoren mengyou ji* 49:806; #17 of 28. Form: 7-j.

405. Source: X73n1456 *Hanshan laoren mengyou ji* 48:794. Form: 5-lü.

406. Source: X73n1456 *Hanshan laoren mengyou ji* 48:795; #6 of 10. Form: 5-lü.

407. Source: X73n1456 *Hanshan laoren mengyou ji* 48:795; #1 of 3. Form: 5-lü.

408. Source: Chen Xiang, *Chanshi liubai shou,* 131. From *Miyun chanshi yulu,* in *Zhonghua Dazangjing* (H01741). Form: 7-j.

409. Bio.: X80n1566 *Wudeng huiyuan xulue* 4:529; X65n1280 *Piwang jiu lueshuo* 9:177; X84n1579 *Xu Zhiyue lu* 18:125.

410. T51n2076 *Jingde Chuandeng lu* 7:254.

411. Source: Chen Xiang, *Chanshi liubai shou,* 131; from *Miyun chanshi yulu,* in *Zhonghua Dazangjing* (H01741). Form: 7-j.

412. Source: X72n1435 *Wuyi Yuanlai chanshi guanglu* 34:376. Form: 5-lü.

413. Bio.: X72n1435 *Wuyi Yuanlai chanshi guanglu* 35:378.

414. Source: X72n1435 *Wuyi Yuanlai chanshi guanglu* 34:374. Form: 5-gu.

415. Source: X72n1437 *Yongjue Yuanxian chanshi guanglu* 24:523; #1 of 4. Form: 5-lü.

416. Bio.: X72n1437 *Yongjue Yuanxian chanshi guanglu* 30:576.

417. Source: X72n1437 *Yongjue Yuanxian chanshi guanglu* 25:529. Form: 7-lü.

418. T48n2003 *Foguo Yuanwu chanshi Biyan lu* 5:180.

419. Source: X72n1437 *Yongjue Yuanxian chanshi guanglu* 24:523. Form: 5-lü.

420. Source: X72n1437 *Yongjue Yuanxian chanshi guanglu* 24:525. Form: 5-gu.

421. Source: X72n1437 *Yongjue Yuanxian chanshi guanglu* 24:525; #2 of 2. Form: 5-lü.

422. T50n2059 *Gaoseng zhuan* 13:415.

423. Source: X72n1437 *Yongjue Yuanxian chanshi guanglu* 24:518. Form: 5-gu.

424. Source: X72n1437 *Yongjue Yuanxian chanshi guanglu* 24:519. Form: 5-gu.

425. Li Fang, *Taiping Guangji* 60:370, from *Shenxian zhuan* 7.

426. Source: X65n1278 *Chanzong za duhai* 4:77. Form: 7-j.

427. Bio.: X82n1571 *Wudeng quanshu* 62:276.

Glossary

aluohan 阿羅漢

anxin 安心

asheli 阿闍梨

bafeng 八風

bailian 白蓮

bailu shating li, luhua xiangdui kai 白鷺沙汀立 蘆花相對開

baima ru luhua 白馬入蘆花

baizhang gantou 百丈竿頭

banruo 般若

baoshen 報身

benlai ren 本來人

benlai 本來

biding 壁定

biguan 壁觀

binang 敝囊

bingzhu yeyou 炳燭夜游, 秉燭夜游

boluomi 波羅密

buli wenzi 不立文字

buqiu 布裘

buranxing 不染性

busi 不死

cao'an 草庵

caotang 草堂

Caoyuan yidi shui 曹源一滴水

chan (Chan Buddhism) 禪

chan (cicada) 蟬

chanding 禪定

chanji 禪機

chanku 禪窟

channa 禪那

chanzong 禪宗

chaoshi 超師

che 車

chen'ai 塵埃

chi 癡

chou pidai 臭皮袋

chuan daoqing 傳道情

chuandeng 傳燈

conglin 叢林

cunsi bugua 寸絲不掛

dafenzhi 大奮志

dan wushen 淡吾身

dao 道

dasheng 大乘

dasi 大死

daxin'gen 大信根

dayiqing 大疑情

ding 定

dong 動

dujue 獨覺

dulong 毒龍

dushe 毒蛇

duyu 杜宇

echu 惡處

edao 惡道

fa 法

fahai 法海

fajie 法界

falun 法輪

fanbai 梵唄

fanben huanyuan 返本還源

fangbian 方便

fangzhang laoren 方丈老人

fannao 煩惱

fansheng 凡聖

fansheng yiru 凡聖一如

fashen 法身

feixin feifo 非心非佛

fo 佛

foxing 佛性

ganlu 甘露

gong'an 公案

guan 觀

guankong 觀空

guanxin 觀心

gushi 古詩

guti shi 古體詩

haizhong 海眾

han 寒

hanxu 含蓄

hao 號

huangye zhiti 黃葉止啼

huashen 化身

huatou 話頭

huiguang fanzhao 迴光返照

huiyan 慧眼

hushen 護身

hushen jiachi 護身加持

ji 跡

jiaowai biechuan 教外別傳

jie 借

jijing 機境

Jin'gangwang baojian 金剛王寶劍

jing (realm) 境

jing (tranquility, stillness) 靜

Jingtu 淨土

jinti shi 近體詩

jiucai 韭菜

jixin jifo 即心即佛

jixin shifo 即心是佛

jiyuan wenda 機緣問答

jueju 絕句

jueshu 覺樹

junchen wuwei 君臣五位

jushi 居士

kanxin 看心

kong 空

kongmen 空門

kongwang 空王

kouguan 叩關

ku 窟

kuchan 枯禪

kumu 枯木

kumu chan 枯木禪

kumu hanhui 枯木寒灰

kumu huakai jiewai chun 枯木花開劫外春

kumu yi hanyan, sandong wu nuanqi 枯木依寒巖 三冬無暖氣

kumu zai shenghua 枯木再生花

li (principle of the absolute) 理

li (unit of distance) 里

liaoyi 了義

linggen 靈根

linian 離念

liuchen jingjie 六塵境界

liudao 六道

liugen 六根

liuqu 六趣

lunhui 輪回

luohan 羅漢

lüshi 律詩

luye Damo 蘆葉達摩

miaoji 妙機

mihou tan shuiyue 獼猴探水月

Mile fo 彌勒佛

mozhao 默照

mozhi 默知

nian 念

niepan 涅槃

niezu zhi ji 齧鏃之機

pian 偏

pidai 皮袋

pidaigu 皮袋骨

Pilu 毗盧

pingchang xin 平常心

pingdan 平淡

pingsheng dao 平生道

pu 普

pubu 瀑布

puliu 瀑流

puqing 普請

pusa 菩薩

qi 氣

qibao 七寶

qie 伽

qietuo 伽陀

qing 清

qingjing 清境

qingjing jiaorong 情景交融

qingliang 清涼

qitong 漆同

ranwuyi 染污意

roushen 肉身

Rulai 如來

rulaizang 如來藏

sandong kumu xiu, jiuxia xuehua fei 三冬枯木
秀 九夏雪花飛

sandu 三毒

sanfayin 三法印

sanjie 三界

sanmei 三昧

sanshi fo 三世佛

sanshi na 三事衲

sanshi zhufo kou gua bishang
三世諸佛口掛壁上

sanxuan sanyao 三玄三要

se 色

sejie 色界

shangfang 上方

sheli 舍利

shengsheng 生生

shengwen 聲聞

shi (phenomena) 事

shi (poem) 詩

shi fajie 十法界

shifang shijie 十方世界

Shijia mouni 釋迦牟尼

shijie 十界

shi'nei yizhan deng 室內一盞燈

shiseng 詩僧

shoujie 守節

shouxin 守心

shu daoqing 抒道情

shuijing 水精/水晶

shuizhong laoyue 水中撈月

shuqing shi 抒情詩

si (thoughts) 思

si (threads) 絲

si binzhu 四賓主

sihai 四海

songmen 松門

sudi 俗諦

suibo zhulang 隨波逐浪

suihan sanyou 歲寒三友

suiyuan jiewu 隨緣接物

taixu 太虛

ti 體

tianren shi 天人師

tianzhen fo 天真佛

tieshu 鐵樹

tongdi tuo 桶底脫

tongsu 通俗

touhe 投和

touji 投機

tuoluoni 陀羅尼

wanxiang 萬象

weiwo duzun 唯我獨尊

wenjin 問津

wenzi chan 文字禪

wu 無

wugen shu 無根樹

wuming 無名

wuming ku 無明窟

wunian 無念

wuqing shuofa 無情說法

wuseding 無色定

wusejie 無色界

wuwei (Five Ranks) 五位

wuwei (nonaction/*nirvāṇa*) 無為

wuwei zhenren 無位真人

wuwo zhi jing 無我之境

wuwu 無物

wuxin 無心

wuyun 五蘊

wuzhu (nonabiding) 無住

wuzhu (unattached) 無著

wuzhuchu 無住處

xinchuan 心傳

xindi 心地

xintian 心田

xinwen 心聞

xinxin 心心

xinxinxin 心心心

xinyin 心印

xiyi 希夷

xuanwei 玄微

xuanzhi 玄旨

xuehai 學海

xun XX buyu 尋 XX 不遇

yanwai zhi yi 言外之意

yaoji 要機

yaomiao 要妙

ye 業

yecha 夜叉

yexing ren 夜行人

yi 疑

yichang santan 一唱三歎

yijing 意境

yiju 一句

yingbing yuyao 應病與藥

yinke 印可

yinuo quanjin 一諾千金

yisi bugua 一絲不掛

yituan 疑團

yixing sanmei 一行三昧

yiyan 一言

yizhu 衣珠

yong 用

yongwu shi 詠物詩

you 有

youwo zhi jing 有我之境

youwu (existence) 有物

youwu (having and not having) 有無

yuan 遠

yujie 欲界

yulu 語錄

yungen 雲根

yunshui seng 雲水僧

yunying 雲影

zangshi 藏識

zhendi 真諦

zhenfo wuli zuo 真佛屋裡坐

zheng 正

zhenru 真如

zhenxin 真心

zhenxing 真性
zhi 指
zhi 止
zhihui 智慧
zhizutian 知足天
zhongzi 種子
zhuan 轉
zhuanchu 轉處

zhuandu 轉讀
zhurengong 主人公
zhurenweng 主人翁
zi 字
zigui 子歸
zongchi 總持
zuochan 坐禪

Bibliography

Abbreviations

Blue Cliff	*Foguo Yuanwu chanshi Biyan lu* (The Blue Cliff Record). T48n2003. For translations, see under Thomas and J. C. Cleary, and Sekida Katsuki.
Eminent Monks	*Song Gaoseng zhuan* (Biographies of Eminent Monks Compiled in the Song Period). T50n2061.
Gateless Pass	*Wumenguan* (The Gateless Pass). T48n2005. For a translation, see under Sekida Katsuki.
QTS	*Quan Tang shi* (The Complete Tang Poems). See under Peng Dingqiu.
T	*Taishō shinshū daizōkyō* (Taisho Era Edition of the Buddhist Canon). See under Takakusu Junjirō.
Transmission	*Jingde Chuandeng lu* (*Record of the Transmission of the Lamp* Compiled in the Jingde Era). T51n2076. For a partial translation, see under Chang Chung-yuan.
X	*Xu zang jing* (Supplement to the Buddhist Canon). See under Maeda Eun.

Awakawa, Yasuichi. *Zen Painting*. Trans. John Bester. Tokyo: Kodansha International, 1970.

Berling, Judith A. "Bringing the Buddha down to Earth: Notes on the Emergence of *Yü-lu* as a Buddhist Genre." *History of Religions* 27, no. 1 (1987): 56–88.

Bielefeldt, Carl. "Ch'ang-lu Tsung-tse's *Tso-Ch'an I* and the 'Secret' of Zen Meditation." In *Traditions of Meditation in Chinese Buddhism*, ed. Peter N. Gregory, 129–161.

———. *Dōgen's Manuals of Zen Meditation*. Berkeley: University of California Press, 1988.

———, trans. "Mountains and Waters Sūtra: *Shōbōgenzō* sansui kyō." Soto Zen Text Project. http://hcbss.stanford.edu/research/projects/sztp/translations/shobogenzo/translations/sansuikyo/sansuikyo.html.

Birnbaum, Raoul. "Thoughts on T'ang Buddhist Mountain Traditions and Their Context." *T'ang Studies* 2 (1984): 5–23.

Blofeld, John, trans. *The Zen Teaching of Huang-po: On the Transmission of Mind*. New York: Grove, 1959.

Bodiford, William, ed. *Going Forth: Visions of Buddhist Vinaya*. Honolulu: University of Hawai'i Press, 2005.

Brinker, Helmut. *Zen in the Art of Painting*. Trans. George Campbell. New York and London: Arkana (Routledge and Kegan Paul), 1987.

Buswell, Robert E. "Chinul's Systematization of Chinese Meditative Techniques in Korean Sŏn Buddhism." In *Traditions of Meditation in Chinese Buddhism*, ed. Peter N. Gregory, 199–242.

——. *The Korean Approach to Zen: The Collected Works of Chinul*. Honolulu: University of Hawai'i Press, 1983.

——. "The 'Short-cut' Approach of *K'an-hua* Meditation: The Evolution of a Practical Subitism in Chinese Ch'an Buddhism." In *Sudden and Gradual: Approaches to Enlightenment in Chinese Thought*, ed. Peter N. Gregory, 321–377.

Buswell, Robert E. and Robert M. Gimello, eds. *Paths to Liberation: The Mārga and Its Transformations in Buddhist Thought*. Honolulu: University of Hawai'i Press, 1992.

Cai, Zong-qi, ed. *How to Read Chinese Poetry: A Guided Anthology*. New York: Columbia University Press, 2008.

Cahill, James. "Tung Ch'i-ch'ang's 'Southern and Northern Schools' in the History and Theory of Painting: A Reconsideration." In *Sudden and Gradual: Approaches to Enlightenment in Chinese Thought*, ed. Peter N. Gregory, 429–446.

Chan'an Jushi. *Gaoseng shanju shi* ("Living in the Mountains" Poems by Eminent Monks). Shanghai: Shangwu, 1934. Also Taipei: Guangwen, 1971.

Chang, Chung-yuan. *Original Teachings of Ch'an Buddhism: Selected from* The Transmission of the Lamp. New York: Random House, 1969.

Chang, Kang-i Sun. "Description of Landscapes in Early Six Dynasties Poetry." In *The Vitality of the Lyric Voice: Shih Poetry from the Late Han to the T'ang*, ed. Shuen-fu Lin and Stephen Owen, 105–129.

Chappell, David W., ed. *Buddhist and Taoist Practice in Medieval Chinese Society*. Honolulu: University of Hawai'i Press, 1987.

——. "From Dispute to Dual Cultivation: Pure Land Responses to Ch'an Critics." In *Traditions of Meditation in Chinese Buddhism*, ed. Peter N. Gregory, 163–197.

——. "The Teachings of the Fourth Ch'an Patriarch Tao-hsin (580–651)." In *Early Ch'an in China and Tibet*, ed. Whalen Lai and Lewis R. Lancaster, 89–129.

Chaves, Jonathan. *Mei Yao-ch'en and the Development of Early Sung Poetry*. New York: Columbia University Press, 1976.

Ch'en, Kenneth S. *The Chinese Transformation of Buddhism*. Princeton: Princeton University Press, 1973.

Chen, Xiang (Ch'en Hsiang), comp. *Chanshi liubai shou* (Six Hundred Chan Poems). Taipei: Guojia, 1982.

Cheng, François. *Chinese Poetic Writing: With an Anthology of T'ang Poetry*. Trans. Donald A. Riggs and Jerome P. Seaton. Bloomington: Indiana University Press, 1982.

Chinese Buddhist Electronic Text Association (CBETA). http://www.cbeta.org/index.htm.

Cleary, Christopher [J. C.], trans. *Swampland Flowers: The Letters and Lectures of Zen Master Ta Hui*. New York: Grove, 1977.

Cleary, Thomas, trans. *Book of Serenity: One Hundred Zen Dialogues*. Boston and London: Shambhala, 1998.

——, trans. *The Flower Ornament Scripture: A Translation of the Avatamsaka Sutra*. Boulder, Colo.: Shambhala, 1984.

Cleary, Thomas and J. C. Cleary, trans. *The Blue Cliff Record*. Boston and London: Shambhala, 1992.

Collcutt, Martin. "The Early Ch'an Monastic Rule: *Ch'ing kuei* and the Shaping of Ch'an Community Life." In *Early Ch'an in China and Tibet*, ed. Whalen Lai and Lewis R. Lancaster, 165–184.

——. *Five Mountains: The Rinzai Zen Monastic Institution in Medieval Japan*. 1981; reprint, Cambridge, Mass.: Harvard University Press, 1996.

Conze, Edward. *Buddhist Thought in India: Three Phases of Buddhist Philosophy*. London: Allen and Unwin, 1962.

——. "The Ontology of the *Prajñāpāramitā*." *Philosophy East and West* 3 (1953).

——, trans. *The Perfection of Wisdom in Eight Thousand Lines and Its Verse Summary*. Bolinas, Calif.: Four Seasons Foundation, 1973.

——. *The Prajñāpāramitā Literature*. 's-Gravenhage (The Hague): Mouton, 1960.

——, trans. *The Short Prajnaparamita Texts*. London: Luzac and Co., 1973.

Demiéville, Paul. "The Mirror of the Mind." Trans. Neal Donner. In *Sudden and Gradual: Approaches to Enlightenment in Chinese Thought*, ed. Peter N. Gregory, 13–40.

Ding, Fubao (Ting Fu-pao). *Foxue da zidian* (Dictionary of Buddhism). 4 vols. Taipei: Huayan lianshe, 1959.

Donner, Neal. "Sudden and Gradual Intimately Conjoined: Chih-i's T'ien-t'ai View." In *Sudden and Gradual: Approaches to Enlightenment in Chinese Thought*, ed. Peter N. Gregory, 201–226.

Du, Songbo (Tu Sung-po). *Chanshi sanbai shou* (Three Hundred Chan Poems). Taipei: Liming, 1981.

——. *Chanxue yu Tang Song shixue* (Chan Studies and Studies on Tang and Song Poetry). Taipei: Liming, 1976.

Ebrey, Patricia Buckley and Peter N. Gregory, eds. *Religion and Society in T'ang and Sung China.* Honolulu: University of Hawai'i Press, 1993.

Faure, Bernard. *Chan Insights and Oversights: An Epistemological Critique of the Chan Tradition.* Princeton: Princeton University Press, 1993.

——. "The Concept of One-Practice Samādhi in Early Ch'an." In *Traditions of Meditation in Chinese Buddhism,* ed. Peter N. Gregory, 99–128.

——. *The Rhetoric of Immediacy: A Cultural Critique of Chan/Zen Buddhism.* Princeton: Princeton University Press, 1991.

——. *The Will to Orthodoxy: A Critical Genealogy of Northern Chan Buddhism.* Trans. Phyllis Brooks. Stanford: Stanford University Press, 1997.

Ferguson, Andrew, trans. *Zen's Chinese Heritage: The Masters and Their Teachings.* Somerville, Mass.: Wisdom, 2000.

Foulk, T. Griffith. "Myth, Ritual, and Monastic Practice in Sung Ch'an Buddhism." In *Religion and Society in T'ang and Sung China,* ed. Patricia Buckley Ebrey and Peter N. Gregory, 147–208.

——. "Religious Functions of Buddhist Art in China." In *Cultural Intersections in Later Chinese Buddhism,* ed. Marsha Weidner, 13–29.

——. "Sung Controversies Concerning the 'Separate Transmission' of Ch'an." In *Buddhism in the Sung,* ed. Peter N. Gregory and Daniel A. Getz Jr., 220–294.

Frankel, Hans H. *The Flowering Plum and the Palace Lady: Interpretations of Chinese Poetry.* New Haven: Yale University Press, 1976.

Frodsham, J. D. *The Murmuring Stream.* Kuala Lumpur: University of Malaya Press, 1967.

——. "The Origins of Chinese Nature Poetry." *Asia Major* 8, no. 1 (1960): 68–104.

Frye, Northrop. *Anatomy of Criticism: Four Essays.* 1957; reprint, Princeton: Princeton University Press, 1973.

Fung, Yu-lan. *A History of Chinese Philosophy.* Trans. Derk Bodde. 2nd ed. Princeton: Princeton University Press, 1952.

Gao, Buying, ed. *Tang Song shi juyao* (Essential Poems of the Tang and Song Dynasties). 1959; reprint, Hong Kong: Zhonghua, 1985.

Gimello, Robert M. "Mārga and Culture: Learning, Letters, and Liberation in Northern Sung Ch'an." In *Paths to Liberation: The Mārga and Its Transformations in Buddhist Thought,* ed. Robert E. Buswell and Robert M. Gimello, 371–437.

Gimello, Robert M. and Peter N. Gregory, eds. *Studies in Ch'an and Hua-yen.* Honolulu: University of Hawai'i Press, 1983.

Gómez, Luis O. "Purifying Gold: The Metaphor of Effort and Intuition in Buddhist Thought and Practice." In *Sudden and Gradual: Approaches to Enlightenment in Chinese Thought,* ed. Peter N. Gregory, 67–165.

——. "Selected Verses from the *Gaṇḍavyūha.*" Ph.D. diss., Yale University, 1967.

Goodrich, L. Carrington and Chaoying Fang, eds. *Dictionary of Ming Biography, 1368–1644.* New York: Columbia University Press, 1976.

Grant, Beata. *Daughters of Emptiness: Poems of Chinese Buddhist Nuns.* Somerville, Mass.: Wisdom, 2003.

——. *Eminent Nuns: Women Chan Masters of Seventeenth-century China.* Honolulu: University of Hawai'i Press, 2008.

——. *Mount Lu Revisited: Buddhism in the Life and Writings of Su Shih.* Honolulu: University of Hawai'i Press, 1994.

——. "Through the Empty Gate: The Poetry of Buddhist Nuns in Late Imperial China." In *Cultural Intersections in Later Chinese Buddhism,* ed. Marsha Weidner, 87–113.

Gregory, Peter N. *Inquiry into the Origin of Humanity: An Annotated Translation of Tsung-mi's Yuan jen lun.* Honolulu: University of Hawai'i Press, 1995.

——, ed. *Sudden and Gradual: Approaches to Enlightenment in Chinese Thought.* Honolulu: University of Hawai'i Press, 1987.

——. "Sudden Enlightenment Followed by Gradual Cultivation: Tsung-mi's Analysis of Mind." In *Sudden and Gradual: Approaches to Enlightenment in Chinese Thought,* ed. Peter N. Gregory, 279–320.

——, ed. *Traditions of Meditation in Chinese Buddhism.* Honolulu: University of Hawai'i Press, 1986.

——. *Tsung-mi and the Sinification of Buddhism.* Honolulu: University of Hawai'i Press, 2002.

Gregory, Peter N. and Daniel A. Getz Jr., eds. *Buddhism in the Sung.* Honolulu: University of Hawai'i Press, 1999.

Guangwen bianyi suo (Guangwen Editorial Committee), ed. *Zhuzi huiyao* (Assembled Essential Writings of the Philosophers). Taipei: Guangwen, 1965.

Hakeda, Yoshito S. *The Awakening of Faith: Attributed to Aśvaghosha.* New York and London: Columbia University Press, 1967.

Hamill, Sam, and Jerome P. Seaton, trans. *The Poetry of Zen.* Boston: Shambhala, 2004.

Hammond, Kenneth J. "Beijing's Zhihua Monastery: History and Restoration in China's Capital." In *Cultural Intersections in Later Chinese Buddhism,* ed. Marsha Weidner, 189–208.

Harvey, Peter. *An Introduction to Buddhism: Teachings, History, and Practices.* Cambridge, U.K.: Cambridge University Press, 1990.

He, Ziquan and Xie Chongguang, eds. *Zhongguo lidai mingseng* (Famous Chinese Monks Through the Dynasties). Henan: Henan renmin, 1995.

Heine, Steven. "A Critical Survey of Works on Zen Since Yampolsky." *Philosophy East and West* 57, no. 4 (Oct. 2007): 577–592.

Heine, Steven and Dale S. Wright, eds. *The Kōan: Texts and Contexts in Zen Buddhism.* Oxford: Oxford University Press, 2000.

——, eds. *The Zen Canon: Understanding the Classic Texts.* Oxford: Oxford University Press, 2004.

Henricks, Robert, trans. *The Poetry of Han-shan: A Complete, Annotated Translation of Cold Mountain*. Albany: State University of New York Press, 1990.

Herrnstein-Smith, Barbara. *Poetic Closure: A Study of How Poems End*. Chicago: University of Chicago Press, 1968.

Hershock, Peter D. *Chan Buddhism*. Honolulu: University of Hawai'i Press, 2004.

Hobson, Peter, trans. *Poems of Hanshan*. Walnut Creek, Calif.: AltaMira Press, 2003.

Horner, Isaline B., ed. *Early Buddhist Poetry: An Anthology*. Colombo, Ceylon: Ananda Semage, 1963.

Hsieh, Ding-hwa E. "Images of Women in Ch'an Buddhist Literature of the Sung Period." In *Buddhism in the Sung*, ed. Peter N. Gregory and Daniel A. Getz Jr., 148–187.

Hsu, Sung-peng. *A Buddhist Leader in Ming China: The Life and Thought of Han-shan Te-ch'ing, 1546–1623*. University Park: Pennsylvania State University Press, 1979.

Huang, Chi-chiang. "Elite and Clergy in Northern Sung Hang-chou: A Convergence of Interest." In *Buddhism in the Sung*, ed. Peter N. Gregory and Daniel A. Getz Jr., 295–339.

Huzi. *Tiaoxi yuyin conghua* (Compendium of Poetry Criticism of the Fisherman Recluse of Tiao Stream). Taipei: Zhonghua, 1965.

Inagaki, Hisao. *A Glossary of Zen Terms*. Kyoto: Nagata Bunshodo, 1991.

Iritani, Sensuke and Matsumura Takashi. *Kanzan shi* (Poems of Hanshan). Zen no goroku 13. Tokyo: Chikuma Shobō, 1970.

Iriya, Yoshitaka. "Chinese Poetry and Zen." *The Eastern Buddhist* 6, no. 1 (1973): 54–67.

——. *Kanzan* (Hanshan). Chūgoku shijin senshū 5. Tokyo: Iwanami Shoten, 1958.

Iriya, Yoshitaka and Koga Hidehiko, eds. *Zengo jiten* (Dictionary of Zen Terms). Kyoto: Shibunkaku, 1991.

Ji, Yun, ed. *Yingyin Wenyuange Siku quanshu* (Photo-reprint of the Wenyuan Library Complete Books of the Four Treasuries). Taipei: Taiwan Shangwu, 1983–1986.

Jin, Jinhua. *The Hongzhou School of Chan Buddhism in Eighth- Through Tenth-century China*. Albany: State University of New York Press, 2007.

Kao, Yu-kung. "Chinese Lyric Aesthetics." In *Words and Images: Chinese Poetry, Calligraphy, and Painting*, ed. Alfreda Murck and Wen Fong, 47–90.

Kao, Yu-kung and Tsu-lin Mei. "Meaning, Metaphor, and Allusion in T'ang Poetry." *Harvard Journal of Asiatic Studies* 38, no. 2 (Dec. 1978): 281–356.

——. "Syntax, Diction, and Imagery in T'ang Poetry." *Harvard Journal of Asiatic Studies* 31 (Dec. 1971): 49–136.

Kieschnick, John. *The Eminent Monk: Buddhist Ideals in Medieval Chinese Hagiography*. Honolulu: University of Hawai'i Press, 1997.

Komazawa daigaku nai Zengaku daijiten hensansho (Komazawa University Zen Studies Dictionary Editorial Committee). *Zengaku daijiten* (Zen Studies Dictionary). 3 vols. Tokyo: Taishūkan shoten, 1977.

Kraft, Kenneth, ed. *Zen: Tradition and Transformation: A Sourcebook by Contemporary Zen Masters and Scholars*. New York: Grove, 1988.

LaFleur, William R. *The Karma of Words: Buddhism and the Literary Arts in Medieval Japan*. Berkeley: University of California Press, 1983.

Lai, Whalen W. "Ch'an Metaphors: Waves, Water, Mirror, Lamp." *Philosophy East and West* 29, no. 3 (July 1979): 243–253.

——. "Sinitic Mandalas: The *Wu-wei-t'u* of Ts'ao-shan." In *Early Ch'an in China and Tibet*, ed. Whalen Lai and Lewis R. Lancaster, 229–257.

——. "T'an-ch'ien and the Early Ch'an Tradition: Translation and Analysis of the Essay 'Wang-shih-fei-lun.'" In *Early Ch'an in China and Tibet*, ed. Whalen Lai and Lewis R. Lancaster, 65–87.

——. "Tao-sheng's Theory of Sudden Enlightenment Re-examined." In *Sudden and Gradual: Approaches to Enlightenment in Chinese Thought*, ed. Peter N. Gregory, 169–200.

——. "The Transmission Verses of the Ch'an Patriarchs." *Han-hsüeh yen-chiu* 1, no. 2 (1983): 593–624.

Lai, Whalen and Lewis R. Lancaster, eds. *Early Ch'an in China and Tibet*. Berkeley, Calif.: Berkeley Buddhist Studies Series, 1983.

Leighton, Daniel and Yi Wu. *Cultivating the Empty Field: The Silent Illumination of Zen Master Hongzhi*. San Francisco: North Point Press, 1991.

Levering, Miriam. "Miao-tao and Her Teacher Ta-hui." In *Buddhism in the Sung*, ed. Peter N. Gregory and Daniel A. Getz, 188–219.

Li, E. *Songshi jishi* (Recorded Events of Song Poets). 4 vols. Shanghai: Shanghai Guji, 1983.

Li, Fang. *Taiping guangji* (Extensive Records of the Taiping Era). 5 vols. Taipei: Xinan, 1983.

Li, Zhao. *Tangguo shibu* (Supplement to the History of Tang). Shanghai: Gudian wenxue, 1957.

Lin, Shuen-fu and Stephen Owen, eds. *The Vitality of the Lyric Voice: Shih Poetry from the Late Han to the T'ang*. Princeton: Princeton University Press, 1986.

Liu, James J.Y. *The Art of Chinese Poetry*. Chicago: University of Chicago Press, 1962.

——. *Language—Paradox—Poetics: A Chinese Perspective*. Ed. Richard John Lynn. Princeton: Princeton University Press, 1988.

Lu K'uan Yü (Charles Luk), trans. *Ch'an and Zen Teaching*. 3 vols. London: Rider, 1960 (vol. 1), 1961 (vol. 2), 1962 (vol. 3).

——, trans. *The Vimalakirti Nirdesa Sutra (Wei mo chieh so shuo ching)*. Berkeley, Calif.: Shambhala, 1972.

Lynn, Richard John. "The Sudden and the Gradual in Chinese Poetry Criticism: An Examination of the Ch'an-Poetry Analogy." In *Sudden and Gradual: Approaches to Enlightenment in Chinese Thought*, ed. Peter N. Gregory, 381–427.

——. "The Talent Learning Polarity in Chinese Poetics: Yan Yu and the Later Tradition." *Chinese Literature: Essays, Articles, Reviews (CLEAR)* 5, nos. 1/2 (June 1983): 157–184.

Maeda, Eun, ed. *Xu zang jing* (Supplement to the Buddhist Canon). Taipei: Xinwenfeng, n.d. Originally published as *Dai Nihon zoku Zōkyō: Dai isshu, Indo, Shina senjutsu* (Japanese Supplement to the Buddhist Canon: Part 1, Indian and Chinese Selections). Kyoto: Zōkyō shoin, 1905–1912.

Mair, Victor. "Script and Word in Medieval Vernacular Sinitic." *Journal of the American Oriental Society* 112, no. 2 (1992): 269–278.

Matsuura, Shūkō. *Zenshū kojitsu gemon no kenkyū* (Researches on the Versified Literature of the Chan School). Tokyo: Sankibō busshorin, 1972.

McNair, Amy. "Buddhist Literati and Literary Monks: Social and Religous Elements in the Critical Reception of Zhang Jishi's Calligraphy." In *Cultural Intersections in Later Chinese Buddhism,* ed. Marsha Weidner, 73–86.

McRae, John R. "Buddhism." *Journal of Asian Studies* 54, no. 2 (May 1995): 354–371.

——. "Encounter Dialogue and the Transformation of the Spiritual Path in Chinese Ch'an." In *Paths to Liberation: The Mārga and Its Transformations in Buddhist Thought,* ed. Robert E. Buswell and Robert M. Gimello, 339–369.

——. *The Northern School and the Formation of Early Ch'an Buddhism.* Honolulu: University of Hawai'i Press, 1986.

——. "The Ox-head School of Chinese Ch'an Buddhism: from Early Ch'an to the Golden Age." In *Studies in Ch'an and Hua-yen,* ed. Robert M. Gimello and Peter N. Gregory, 169–252.

——. *The Platform Sutra of the Sixth Patriarch.* Berkeley, Calif.: Numata Center for Buddhist Translation and Research, 2000.

——. *Seeing Through Zen: Encounter, Transformation, and Genealogy in Chinese Chan Buddhism.* Berkeley: University of California Press, 2003.

——. "Shen-hui and the Teaching of Sudden Enlightenment in Early Ch'an Buddhism." In *Sudden and Gradual: Approaches to Enlightenment in Chinese Thought,* ed. Peter N. Gregory, 227–278.

——. "The Story of Early Ch'an." In *Zen: Tradition and Transformation: A Sourcebook by Contemporary Zen Masters and Scholars,* ed. Kenneth Kraft, 125–139.

Miao, Ronald C., ed. *Studies in Chinese Poetry and Poetics.* Vol. 1. San Francisco: Chinese Materials Center, 1978.

Miaofeng, ed. *Caoxi Chan yanjiu* (Caoxi: the Symposium on Chan Buddhism in China). Beijing: Zhongguo shehui kexue, 2002.

Mill, John Stuart. *Essays on Poetry.* Ed. F. Parvin Sharpless. Columbia: University of South Carolina Press, 1976.

Miura, Isshū and Ruth Fuller Sasaki. *Zen Dust: The History of the Koan and Koan Study in Rinzai (Linchi) Zen.* New York: Harcourt, Brace and World, 1967.

Mueller, F. Max, trans. "The Larger Sukhavativyuha Sutra, or the Sutra on the Buddha of Eternal Life." Ed. Richard St. Clair. http://web.mit.edu/stclair/www/larger.html. Last modified December 11, 2000.

Muller, A. Charles, ed. *Digital Dictionary of Buddhism.* http://buddhism-dict.net/ddb. Last modified March 31, 2009.

Murck, Alfreda and Wen Fong, eds. *Words and Images: Chinese Poetry, Calligraphy, and Painting.* Princeton: Princeton University Press, 1991.

Nakamura, Hajime. *Bukkyōgo daijiten* (Encyclopedia of Buddhist Terms). Tokyo: Tōkyō shoseki, 1981.

Nielson, Thomas P. "The T'ang Poet-monk Chiao-jan." Occasional Paper no. 3. Tempe: Center for Asian Studies, Arizona State University, 1972.

Nienhauser, William H., ed. *The Indiana Companion to Traditional Chinese Literature.* Bloomington: Indiana University Press, 1986.

O'Donnell, Patrick S., comp. "Buddhism: A Select Bibliography (Books in English)." Buddha Dharma Association and Buddhanet, http://www.buddhanet.net/e-learning/buddhism/bibliography.htm. Last modified February 1, 2008.

Owen, Stephen. *Readings in Chinese Literary Thought.* Cambridge, Mass.: Council on East Asian Studies, Harvard University, 1992.

Peng, Dingqiu, ed. *Quan Tangshi* (Complete Tang Poems). Taipei: Zhonghua, 1985.

PripMøller, Johannes. *Chinese Buddhist Monasteries; Their Plan and Its Function as a Setting for Buddhist Monastic Life.* 1937; reprint, Hong Kong: Hong Kong University Press, 1982.

Pulleyblank, E. G. "Linguistic Evidence for the Date of Han-shan." In *Studies in Chinese Poetry and Poetics,* vol. 1, ed. Ronald C. Miao, 163–185.

Red Pine (Bill Porter), trans. *Collected Songs of Cold Mountain.* Port Townsend, Wash.: Copper Canyon Press, 2000.

——, trans. *The Zen Works of Stonehouse: Poems and Talks of a Fourteenth-Century Chinese Hermit.* San Francisco: Mercury House, 1999.

Red Pine (Bill Porter) and Mike O'Connor, eds. *The Clouds Should Know Me By Now: Buddhist Poet Monks of China.* Boston: Wisdom, 1990.

Robinson, Richard H., trans. *Chinese Buddhist Verse.* 1954; reprint, Westport, Conn.: Greenwood, 1980.

Sasaki, Ruth Fuller, Yoshitaka Iriya, and Dana R. Fraser, trans. *A Man of Zen: The Recorded Sayings of Layman P'ang.* New York: Weatherhill, 1971.

Sawada, Mizuho. *Bukkyō to Chūgoku bungaku* (Buddhism and Chinese Literature). Tokyo: Kokusho kankōkai, 1975.

Schlütter, Morten. *How Zen Became Zen: The Dispute Over Enlightenment and the Formation of Chan Buddhism in Song-Dynasty China.* Honolulu: University of Hawai'i Press, 2008.

——. "Silent Illumination, Kung-an Introspection, and the Competition for Lay Patronage in Sung Dynasty Ch'an." In *Buddhism in the Sung,* ed. Peter N. Gregory and Daniel A. Getz, 109–147.

——. "Vinaya Monasteries, Public Abbacies, and State Control of Buddhism Under the Sung Dynasty (960–1279)." In *Going Forth: Visions of Buddhist Vinaya,* ed. William Bodiford, 136–160.

Schmidt, J. D. "Ch'an, Illusion, and Sudden Enlightenment in the Poetry of Yang Wan-li." *T'oung Pao* 60, nos. 4–5 (1974): 230–281.

——. *Yang Wan-li*. Boston: Twayne, 1976.

Seaton, Jerome and Dennis Maloney, eds. *A Drifting Boat: An Anthology of Chinese Zen Poetry*. Fredonia, N.Y.: White Pine Press, 1994.

Sekida, Katsuki. *Two Zen Classics: Mumonkan and Hekiganroku*. Ed. A. V. Grimstone. New York and Tokyo: Weatherhill, 1996.

Snyder, Gary. "Cold Mountain Poems." *Evergreen Review* 2, no. 6 (1958): 69–80.

——. *Riprap; and, Cold Mountain Poems*. San Francisco: North Point Press, 1990.

Sponberg, Alan. "Meditation in Fa-hsiang Buddhism." In *Traditions of Meditation in Chinese Buddhism*, ed. Peter N. Gregory, 15–43.

Stein, R. A. "Sudden Illumination or Simultaneous Comprehension: Remarks on Chinese and Tibetan Terminology." Trans. Neal Donner. In *Sudden and Gradual: Approaches to Enlightenment in Chinese Thought*, ed. Peter N. Gregory, 41–65.

Stevenson, Daniel B. "The Four Kinds of Samādhi in Early T'ien-t'ai Buddhism." In *Traditions of Meditation in Chinese Buddhism*, ed. Peter N. Gregory, 45–97.

Stryk, Lucien and Takashi Ikemoto, trans. *The Penguin Book of Zen Poetry*. London: Allen Lane, 1977.

——, trans. *Zen Poetry: Let the Spring Breeze Enter*. New York: Grove, 1995.

Stryk, Lucien, Takashi Ikemoto, and Taigan Takayama, trans. *Zen Poems of China and Japan; The Crane's Bill*. Garden City, N.Y.: Anchor Press, 1973.

Sun, Changwu. *Chansi yu shiqing* (Chan Thought and Poetic Emotion). Beijing: Zhonghua, 1997.

Sun, Qi (Sun Ch'i). *Hanshan yu xipi* (Hanshan and the Hippies). Taizhong, Taiwan: Putian, 1974.

Suzuki, D. T. *Manual of Zen Buddhism*. New York: Grove, 1960.

Sze, Mai-mai. *The Tao of Painting; a Study of the Ritual Disposition of Chinese Painting: with a Translation of the Jie tzu yuan hua zhuan; or, Mustard Seed Garden Manual of Painting, 1679–1701*. 2nd ed. Princeton: Princeton University Press, 1967.

Takakusu, Junjirō and Watanabe Kaikyoku, eds. *Taishō shinshū daizōkyō* (Taisho Era Edition of the Buddhist Canon). Tokyo: Nihon Tōkyō Daizōkyō Kankōkai, 1924–1932.

Tan, Wei. *Pang jushi yanjiu* (Researches on Layman Pang). Chengdu: Sichuan minzu, 2002.

Tang, Yanfang. "Language, Truth, and Literary Interpretation: A Cross-cultural Examination." *Journal of the History of Ideas* 60, no. 1 (Jan. 1999): 1–20.

Thurman, Robert, trans. *The Holy Teaching of Vimalakirti: A Mahayana Scripture*. University Park: Pennsylvania State University Press, 1976.

Tu, Ching-I. "Some Aspects of the *Jen-chien tz'u-hua*." *Journal of the American Oriental Society* 93, no. 3 (July–Sept. 1973): 306–316.

Wagner, Marsha L. *Wang Wei*. Boston: Twayne, 1981.

Waley, Arthur, trans. *The Analects of Confucius*. New York: Vintage, 1938.

———, trans. *Ballads and Stories from Tun-huang*. London: Allen and Unwin, 1960.

———, trans. *The Book of Songs: The Ancient Chinese Classic of Poetry*. Ed. with additional trans. Joseph Allen. New York: Grove, 1996.

———, trans. "27 Poems by Han-shan." *Encounter* 3, no. 3 (Sept. 1954): 3–8.

———, trans. *The Way and Its Power: A Study of the Tao Te Ching and Its Place in Chinese Thought*. New York: Grove, 1934.

Watson, Burton, trans. *Cold Mountain: 100 Poems by the T'ang Poet Han-shan*. 1962; reprint, New York and London: Columbia University Press, 1970.

———, trans. *The Complete Works of Chuang Tzu*. New York: Columbia University Press, 1968.

———, trans. *The Lotus Sutra*. New York: Columbia University Press, 1993.

———. "Zen Poetry." In *Zen: Tradition and Transformation: A Sourcebook by Contemporary Zen Masters and Scholars*, ed. Kenneth Kraft, 105–124.

———, trans. *The Zen Teachings of Master Lin-chi: A Translation of the Lin-chi lu*. 2nd ed. New York: Columbia University Press, 1999.

Wei, Qingzhi. *Shiren yuxie* (Jade Splinters of the Poets). Taipei: Shangwu, 1972.

Weidner, Marsha, ed. *Cultural Intersections in Later Chinese Buddhism*. Honolulu: University of Hawai'i Press, 2001.

Weinstein, Stanley. *Buddhism Under the T'ang*. Cambridge, U.K.: Cambridge University Press, 1987.

Welter, Albert. *Monks, Rulers, and Literati: The Political Ascendancy of Chan Buddhism*. Oxford: Oxford University Press, 2006.

Williams, Paul. *Mahāyāna Buddhism: The Doctrinal Foundations*. London and New York: Routledge, 1989.

Williams, Paul and Anthony Tribe. *Buddhist Thought: A Complete Introduction to the Indian Tradition*. London and New York: Routledge, 2000.

Wright, Dale S. "The Discourse of Awakening: Rhetorical Practice in Classical Ch'an Buddhism." *Journal of the American Academy of Religion* 61, no. 1 (Spring 1993): 23–40.

Wu, Chi-yu. "A Study of Han-shan." *T'oung Pao* 45 (1957): 392–450.

Wu, Yansheng. *Chanzong shige jingjie* (The Position of Poetry in Chan). Beijing: Chung-hua, 2001.

Xiang, Chu and Zhang Zikai, Tan Wei, and He Jianping. *Tangdai baihua shipai yanjiu* (Researches on Tang Dynasty Vernacular Poetry). Chengdu: Sichuan chuban jituan, 2004.

Xu, Jinfu (Hsü, Chin-fu), ed. *Chanlin qingyun* (Pure Rhymes of the Chan Forest). Taipei: Xin wenfeng, 1979.

Yampolsky, Philip. "New Japanese Studies in Early Ch'an History." In *Early Ch'an in China and Tibet*, ed. Whalen Lai and Lewis R. Lancaster, 1–11.

———. *The Platform Sutra of the Sixth Patriarch: The Text of the Tun-huang Manuscript, Translated, with Notes*. New York: Columbia University Press, 1967.

Yanagida, Seizan. "The Li-tai fa-pao chi and the Ch'an Doctine of Sudden Awakening." Trans. Carl Bielefeldt. In *Early Ch'an in China and Tibet,* ed. Whalen Lai and Lewis R. Lancaster, 13–49.

——. "The 'Recorded Sayings' Texts of Chinese Ch'an Buddhism." Trans. John R. McRae. In *Early Ch'an in China and Tibet,* ed. Whalen Lai and Lewis R. Lancaster, 185–205.

——. *Zen no yuige* (The Departing Verses of Chan/Zen). Tokyo: Chōbunsha, 1973.

Yang, Guanlin, et al., eds. *Zhongguo mingsheng zidian* (Dictionary of Chinese Scenic Places). 2nd ed. Shanghai: Shanghai zishu, 1989.

Yifa. *The Origins of Buddhist Monastic Codes in China: An Annotated Translation and Study of the Chanyuan qinggui.* Honolulu: University of Hawai'i Press, 2002.

Yokoi, Yūhō. *The Japanese-English Zen Buddhist Dictionary.* Tokyo: Sankibō Buddhist Bookstore, 1991.

Yoshizawa, Katsuhiro, ed. *Gōko Fūgetsushū yakuchū* (Wind and Moon Over Rivers and Lakes Collection, Annotated and Translated). Kyoto: Zen Bunka Kenkyūjo, 2003.

Yoshizu, Yoshihide. "The Relation Between Chinese Buddhist History and Soteriology." Trans. Paul Groner. In *Paths to Liberation: The Mārga and Its Transformations in Buddhist Thought,* ed. Robert E. Buswell and Robert M. Gimello, 309–338.

Yu, Pauline. *The Poetry of Wang Wei: New Translations and Commentary.* Bloomington: Indiana University Press, 1980.

Yuan, Bin, ed. *Chanzong zidian* (Dictionary of the Chan Sect). Wuhan: Hubei renmin, 1994.

Zeuschner, Robert B. "The Concept of *li nien* ('Being Free from Thinking') in the Northern Line of Ch'an Buddhism." In *Early Ch'an in China and Tibet,* ed. Whalen Lai and Lewis R. Lancaster, 131–148.

——. "A Selected Bibliography on Ch'an Buddhism in China." *Journal of Chinese Philosophy* 3 (1976): 229–311.

Zhang, Qiyun (Chang Ch'i-yun), et al., eds. *Zhongwen da cidian* (The Encyclopedic Dictionary of the Chinese Language). Taipei: Zhongguo Wenhua Yanjiusuo, 1973.

Zhongguo Fojiao renming dazidian (Dictionary of Names of Chinese Buddhist Personages). Shanghai: Shanghai zishu, 1999.

Zhou, Fagao (Chou Fa-Kao). *Hanzi gujin yinhui* (A Pronouncing Dictionary of Chinese Characters in Archaic and Ancient Chinese, Mandarin and Cantonese). Hong Kong: Chinese University Press, 1974.

Zhou, Yukai. *Zhongguo Chanzong yu shige* (Chinese Chan and Poetry). Shanghai: Renmin, 1992.

Zhu, Fengyu (Chu Feng-yü). *Wang Fanzhi shi yanjiu* (Research in the Poetry of Wang Fanzhi). 2 vols. Taipei: Xuesheng, 1987.

Zürcher, Erik. *The Buddhist Conquest of China: The Spread and Adaptation of Buddhism in Early Medieval China.* 2 vols. Leiden: E. J. Brill, 1959.

Index

Translations from the Asian Classics

Records of the Historian: Chapters from the Shih chi of Ssu-ma Ch'ien, tr. Burton Watson. Paperback ed. only. 1969

Cold Mountain: 100 Poems by the T'ang Poet Han-shan, tr. Burton Watson. Also in paperback ed. 1970

Twenty Plays of the Nō Theatre, ed. Donald Keene. Also in paperback ed. 1970

Chūshingura: The Treasury of Loyal Retainers, tr. Donald Keene. Also in paperback ed. 1971; rev. ed. 1997

The Zen Master Hakuin: Selected Writings, tr. Philip B. Yampolsky 1971

Chinese Rhyme-Prose: Poems in the Fu Form from the Han and Six Dynasties Periods, tr. Burton Watson. Also in paperback ed. 1971

Kūkai: Major Works, tr. Yoshito S. Hakeda. Also in paperback ed. 1972

The Old Man Who Does as He Pleases: Selections from the Poetry and Prose of Lu Yu, tr. Burton Watson 1973

The Lion's Roar of Queen Śrīmālā, tr. Alex and Hideko Wayman 1974

Courtier and Commoner in Ancient China: Selections from the History of the Former Han by Pan Ku, tr. Burton Watson. Also in paperback ed. 1974

Japanese Literature in Chinese, vol. 1: *Poetry and Prose in Chinese by Japanese Writers of the Early Period*, tr. Burton Watson 1975

Japanese Literature in Chinese, vol. 2: *Poetry and Prose in Chinese by Japanese Writers of the Later Period*, tr. Burton Watson 1976

Love Song of the Dark Lord: Jayadeva's Gītagovinda, tr. Barbara Stoler Miller. Also in paperback ed. Cloth ed. includes critical text of the Sanskrit. 1977; rev. ed. 1997

Ryōkan: Zen Monk-Poet of Japan, tr. Burton Watson 1977

Calming the Mind and Discerning the Real: From the Lam rim chen mo of Tsoṅ-kha-pa, tr. Alex Wayman 1978

The Hermit and the Love-Thief: Sanskrit Poems of Bhartrihari and Bilhaṇa, tr. Barbara Stoler Miller 1978

The Lute: Kao Ming's P'i-p'a chi, tr. Jean Mulligan. Also in paperback ed. 1980

A Chronicle of Gods and Sovereigns: Jinnō Shōtōki of Kitabatake Chikafusa, tr. H. Paul Varley 1980

Among the Flowers: The Hua-chien chi, tr. Lois Fusek 1982

Grass Hill: Poems and Prose by the Japanese Monk Gensei, tr. Burton Watson 1983

Doctors, Diviners, and Magicians of Ancient China: Biographies of Fang-shih, tr. Kenneth J. DeWoskin. Also in paperback ed. 1983

Theater of Memory: The Plays of Kālidāsa, ed. Barbara Stoler Miller. Also in paperback ed. 1984

The Columbia Book of Chinese Poetry: From Early Times to the Thirteenth Century, ed. and tr. Burton Watson. Also in paperback ed. 1984

Poems of Love and War: From the Eight Anthologies and the Ten Long Poems of Classical Tamil, tr. A. K. Ramanujan. Also in paperback ed. 1985

The Bhagavad Gita: Krishna's Counsel in Time of War, tr. Barbara Stoler Miller 1986

The Columbia Book of Later Chinese Poetry, ed. and tr. Jonathan Chaves. Also in paperback ed. 1986

The Tso Chuan: Selections from China's Oldest Narrative History, tr. Burton Watson 1989

Waiting for the Wind: Thirty-six Poets of Japan's Late Medieval Age, tr. Steven Carter 1989

Selected Writings of Nichiren, ed. Philip B. Yampolsky 1990

Saigyō, Poems of a Mountain Home, tr. Burton Watson 1990

The Book of Lieh Tzu: A Classic of the Tao, tr. A. C. Graham. Morningside ed. 1990

The Tale of an Anklet: An Epic of South India — The Cilappatikāram of Iḷaṇkō Aṭikaḷ, tr. R. Parthasarathy 1993

Waiting for the Dawn: A Plan for the Prince, tr. with introduction by Wm. Theodore de Bary 1993

Yoshitsune and the Thousand Cherry Trees: A Masterpiece of the Eighteenth-Century Japanese Puppet Theater, tr., annotated, and with introduction by Stanleigh H. Jones, Jr. 1993

The Lotus Sutra, tr. Burton Watson. Also in paperback ed. 1993

The Classic of Changes: A New Translation of the I Ching *as Interpreted by Wang Bi*, tr. Richard John Lynn 1994

Beyond Spring: Tz'u Poems of the Sung Dynasty, tr. Julie Landau 1994

The Columbia Anthology of Traditional Chinese Literature, ed. Victor H. Mair 1994

Scenes for Mandarins: The Elite Theater of the Ming, tr. Cyril Birch 1995

Letters of Nichiren, ed. Philip B. Yampolsky; tr. Burton Watson et al. 1996

Unforgotten Dreams: Poems by the Zen Monk Shōtetsu, tr. Steven D. Carter 1997

The Vimalakirti Sutra, tr. Burton Watson 1997

Japanese and Chinese Poems to Sing: The Wakan rōei shū, tr. J. Thomas Rimer and Jonathan Chaves 1997

Breeze Through Bamboo: Kanshi of Ema Saikō, tr. Hiroaki Sato 1998

A Tower for the Summer Heat, by Li Yu, tr. Patrick Hanan 1998

Traditional Japanese Theater: An Anthology of Plays, by Karen Brazell 1998

The Original Analects: Sayings of Confucius and His Successors (0479–0249), by E. Bruce Brooks and A. Taeko Brooks 1998

The Classic of the Way and Virtue: A New Translation of the Tao-te ching *of Laozi as Interpreted by Wang Bi*, tr. Richard John Lynn 1999

The Four Hundred Songs of War and Wisdom: An Anthology of Poems from Classical Tamil, The Puṛanāṇūṛu, ed. and tr. George L. Hart and Hank Heifetz 1999

Original Tao: Inward Training (Nei-yeh) *and the Foundations of Taoist Mysticism*, by Harold D. Roth 1999

Lao Tzu's Tao Te Ching: A Translation of the Startling New Documents Found at Guodian, by Robert G. Henricks 2000

The Shorter Columbia Anthology of Traditional Chinese Literature, ed. Victor H. Mair 2000

Mistress and Maid (Jiaohongji), by Meng Chengshun, tr. Cyril Birch 2001

Chikamatsu: Five Late Plays, tr. and ed. C. Andrew Gerstle 2001

The Essential Lotus: Selections from the Lotus Sutra, tr. Burton Watson 2002

Early Modern Japanese Literature: An Anthology, 1600–1900, ed. Haruo Shirane 2002; abridged 2008

The Columbia Anthology of Traditional Korean Poetry, ed. Peter H. Lee 2002

The Sound of the Kiss, or The Story That Must Never Be Told: Pingali Suranna's Kalapurnodayamu, tr. Vecheru Narayana Rao and David Shulman 2003

The Selected Poems of Du Fu, tr. Burton Watson 2003

Far Beyond the Field: Haiku by Japanese Women, tr. Makoto Ueda 2003

Just Living: Poems and Prose by the Japanese Monk Tonna, ed. and tr. Steven D. Carter 2003

Han Feizi: Basic Writings, tr. Burton Watson 2003

Mozi: Basic Writings, tr. Burton Watson 2003

Xunzi: Basic Writings, tr. Burton Watson 2003

Zhuangzi: Basic Writings, tr. Burton Watson 2003

The Awakening of Faith, Attributed to Aśvaghosha, tr. Yoshito S. Hakeda, introduction by Ryuichi Abe 2005

The Tales of the Heike, tr. Burton Watson, ed. Haruo Shirane 2006

Tales of Moonlight and Rain, by Ueda Akinari, tr. with introduction by Anthony H. Chambers 2007

Traditional Japanese Literature: An Anthology, Beginnings to 1600, ed. Haruo Shirane 2007

The Philosophy of Qi, by Kaibara Ekken, tr. Mary Evelyn Tucker 2007

The Analects of Confucius, tr. Burton Watson 2007

The Art of War: Sun Zi's Military Methods, tr. Victor Mair 2007

One Hundred Poets: One Poem Each: A Translation of the Ogura Hyakunin Isshu, tr. Peter McMillan 2008

Zeami: Performance Notes, tr. Tom Hare 2008

Zongmi on Chan, tr. Jeffrey Lyle Broughton 2009

Scripture of the Lotus Blossom of the Fine Dharma, revised edition, tr. Leon Hurvitz, preface and introduction by Stephen R. Teiser 2009

Mencius, tr. Irene Bloom, edited and with an introduction by Philip J. Ivanhoe